A Theory of Social Interaction

A Theory of
Social Interaction

Jonathan H. Turner

Stanford University Press
Stanford, California
1988

Stanford University Press, Stanford, California

© 1988 by the Board of Trustees of the
Leland Stanford Junior University

Printed in the United States of America

Library of Congress Cataloging-in-Publication Data

Turner, Jonathan H.
    A theory of social interaction / Jonathan H. Turner.
      p.   cm.
    Bibliography: p.
    Includes index.
    ISBN 0-8047-1463-0 (alk. paper). ISBN 0-8047-1479-7
(pbk.: alk. paper)
    1. Social interaction.   I. Title.
HM291.T87 1988   87-32531
302—dc19   CIP

To my sister, SUSAN FLORES

Preface

THIS IS a theoretical work on the process of social interaction among individuals. My goal is to conceptualize the structure of social interaction and the play here on the title of Talcott Parsons's famous work, *The Structure of Social Action*, is deliberate, for the pages that follow represent a critique of Parsons's analysis of "the act" and an alternative to his analysis of micro processes. In conceptualizing "unit acts" as the most basic elements of sociological analysis and in moving rapidly to an ever more macro functionalism, Parsons underemphasized what I believe to be the most fundamental unit of sociological analysis—social interaction. And so, contrary to many who have viewed Parsons's first work as a "promising beginning," my own view is that this was not the best place to begin sociological theory. Indeed, for all of its deficiencies, Parsons's macro structuralism is more theoretically interesting than this early micro approach.

Despite my criticism of Parsons's early analysis, I follow in this book the general strategy he used in *The Structure of Social Action*: assessing existing works, extracting their useful concepts, and combining them in new ways to produce a synthetic conceptualization. I share Parsons's assumption that there are invariant properties of the social world and that it is possible to denote these properties and map their interrelations with analytical schemes. The difference comes in just how one "structures" an analytical scheme. In my view, analytical schemes are only the first step in theory building. One must also translate the elements of the scheme into more exact causal models that indicate the dynamic relationships among clearly conceptualized variables. Such an exercise should not reduce the level of abstraction, as many in sociology contend; rather, it should increase the level of precision. Moreover, once models are constructed, they can be translated into abstract theoretical propositions that, in principle, are testable. Such propositions are still abstract, but they do break a complex model down into a more manageable number of variables.

Although I do not offer tests or summarize empirical literatures to illustrate my models and propositions, I hope that the variables, models, and propositions of my purely theoretical effort may stimulate empirical work by others. Too often in sociology we try to make theorists into researchers and researchers into theorists, but I believe that there can be a productive division of labor between the two. Therefore I welcome efforts by others to test the ideas presented here.

My analysis of interaction is decidedly micro in tone. Sociologists have agonized over whether micro or macro levels of reality are theoretically more important, and they have desperately tried to link one level of analysis to the other, in hopes of closing the micro-macro gap. All of this effort seems premature; rather than arguing for the primacy of one over the other or seeking to plug apparent gaps between them, perhaps we ought to ignore the issue, at least for the time being. Let us instead develop precise micro theories of interaction, on the one side, and macro theories of social structure, on the other. Only then will we be able to determine what points, if any at all, of theoretical reconciliation between these levels are evident. Thus, in concentrating on the process of social interaction, I am not asserting that micro takes precedence over macro and that one is reducible to the other. Moreover, if pressed on this issue, I believe that micro and macro analysis will always remain theoretically disconnected. Neither is more important; each simply provides a different kind of insight into human affairs.

In approaching the topic of interaction, I have divided it into three constituent properties: motivational, interactional, and structuring. Motivational processes are those that energize and mobilize actors to interact; interactional processes concern how actors use gestures to signal and interpret; and structuring processes are those behaviors among motivated individuals that allow them to repeat and organize interactions across time and space. I am not asserting, of course, that this is the only approach, but I would argue that most theories of interaction are too global. That is, they collapse discrete processes into one grand scheme, with the result that the full complexity of social interaction is not adequately conceptualized. For each of these three properties of interaction—that is, motivational, interactional, and structuring—early and more contemporary works are summarized and modeled with an eye to what they offer to a more synthetic or composite model. Using this composite model I propose "laws," or abstract principles, about motivational, interactional, and structural dynamics. And then, in conclusion, I try to pull together the three composite models and recast the abstract principles in a way that emphasizes the relationships among the three properties of social interaction.

The models and propositions offered in the chapters to follow are only provisional. I have sought to state them with sufficient precision to encourage not only empirical tests by researchers but also modifications by theorists. My goal is to stimulate theoretical cumulation, though it may be at the cost of repeated revision or even refutation.

My thanks for support received during my work on this project go first of all to the Academic Senate of the University of California at Riverside, which has provided funds for the research presented in these pages. Second, I want to express, once again, my gratitude for the help and friendship of my typist for the last eighteen years, Clara Dean. As always, she has worked very hard to read my difficult (and degenerating) handwriting, checked my horrible spelling, and called attention to my many errors of inattention to detail. And third, I wish to thank those who read all or various portions of the manuscript, offering constructive advice. Among these, my colleague Randall Collins deserves special mention because he read the manuscript in its various stages and provided detailed comments and commentary on all phases of my thinking. He has also been a constant source of friendly debate and dialogue during the course of preparing the manuscript. Murray Webster, Anthony Giddens, and Lee Freese also offered encouragement, even in their points of disagreement. Others have read portions of the book in the various articles that have come from this research. Their comments have helped me to focus and refine my ideas, thereby making the arguments in this volume much stronger than they would otherwise have been. Thus, a thank you to Sheldon Stryker, Norbert Wiley, Michael Schwalbe, Victor Gecas, Morris Rosenberg, David Morgan, and several anonymous reviewers.

J.H.T.

Contents

Figures and Tables

Figures

Tables

I

Introduction

1

Do People Interact in Action Theory?

"WHO NOW READS PARSONS?" It is difficult for us to realize how great a stir he made in the world. He was the intimate confidant of a strange and rather unsatisfactory god, whom he called Action Theory. His god has betrayed him. We (should) have moved beyond Parsons.

It may seem outrageous for me to insert Parsons's name for that of Herbert Spencer in this question from the first paragraph of *The Structure of Social Action* (1937: 3). Indeed, it may seem a cheap shot, especially against a scholar whom I have always admired, even in disagreement. Yet, the intent behind my paraphrasing is an important theme of this book. Parsons pronounced Spencer "dead"; and although Parsons's approach is not certifiably dead, it is dying, despite creative efforts at resuscitation in the United States and in Germany (e.g., Alexander, 1984, 1987; Münch, 1982a). Much of Parsons's work has, of course, filtered into mainstream sociology, so his genius will live on, but—we may hope—in dramatically transmuted form. My argument is that Parsons's starting point—a conceptualization of action—and his end point—a requisite functionalism—took sociology off the mark.[1] The basic unit of sociological analysis is not action, but *inter*action; and the presumption that one can begin with elementary conceptualizations of action and then progressively move up to the analysis of interaction and structure is highly questionable. Parsons's great error, then, was to begin with an analysis of "acts" (Parsons, 1937) and to move hurriedly toward conceptualizations of structure and social systems (Parsons, 1951), leaving behind serious consideration of the process of social interaction. To paraphrase George Homans, the result was a theory of action with darn little action.

This book represents an effort to correct this error made by Parsons and many others. I start over by beginning with the most basic unit of sociology: social interaction. In effect, I then parallel Parsons's first great work,

[1] In a number of places, I have wrestled with the concept of "action" (see J. Turner, 1983b, 1985c). Though it can be argued that a conceptualization of action must precede one of interaction, I am now convinced that the result is either regression back into psychology or a leap into the macro analysis of social structure—without paying much attention to the dynamics of *inter*action.

reviewing and synthesizing the ideas of others, with the major difference that I borrow from those who have conceptualized the process of inter-action rather than action.[2] The result is a theoretical analysis of the struc-ture of social *inter*action instead of acts and action.

But first let me review in more detail the strategic miscalculation of Par-sons and his intellectual mentor, Max Weber. Their errors in conceptual-izing interaction have been repeated many times over the last fifty years, so what is said about them applies to others as well. In the next chapter, I propose an alternative strategy that, like Parsons's, seeks to highlight the structure of micro processes but, unlike Parsons's, does not preclude the dynamic properties of interaction.

The Parsonian Strategy

Parsons as a Weberian

To understand Parsons's approach to a theory of action, it is necessary first to examine Max Weber's theoretical strategy. Weber recognized that the problems selected for study by sociologists will, to some degree, reflect their bias, but he also believed that a "value-free" sociology is possible if "rational procedures" are used for developing knowledge about "historical phenomena." Such procedures must involve an "interpretive understand-ing of social action and . . . a causal explanation of its course and conse-quences." He saw the highly abstract laws of positivistic sociology as "de-void of content"; in their place "knowledge of historical phenomena in their concreteness" was to be inserted. The methodological tool for real-izing this effort is Weber's "ideal type," which analytically accentuates the key features of social action and social forms in their historical context. Yet, despite this emphasis on the historical and empirical embeddedness of sociological analysis, some of Weber's ideal types are highly abstract and analytical, apparently seeking to extract and categorize the essence of more generic and less time-bound phenomena. Such is the nature of his belated and brief discussion of action and social organization in the opening sec-tions of *Economy and Society* (Weber, 1978: 3–62).

The basic model developed in those pages is depicted in Fig. 1.1, which

---

[2] The very fact that I have opened this book with a review of Parsons's initial effort will underscore, I hope, the great respect that I hold for the scholarship in *The Structure of Social Action*. Indeed, to be discussing a book that is over 50 years old attests to its importance. See Alexander (1987) for a review of how sociology after the Second World War has represented a reaction to weaknesses in Parsonian theory. Although this book is itself a reaction to Par-sons's failure to conceptualize interaction, in no way should I be seen as part of an anti-Parsons camp; I have too much respect for Parsons's work and for those carrying forward the action-theoretic tradition.

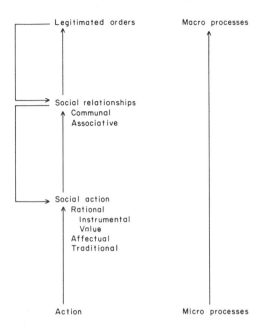

Fig. 1.1. Weber's conceptualization of action, interaction, and organization.

outlines the broad contours of Weber's discussion. Even if one disagrees with my array of definitions and would insert new terms here and there, the logic of his argument is nonetheless the same. Weber appears to equate "action" with the concept of simple movement in the environment. Action is sociologically relevant when it is "social" or "meaningfully oriented to that of others" (Weber, 1978: 23). Moreover, as is typical of Weberian sociology, a typology is offered to denote the ways the action can be oriented: (1) "rational," which is subdivided into "instrumental-rational," or calculated use of the most efficient means to an end, and "value-rational," or use of those means relevant for realizing some moral standard; (2) "affectual," or orientations determined by feelings and emotions; and (3) "traditional," or orientations dictated by custom and habit.

These distinctions are well known, and I need not elaborate on them, especially since it is the logic rather than the substance of Weber's argument that I want to emphasize. Rather than discuss the *process* of orientation— that is, the actual interpersonal practices that actors use to develop orientations toward each other—Weberian sociology gives us these descriptive categories. The same is true of social relationships, or systems of mutual orientations among pluralities of actors. I could enumerate more than two types of relationships, but the two highlighted here, "communal" and "associative," appear more frequently than other distinctions throughout

Weber's sociology. Moreover, they represent more structured manifestations of the types of social action. But whether it is two, four, or six types of relationships, the logic is the same: the basic processes by which social relations are created, sustained, or changed are not discussed; instead, Weber offers a typology of relations. For Weber, communal relations are based upon either affect or tradition; associative relations rest on the "rationally motivated adjustment of interests" (whether value-rational or instrumental-rational) and "agreement by mutual consent." Thus, this typology of relations incorporates the types of social action.

The next level of social organization is the "legitimated order," or "the order" (Weber, 1978: 31). "Orders" appear to be Weber's blanket term denoting macrostructures that are "legitimated," or made "valid," in the eyes of their members by virtue of being organized around one or more of the three types of action orientation. In turn, there are various types of legitimated orders, although Weber's discussion of these is rather ambiguous and appears to delineate a variety of overlapping forms. For this reason, I will not discuss them, but as Collins (1975) suggests, the two most important appear to be "organizations" and "stratification systems."

By the time Weber defines "orders," he has become a macro sociologist.[3] But this macro sociology does not specify the micro process from which it is constructed, changed, and reproduced. Weber makes many assertions that such structures are indeed the end product of individual actions and interactions (e.g., Weber, 1978: 3, 5–6, 11, 13–15, 19, 22–28, 46), but he does not provide an analysis of the process of action and interaction. (As is well known, Alfred Schutz [1932] made a similar critique.) Only when Weber becomes a macro sociologist, which is almost immediately after the opening chapter of *Economy and Society*, do we get a sense for social process. But, again, his analysis has little to do with the micro realm from which these macro social processes are presumably constructed.

Thus, without belaboring the point, Weber's typological approach can provide little in the way of understanding the topic of this book, social interaction. Weber did not discuss processes at the micro level, and despite his proclamations that sociology is the study of social action, his actual analysis of most topics is decidedly macrostructural. To the extent that Weber's typological strategy is employed, not only will analysis of interaction be static, but it will also move rather quickly to macrostructures where the

---

[3] I should emphasize, of course, that Weber wrote much of his macro sociology before he turned to the analysis of action, especially rational action. Thus, Fig. 1.1 would have the arrows reversed if it represented the sequence of Weber's work. But the *substance* of these later essays in part I of *Economy and Society* communicates the image delineated here. Moreover, this image is what Parsons implicitly advocated—that is, theorists should first analyze acts and action, and then, move on to an ever more macrostructural level of analysis.

processes of interaction among people are ignored. Such was also to be true of Talcott Parsons's effort to develop "action theory."

Parsonian "Inaction" Theory

There has been considerable debate (e.g., Scott, 1963; Gerstein, 1976; Münch, 1981, 1982b) over whether or not Talcott Parsons abandoned a promising analysis of interpersonal processes in his *The Structure of Social Action* (1937) in favor of a more macrostructural and functional approach in *The Social System* (1951). My own view (Turner and Beeghley, 1974) is that Parsons's movement away from the micro "unit act" to macrostructural analysis was much like Weber's. For Parsons adopted Weber's ideal type or typological methodology, but unlike Weber, he advocated a form of positivism or a commitment to discovering the invariant properties of the empirical world. In Parsons's view, theory must develop a "generalized system of concepts" that "adequately 'grasp' aspects of the objective external world. . . . These concepts correspond not to concrete phenomena, but to elements in them which are analytically separable from other elements" (Parsons, 1937: 730). Parsons was thus committed to developing a system of categories that analytically accentuates universal and generic properties of the social universe (Parsons, 1970); and on this score, I am more sympathetic with his position than with Weber's.

Parsons began with the "unit act" (Parsons, 1937), moved to systems of interaction, or "social systems" (Parsons, 1951), and then to ever more inclusive visions of action systems, (Parsons, 1961; Parsons, Bales, and Shils, 1953). And in a final burst of activity more reminiscent of Herbert Spencer than Max Weber, he conceptualized the whole universe, or "human condition" (Parsons, 1978).[4] Unlike Weber's, Parsons's typologies were not restricted or constrained by the specific historical events and contexts; rather, they were designed to denote more generic and universal properties of human action, interaction, and organization. Yet, much like Weber's more analytical ideal types, Parsons moved rather quickly from "unit acts" to "social systems" and beyond. And, given his commitment to classification of phenomena, once he had defined the elements of unit acts in *The Structure of Social Action*, he apparently concluded that there was nothing left for him to do but move on to classification of interaction, social system, systems of action, and the human condition.

Fig. 1.2 summarizes Parsons's model in *The Structure of Social Action*, in which he visualized unit acts as involving a process of making decisions concerning alternative means to ends or goals. These decisions are not ra-

---

[4] Indeed, though Parsons began his career by asking "who now reads Spencer?" he obviously did, since his later work rediscovers Spencer's Synthetic Philosophy. See Turner, 1985b, for details.

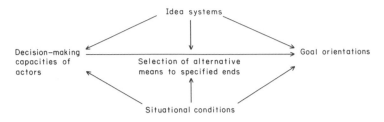

Fig. 1.2. Parsons's conceptualization of unit acts.

tional, in the sense emphasized by utilitarian economics; rather, individuals are constrained by ideas and by the material conditions of a situation. Values, beliefs, norms, and other symbols constrain what actors see as appropriate goals and what alternatives are perceived as relevant. Similarly, the ecology of a situation and the biology of the actors circumscribe the perception of both goals and means.

This model reconciles, as is well known, Parsons's synthesis of diverse intellectual traditions—particularly idealism, utilitarianism, and positivism. As is evident, this is a model of human behavior or action, not *inter*action. It is an improvement over Weber, because one can visualize something actually occurring in unit acts. However, although it classifies elements of action, it tells us nothing of how people use these and other capacities to *inter*act. Parsons recognized this limitation near the end of *The Structure of Social Action* when he wrote "any atomistic system that deals only with the properties identifiable in the unit act . . . will of necessity fail to treat these latter elements adequately and be indeterminate as applied to complex systems" (Parsons, 1937: 748–49).[5] I doubt if he knew then just how far he was to go, but he saw the problem; and by 1949 he recognized that "the structure of social systems cannot be derived directly from the actor-situation frame of reference. It requires functional analysis of the complications introduced by the interaction of a plurality of actors" (Parsons, 1949: 229). This transition from "unit acts" to "systems of interaction" was made in *The Social System*. In Fig. 1.3, I have represented Parsons's argument in a way that facilitates comparison with Weber's similar model in Fig. 1.1.

Much like Weber, Parsons defines the process of action as involving "orientations" that can be classified as "motivational" and "value." In true ideal-type fashion, Parsons then classifies each of these orientations,

---

[5] Unfortunately, elements of the "unit act" portrayed in Fig. 1.2 became full blown action systems *before* Parsons had adequately conceptualized interaction. Idea systems became the cultural system; decision-making and goal-orienting dynamics became the psychological system, as later embellished by Freudian concepts; situational conditions became the organismic and, later, the behavioral system; and elements of situational conditions (positions) and idea systems (norms) became the social system.

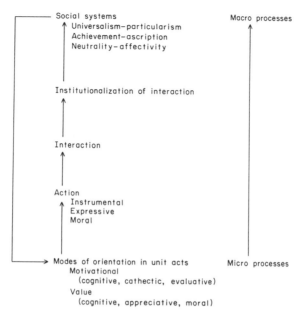

Fig. 1.3. Parsons's conceptualization of action, interaction, and institutionalization.

which, when combined, produce three types of action that look very much like Weber's three types of "social action." Action becomes "interaction" when variously oriented actors must reconcile their respective orientations; and when such reconciliations become more stable, or "institutionalized," then a "social system" can be said to exist. Such social systems can be classified, or typified, in terms of Parsons's famous "pattern variables," which, once again, are very similar to the distinctions that Weber makes for types of social relations and legitimated orders.

The substantive details of Parsons's argument are not my main concern, but rather the logic of his argument. Parsons merely classifies orientations, actions, and social systems. He does not inform us about the *processes* involved in motivation,[6] in forming value orientations, in developing a line of action, in interacting with others, and in structuring social relations. Moreover, he does not even offer a typology of interaction, though, curiously, he offers typologies for everything else—orientations, actions, and social systems. He simply jumps over interaction in much the same way as Weber did; and as with Weber, he never looks back as he moves into ever more macro conceptualization of social reality.

[6] Even Parsons's perceptive Freudian analysis of cathexis and internalization becomes more classificatory than process oriented. See Parsons and Shils, 1951.

Toward a New Strategy

In light of all this, I do not think that Parsons's approach ever marked a promising beginning for the analysis of micro processes. Static typologies do not easily allow for the analysis of processes; and as noted, they have a tendency to move rather quickly into macro analysis, without specifying the underlying micro processes.[7] I am not arguing that theory must necessarily be micro before it can legitimately be macro. But both Weber and Parsons asserted the primacy of social action (i.e., meaningful orientations of individuals) as *the* subject matter of sociology; and of course Parsons called his approach the "theory of action." And so it is their failure to practice what they preached that makes them both open to criticism.

I should also emphasize that it is equally reasonable to move from macro to micro; and in fact, Parsons and Weber did this more than their avowed advocacy of going from micro to macro. More fundamentally, however, I do not believe that it is necessary to reconcile micro and macro or to move back and forth between these two realms, at least at this stage in the development of sociological theory. It is perfectly reasonable to perform analysis of micro interactive processes, taking macrostructures as a given. Alternatively, it is equally reasonable to examine macrostructures, taking the process of interaction as a given. And to the extent that Parsons and Weber did the latter in most of their work, I do not see this as problematic. It is only problematic to the degree that both thought they were adequately conceptualizing the process of interaction.

Perhaps too much effort and attention has been devoted to reconciling micro and macro analysis *before* we have adequate models and theories of either (J. Turner, 1983a, 1986a, 1986b). The result is often dogmatic and/ or metaphorical assertions that macro is nothing but micro processes (Collins, 1975; Blumer, 1969), or vice versa (Mayhew, 1981, 1972; Blau, 1977), without specifying just how such is the case. Or, as is evident with Weber and Parsons, one simply slips past the process of interaction on the way from a typological analysis of action to a typological analysis of social systems.

My critique of Parsons's approach to social interaction is not a new one. Besides Schutz (1932), a wide variety of scholars, from behaviorists (Homans, 1974) to phenomenologists (Garfinkel, 1967) and symbolic interactionists (Blumer, 1969), have been making the same criticism for de-

[7] In contrast, an analysis of processes forces the question of how they flow into each other. Thus, if one begins with a concern with explaining processes, rather than constructing typologies, there is less of a tendency to leap conceptually across critical social dynamics, such as the process of interaction.

cades. Yet the many critics of those static and typological biases have been reluctant to follow the most useful part of Parsons's *The Structure of Social Action*: the analysis of a process in terms of its structural elements. Though Parsons emphasized the wrong process—action as opposed to interaction—and was committed to a typological approach rather than a dynamic modeling strategy, he was at least willing to analyze the generic elements in the structure of a process. In that sense, then, this book is in the Parsonian tradition. I seek to understand the invariant properties in the structure of the most elemental process in sociological analysis, social interaction. In addition, much like Parsons, I will examine nineteenth-century and early twentieth-century thinkers—but I concentrate on those who analyzed *inter*action as opposed to action, behavior, or acts. And I will construct dynamic models about the processes of interaction, rather than static typologies. Before proceeding to the analysis of social interaction, however, let me pause to outline the theoretical strategy that I will employ.

2

A Strategy for Analyzing
Micro Dynamics

As I HAVE ARGUED in many places (J. Turner, 1979, 1981, 1984a, 1984b, 1985a, 1985b, 1985c, 1986a, 1986b), sociology can, and should, be a natural science. It can isolate basic and generic properties of the social universe in much the same manner as other "hard sciences," and it can develop highly abstract laws and models that explain the operative dynamics of these properties. Of course, many social theorists disagree with these assertions; and the burden of proof rests on me to demonstrate the viability of this advocacy.[1]

Nowhere is suspicion of "positivism" greater than in the analysis of interaction. Perhaps more than any other topic in sociology, the process of interaction among individuals is considered to involve spontaneity and indeterminacy, thereby rendering it immune to positivists' assertions. My belief is that at the most fundamental level, social interaction reveals invariant properties that always exist when people interact; and though the substantive flow of interaction in any specific situation can change, it does so in terms of lawlike processes. In this chapter, I outline briefly a strategy for isolating these generic or invariant properties of interaction and for developing abstract theoretical principles and laws that can explain the dynamics of these properties.

Theoretical Versus Historical Explanation

Theory must simplify and pull away from the details of any substantive context. Rather than explaining what makes empirical situations unique, the goal of theory is to understand what they have in common. To understand the unique and idiosyncratic features of an empirical situation, one needs to perform an "historical explanation," or a description of the causal sequence of empirical events leading up to the phenomena under investigation. Most analysts prefer such historical explanations, because they are

[1] Of course, much more than advocacy is involved. Just how a discipline is bureaucratically organized determines whether or not it will see itself as a "hard science." For my argument along these lines, see Fuchs and Turner, 1987.

attuned to substance, content, and context. In contrast, a "theoretical explanation" involves efforts to visualize a particular phenomenon as an instance or example of a more fundamental process that is depicted in abstract models and propositions. Obviously, there are long-term philosophical debates over such distinctions, and I do not wish to become embroiled in them here. Instead, my purpose is to outline a strategy for developing theoretical explanations that use abstract laws and models to understand social phenomena. I should note that historical and theoretical explanations are not contradictory; they simply yield different types of knowledge, although the knowledge sought by science must, in the end, constitute a storehouse of theoretical principles and models. Yet I will not argue that scientific knowledge is inherently superior; I only emphasize that it is the kind of knowledge that is sought in this book.

Developing Theoretical Explanations

Much sociological theory is heavily encumbered with philosophical baggage. Far too often, I believe, the great debates over epistemology, ontology, and the like are rekindled and become the major topic in "theorizing." But philosophizing is best left to the philosophers; and while any strategy for building theory has philosophical implications, a great deal of energy in sociology has been devoted to agonizing over what are, in essence, unresolvable philosophical issues. Indeed, we have more meta-theory than theory in sociology; and so, at the outset, let me caution that I will simply ignore the philosophical questions that my approach raises.[2]

My strategy is simple (J. Turner, 1985c): (1) define a generic property of the social universe, which in the present case is social interaction; (2) construct a broad sensitizing scheme to denote its fundamental elements; (3) develop analytical models delineating the operative processes for each of these elements; and (4) articulate abstract laws that express the relations among these operative processes. Let me elaborate on each of these points.

A Definition of Social Interaction

Theory must begin with a definition that denotes a timeless and invariant property of the universe. Such a property is "social interaction," which is defined as a situation where the behaviors of one actor are consciously

---

[2] If I am asked to make a critique of Jeffrey C. Alexander's (1984, 1987) most scholarly and provocative work, it is this: overconcern with presuppositions tends to prevent scholars from actually theorizing—that is, telling us how things work. True, after someone has theorized, we can extract implicit assumptions; but when one begins theoretical activity agonizing over presuppositions, it is difficult to ever get around to the actual theorizing. (Who knows? If I am lucky, perhaps, I can be included as part of Alexander's "twenty-first lecture.")

reorganized by, and influence the behaviors of, another actor, and vice versa. I am using the term "behavior" in the broadest sense to include the overt movements of individuals in space, the covert or "mental" deliberations of individuals, and the physiological processes of individuals. At its most intense level, then, social interaction is the process whereby the overt movements, covert deliberations, and basic physiology of one individual influence those of another, and vice versa. Less intense social interaction would, of course, have lower values for one or all of these basic dimensions of behavior.

Social interaction is the most elementary unit of sociological analysis. The study of behavior per se is the proper subject matter of psychology, whereas sociology studies the *organization* of individuals, which can only begin with social interaction. Thus, the theoretical ideas that I will propose do not seek to explain behavior per se, but only as it is implicated in the process of social interaction.

Although social interaction is the elementary process in all social organization, I am not asserting that social structure can only be understood in these terms. I believe that micro and macro sociology are separate kinds of analyses, each equally valid in its own right. Micro sociology examines the properties of social interaction, whereas macro sociology studies the properties of populations of individuals. For most purposes, micro sociology brackets out of consideration macro dynamics, while the latter takes the fact that individuals interact as a given. This is a reasonable division of intellectual activity; and in fact, until more mature theories of micro and macro processes are developed, it is wise to sustain this division. Hence, the theoretical strategy that I am proposing makes little effort to bridge the micro-macro gap; it is simply a proposal for figuring out how social interaction among individuals operates.[3]

A Sensitizing Scheme

To be a topic of theorizing, a basic social process must be broken down into its constituent elements. In my view, social interaction is a series of processes, each of which requires separate theoretical principles. Indeed, theorizing about social interaction has tended to be rather global in that one scheme is often proposed for all aspects of this process. I suspect that this is why action theory (Parsons, 1951) retreated into static typologies of interaction, for in this way, one could avoid the detailed analysis of its con-

---

[3] However, once one has a more precise theory of social interaction, it is reasonable to examine how macrostructural processes influence the weights and values of the variables in the micro theory. Such an exercise requires an explicit theory of both micro and macro dynamics. This volume is about the micro, another in preparation (J. Turner, n.d.*a*.) is about macro dynamics, and perhaps a third will seek to bridge the gap.

Fig. 2.1. The elements of social interaction.

stituent properties. Similarly, those approaches that have emphasized the process of interaction have tended to be chauvinistic in that they view interaction as understandable in terms of only *one* process, whether this be exchange (Homans, 1961), ethnomethods (Garfinkel, 1967), symbolic interaction (Blumer, 1969), dramaturgy (Goffman, 1959), or interaction rituals (Collins, 1986). These approaches do, of course, conceptualize a variety of processes, but these various processes are rarely viewed as separate topics of theorizing. As a result, social interaction is often seen as a unitary phenomenon.

My sense is that social interaction can be broken down into three separate processes, each of which requires different theoretical models and principles. One might wish to perform further partitioning, but Fig. 2.1 presents the sensitizing scheme that will guide my analysis in subsequent chapters. Fig. 2.1 asserts that social interaction should be viewed as three separate, but obviously interrelated, processes: motivational, interactional, and structuring. At a minimum, then, we need to develop separate models and principles for these three processes.

By motivational processes, I simply mean that, to varying degrees and in diverse ways, individuals are energized and mobilized in their interactions with others. People are willing, or unwilling, to deposit energy in their dealings with each other; and this fact is what I am denoting by the term "motivation." The issue of motivation has, of course, been highly problematic in the social sciences, but we must nonetheless analyze the processes denoted by this rubric. For people *are* mobilized, energized, compelled, and driven to behave in various ways; we cannot ignore this dimension of reality. My approach will be limiting in the sense that, for a sociologist, motivation is only relevant to the degree that it influences the process of interaction. I will not develop a theory of motivation per se, but only models and propositions that allow us to understand what mobilizes people as they interact with each other (J. Turner, 1987).

By interactional processes, I denote what people actually do when they influence each other's behavior. Elsewhere, I have called this phase "the mechanics" of interaction (J. Turner, 1986c), because it involves the controlled operation of humans' behavioral capacities. In broad strokes, these capacities involve signaling a course of behavior and, at the same time, interpreting both one's own behavioral signals and those of others.

I separate motivational and interactional processes, because if they are collapsed together into one process, our understanding of social interaction is reduced. For example, as will be emphasized in later chapters, exchange theory in both its behaviorist (Homans, 1961) and utilitarian (Coleman, 1972) forms is a theory of motivation, because it says little about what people actually do when they interact. Instead, it tells us why they mobilize varying degrees of energy in an interaction situation. And so, to the extent that one views social interaction only in exchange-theoretic terms, a theory of motivation will be imposed upon other critical processes, with the result that our understanding of these other processes will be very limited. Conversely, symbolic interactionism (Blumer, 1969) is primarily a theory of interactional processes, providing only a limited conceptualization of motivational dynamics. Thus, again, to the degree that symbolic interactionism is forced to be a theory of motivation, understanding of both motivational and interactional processes will decrease.

This same line of argument applies to the third element in the sensitizing scheme in Fig. 2.1: we should view the process of structuring as a separate topic of theory. My use of the term "structuring" is intended to denote the fact that social interactions are often repeated across time as well as organized in physical space. As I will argue, these structuring processes cannot be conceptualized solely in terms of motivational and interactional dynamics. Theories of motivation as well as of signaling and interpreting are rather inadequate when it comes to informing us how and why social interactions become structured. We should not, therefore, try to make a theory of motivation or signaling and interpreting also a theory of structuring.

Motivational, interactional, and structuring processes are interrelated in the pattern delineated by the arrows in Fig. 2.1. Just how people signal and interpret is related to their motivational energies; in turn, motivation is circumscribed by prevailing structural arrangements as well as by the course of signaling and interpreting; and the structure of an interaction is very much determined by the motivational profiles of individuals as these affect their signaling and interpreting activities. Thus, the point of developing separate propositions and models is, in the end, to see how they causally influence each other. Without separating them as suggested in Fig. 2.1, we cannot fully appreciate the operative dynamics of social interaction.

Developing Analytical Models

The key to understanding each of the three processes delineated in Fig. 2.1, and, at the same time, appreciating their mutual causal effects, is the construction of what I have termed "analytical models" (J. Turner, 1985c, 1986a, 1986b). While the notion of "model" is ambiguous, especially in the social sciences, the term is used here to mean the visual representation in space of variables and their interrelations. An analytical model is one that is highly abstract and represents general classes of variables and their causal relations. Thus, for each of the three constituent processes of social interaction—motivational, interactional, structuring—it is useful to construct a model delineating the relevant classes of variables and their most important causal relations.

Such models, I believe, can provide a picture of process—that is, of how variables influence each other across time. Moreover, they can also give us a view of complex causal processes. Too often in sociology, we employ simple causal models (Duncan, 1966; Blalock, 1964) that document one-way causal chains among empirical indicators of independent, intervening, and dependent variables. But actual social processes are much more complex, involving feedback loops, reciprocal causal effects, lag effects, threshold effects, and the like. Analytical models seek to capture this complexity by accentuating *configurations* of causal effects among generic classes of variables implicated in a basic social process.[4]

Despite their utility in delineating complex causal processes, analytical models are difficult to test empirically. Their very strength—providing a picture of complex configurations of causality—makes them too global to test as a whole. No one research project, or series of projects, could possibly test the validity of the entire model, and as a result, analytical models can become excessively detached from the empirical processes that they supposedly help us understand. Hence, analytical models must be translated into abstract propositions or principles—the last element of the theoretical strategy that I will pursue in the following chapters.

Formulating Abstract Principles

The ultimate goal of scientific activity is, I believe, to formulate abstract laws about the basic properties of the universe, including the social universe. These laws articulate the relationships among variable processes in the universe; and while mathematical languages can specify relationships more precisely (J. Turner, 1984a, 1984b), we will have to limp along with words, at least for the time being.

I think there is creative synergy between abstract analytical models and propositions. An abstract proposition informs us about how variation in one property is caused by variations in another or others, but it does not specify the processes by which this connection operates. A model can do

[4] I think that many of the pointed remarks in Stanley Lieberson's *Making It Count* (1986) are relevant here. However, he criticizes as a methodologist-theorist; my critique comes as a theorist who sees a great deal of ritualism in the conduct of social research. I hope I will provide some hypotheses that researchers might wish to test in a somewhat less ritualistic way.

this, but unlike a law, it cannot state relationships among variables with sufficient parsimony. By working back and forth between abstract principles and models, then, we formulate testable propositions and, at the same time, visualize social reality in its more robust and complex patterns. A principle gives us a testable statement, whereas an analytical model provides a description of the causal processes that connect the variables in the principle. By formulating laws and then asking what processes are involved, we are moved to create analytical models; and conversely, by developing models depicting configurations of causal processes, we are led to translate these into more parsimonious and testable propositions.

It does not matter where one begins in this creative process; one can start with either models or propositions. The important task is to move back and forth between the two. The end result is a better explanation of how the universe is structured and how it operates. In the chapters to follow, I begin with models, then see how they can be used to formulate abstract laws of motivational, interactional, and structuring processes. I could have begun with the laws, as I have elsewhere (J. Turner, 1984a, 1984b, 1986b), but for this project, I find the models a more satisfactory place to initiate theorizing.

Conclusion and Preview

Theory building is, of course, a creative process; and the strategy that I will employ here is simply my own approach. I am not asserting that this is the only possible strategy, just that it is the one that I tend to follow. However, I do contend that the goal of theory is to develop abstract laws about timeless and generic properties of the social universe. Many will disagree with this advocacy, especially a large proportion of those who study the process of interaction. Yet, even if one does not share my goal, or the strategy for pursuing it, the analysis in the next chapters may still prove interesting. Let me anticipate these chapters by offering a brief preview of their contents.

Chapters 3 and 4 begin my analysis of motivational processes in interaction. In these chapters, I extract the basic theoretical ideas from a variety of general theoretical perspectives, including utilitarianism, behaviorism, exchange, and interactionism. I also borrow key ideas from the works of specific individuals, including George Herbert Mead, Emile Durkheim, Sigmund Freud, Anthony Giddens, Randall Collins, and Harold Garfinkel. In these and other works are to be found important concepts, models, and propositions; but I extract selectively from their texts. Then in Chapter 5, I put these selected concepts back together again by developing a composite model of motivational processes and several synthesizing principles.

Perhaps I should pause to explain my eclecticism, since it is a part of the theoretical strategy that I will employ. One of the great problems in sociological theory, I believe, is the often inflexible encampment of theorists in a "school" or in the work of one or two "great masters." Much in-depth and creative work has, of course, emerged from various camps, but so has a great deal of acrimony and intellectual stubbornness. My approach seeks to break down these barriers through the selective and eclectic use of ideas from what are often perceived as incompatible viewpoints. I find these diverse perspectives highly compatible in the sense that they complement each other: each adds something that the others ignore or miss; together, they provide a more robust explanation of motivational processes. This is true of the mixing of different viewpoints for all three of the elements of social interaction.

I will, no doubt, be accused of taking ideas out of their original context and of violating the sacred presuppositions of important thinkers. Exactly, but I see this intellectual "sin" of de-contextualization as the strength of my approach. I will indeed rip (and tear, grab, and otherwise extract) ideas from their context, especially if I believe that the context is incorrect. Too often, we feel obligated to examine ideas only as they were originally formulated. In contrast, I suggest that if only some ideas of a thinker or school of thought are insightful and the rest are wrong, then we should have no reservations about excising ideas and using them for our own purposes. In fact, such efforts liberate ideas and set them free so that their power can be more fully appreciated. Thus, I should forewarn that no perspective or thinker is sacred;[5] and to maintain intellectual barriers by using ideas only in their original proponents' scheme is, in my view, intellectual folly. It commits us to dogmatism and chauvinism, while partitioning and diluting our theoretical efforts.

Chapters 6, 7, and 8 are thus very much like Chapters 3, 4, and 5 in their eclecticism. They focus on the second element of social interaction, the process of signaling and interpreting. I open where I think Parsons should have paused, if he was to be serious about social action. In Chapter 6, the conceptual canopy provided by George Herbert Mead is examined and then some of the phenomenological refinements in Alfred Schutz's work are introduced. Mead's and Schutz's efforts are seen as the theoretical base for all subsequent theoretical analyses of signaling and interpreting. Using this base, I then introduce in Chapter 7 the conceptual refinements developed

[5] Indeed, as one reviewer of this manuscript noted, perhaps I should indicate that in using others' works, I selectively translate and impose my views. Such is, no doubt, the case. Yet, if we are really to stand on the shoulders of giants, we often need to restructure their conceptual torsos.

in Erving Goffman's dramaturgy as well as his analysis of frames and ritual, Ralph H. Turner's role theory, Jürgen Habermas's analysis of speech acts and communicative action, and Harold Garfinkel's ethnomethodology. Other theorists are discussed, but my view is that this group developed the most important conceptual refinements to Mead's and Schutz's seminal analysis. With these refinements, I propose in Chapter 8 a composite model and a number of abstract laws on the processes of signaling and interpreting.

Chapters 9 and 10 turn to the process of structuring. Here, too, I borrow heavily from others but recombine their ideas in new ways. The emphasis is on how signaling and interpreting are used to organize interactions in space and to stretch them across time. In analyzing these questions, I examine early theories of structure, such as those presented by Durkheim, Spencer, Weber, Mead, and Schutz. Then I supplement these early approaches by reexamining Parsonian functionalism in the context of other modern approaches, including those developed by Erving Goffman, Anthony Giddens, Randall Collins, and various symbolic interactionists.

Finally, in Chapters 12 and 13, I offer some propositions that are suggested by the models of motivational, interactional, and structuring processes, especially as these flow into each other in the pattern outlined in Fig. 2.1. These propositions are, in one sense, "the laws of interaction" as I see them; yet, in a more realistic sense, they are only provisional hypotheses that I offer to my fellow theorists and, perhaps more importantly, to researchers, who often view the work of theorists as irrelevant to their work.

II

Motivational Processes

3

Early Models of Motivation

FEW WOULD DISAGREE with the observation that, to some degree, internal psychological forces mobilize, drive, energize, and organize individual perceptions, actions, and interactions. Yet conceptualization of these processes remains highly problematic; and in fact, the inability to determine just what "motivation" is, and how it operates, has led many to abandon the topic. This is a mistake, since motivation is one of the most fundamental properties of the social universe. Moreover, to avoid the topic is also unrealistic, because most theories of human behavior, interaction, and organization reveal an implicit model of motivation, though this is often unrecognized for what it is or is disguised by new terms and concepts. Thus, we cannot avoid addressing the topic of motivation; it is too basic and fundamental to human interaction for us to tiptoe around it.

Motivation as a Property of Human Interaction

My orientation to the question of motivation is limited by the purpose of this book: to understand human interaction. I do not seek to develop a conceptualization of motivation per se, but rather a more delimited view of what energizes and organizes individuals' responses during the course of their interaction. I leave it to psychology to provide a more encompassing analysis; my goal in this and the next two chapters is sociological, although I suspect that much of what I have to say is relevant to psychology and social psychology.

In this chapter, I will perform a hypothetical exercise: at the time that Talcott Parsons was writing *The Structure of Social Action* (1937), what models of motivation were available to him? Parsons concentrated on the utilitarian model, as modified by Weber's and Durkheim's more sociological approaches. But what other models existed in the 1930's? What if Parsons had examined these? The point is more than historical. In many ways, we still use these early models in contemporary theorizing, although they are altered somewhat from their original profile.

What, then, was the range of theoretical approaches to motivation in the late 1930's? There was, of course, the utilitarian model of Adam Smith, Jeremy Bentham, John Stuart Mill, and others. There was also the behaviorist model, first developed by Ivan Petrovich Pavlov and Edward Lee Thorndike and then translated into methodological dogma by John B. Watson and later B. F. Skinner. Additionally, there were the two social behaviorist models developed by George Herbert Mead, one focusing on the phases of acts and the other on a social interaction. There existed—virtually unrecognized—an exchange model developed by Georg Simmel's critique of Marx. There was the emerging psychoanalytic model, inspired by Freud, that delved into the unconscious parameters of human behavior. And finally, there was a social solidarity model developed by Emile Durkheim and members of the Année School.

Other models existed at this time, but these were the most relevant to sociology. And if we look at contemporary theories of motivation, especially the implicit and unrecognized ones, these models remain the most widely used by present-day sociologists. It is useful, therefore, to review each of these approaches by extracting their key elements and arranging them into dynamic models. In this way, we can better appreciate their importance to contemporary sociological theories of motivation, which are examined in the next chapter.

Utilitarian, Behaviorist, and Exchange Models

The most dominant model of motivation in the Western world is utilitarianism, though, as Parsons (1937) emphasized and as more contemporary critics (e.g., Granovetter, 1986) have stressed, it is a highly deficient account of human behavior. And yet, among some contemporary sociologists (e.g., Coleman, 1975, 1973, 1972, 1966) who should know better, it is becoming the underlying model of what motivates human interaction. Even its early advocates, such as Adam Smith, David Ricardo, John Stuart Mill, and Jeremy Bentham, were more likely than some present-day sociologists to recognize the limitations of utilitarian explanations.

Despite its limitations and the seemingly unreflective incorporation of purely economic models into sociology, the utilitarian approach does capture some of the motivational dynamics in human behavior and interaction. Fig. 3.1 presents the essential elements of the utilitarian model as it stood in the early decades of this century (and as it still stands today).

There is always the assumption in utilitarian models that actors are "rational," that they weigh and assess alternative lines of conduct in terms of their payoffs, or "utilities." Early formulations also assumed that actors had access to all the relevant information necessary to assess payoffs and that they would seek to maximize their utilities. In turn, an individual's hierarchy of values, or preferences, determines whether or not an action

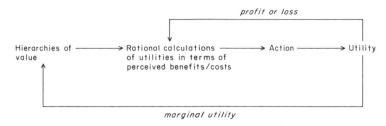

Fig. 3.1. The utilitarian model of motivation.

will bring utility, or gratifications. In some early versions of utilitarianism, and even in some of the more recent versions, there is a presumption that people do possess well-ordered hierarchies of value and that rational calculations are conducted in terms of this hierarchy. Actors thus seek to maximize utilities in the sense of realizing those preferences high in their hierarchies of value, with the result that their calculations of costs and benefits as well as their eventual actions are measured against ordered sets of preferences.

Utilitarian models are cybernetic in that they include two kinds of feedback loops. First, there is always a principle of "marginal utility" that changes an actor's hierarchy of values. The more of a given utility that actors receive, the less valuable it becomes and the lower will be its rank ordering in an actor's preference structure. Second, there is an assessment of "profit or loss" for each act, which is incorporated into the rational calculations for future actions. Moreover, calculations will also involve assessments about the probability of receiving a given utility, based on past experiences and/or access to relevant information about obstacles and options. Action will, therefore, be a function of rational calculations circumscribed by four interrelated forces: hierarchies of value, alterations in these hierarchies by marginal utility, experiences in receiving profits or losses in situations, and access to relevant information about probabilities of receiving varying utilities for different courses of action.

The criticisms of utilitarian models are well known, and I need not offer a complete listing here. For my more limited purposes, a few objections are most relevant. First, utilitarian models tend to be *a*social in that other actors are not present, or, when they are inserted into the model, they are part of an amorphous and competitive marketplace. Hence, utilitarianism is a theory of behavior or action, but not interaction. Yet, as we will see, the development of exchange theory greatly obviated this criticism. Second, in reality, actors do not have well-ordered hierarchies of value. In fact, I suspect that preferences are not highly structured; instead, as Emerson (1986) noted, humans possess domains of value that are *not* rank ordered or highly structured. Action is, therefore, rarely conducted with reference to a clear yardstick of value. Third, calculations are hardly ever "rational," for several reasons: hierarchies of value are not clear-cut; access to relevant information is rarely complete; experience with profits and losses in past situations is often difficult to remember or use in new situations; and maximization of utilities is rarely sought by actors.

Yet, despite these and many other flaws, the model in Fig. 3.1 has, to make a bad pun, some utility. Interaction does involve, at times, calculations and assessments of costs and rewards; it does involve efforts to realize some utility and to avoid costs or losses; it does involve, in a rather loose and amorphous manner, the invocation of preferences; it always reveals feedback processes where the utilities received at time$_1$ circumscribe actions and the effort to receive rewards at time$_2$. This is, of course, pretty much the same conclusion that Parsons reached in *The Structure of Social Action*, although he failed to develop a very sophisticated alternative in light of these qualifications (see Fig. 1.2).

More tangential, but nonetheless evident in Parsons's early analysis of action, was behaviorism, which presented a model very similar to that of utilitarianism. The model was originally developed independently by the Russian physiologist Ivan Petrovich Pavlov (1928) and the American psychologist Edward Lee Thorndike (1932). Pavlov's fortuitous observations with experimental dogs and his subsequent controlled experiments led to the formulation of several basic principles: (1) a stimulus consistently associated with another stimulus producing a given physiological response will, by itself, elicit that response ("conditioned response"); (2) these conditioned responses can be "extinguished" when gratifications associated with stimuli are no longer forthcoming; (3) stimuli that are similar to those producing a conditioned response can also elicit the same response as the original stimulus ("response generalization"); and (4) stimuli that increasingly differ from those used to condition a particular response will decreasingly be able to elicit this response ("response discrimination"). In contrast to Pavlov's controlled experiments, primarily on physiological responses to stimuli, Thorndike's initial studies were on trial and error behavior of animals, but the results were much the same, as can be seen from Thorndike's three principles: (1) the "law of effect," which holds that acts in a situation producing gratification will be more likely to occur in the future when that situation recurs; (2) the "law of use," which states that a situation-response connection is strengthened with repetition and practice; and (3) the "law of disuse," which argues that the connection will weaken when the gratifications associated with a situation-response situation decrease.

These basic ideas, which are very close to utilitarian views of actors as behaving in ways so as to seek rewards or utilities and avoid costs and pun-

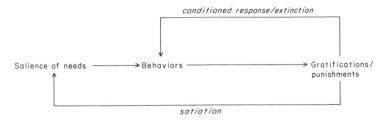

Fig. 3.2. The behaviorist model of motivation.

ishments, were first molded into extreme behaviorism by John B. Watson (1913, 1919), and later by B. F. Skinner (1938, 1953). For Watson abandoned the utilitarian emphasis on rational calculation with the dogmatic assertion that "introspection forms no essential part of [behaviorism's] method, nor is the scientific value of its data dependent upon the readiness with which they lend themselves to interpretation in terms of consciousness" (Watson, 1913: 158). Instead, emphasis was to be on observable responses associated with observable stimuli, with psychologists staying out of the "mystery box" of human cognition.

Later behaviorists were to be less dogmatic and more willing to entertain a limited view of human cognition. Moreover, even extreme behaviorism implicitly invoked cognitive processes, since it assumed that responses that brought gratifications would be retained. Notions of gratification and reward reintroduced utilitarian concerns about hierarchies of value, although behaviorists minimized this concern by structuring an organism's hierarchy of value in terms of imposed deprivations of valued rewards (such as water and food). But the very imposition of deprivations assumes that there is a hierarchy, or at least a varying salience of needs, that can change in light of gratifications or punishments. And as one moves to the analysis of human behavior, one must assume complex systems of needs as mediating stimuli and responses. Thus, while the behaviorists did not explicitly introduce the process of calculation into their models, the other elements of those models are virtually the same as those in utilitarianism formulations. This can be seen by comparing the behaviorist model depicted in Fig. 3.2 to the utilitarian model of Fig. 3.1.

Instead of utilities, behaviorism stresses gratifications or punishments; rather than marginal utility, behaviorism refers to satiation; as an alternative to calculations of costs and profits, behaviorism analyzes conditioned responses and extinction; and instead of utilitarian concerns over hierarchies of value, behaviorism introduces inferences about the salience of needs (as determined by levels of deprivation).

All the criticisms of utilitarianism are also relevant for behaviorism, with the additional proviso that behaviorism tends to ignore what is dis-

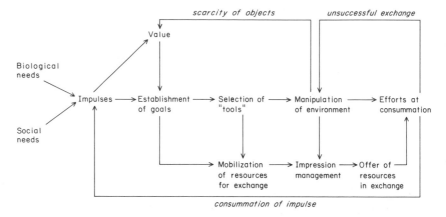

Fig. 3.3. Simmel's early exchange model of action and interaction.

tinctly human: complex cognitive capacities. While utilitarians fail to recognize fully this complexity, they have at least acknowledged the importance of mental processes.

As we will see in the next chapter, utilitarianism and behaviorism have become blended into theories of *inter*action, as opposed to behavior or action, with the emergence of modern exchange theory. But even at the time that Parsons was writing, Georg Simmel (1907) had articulated all the elements of contemporary exchange theory. Parsons was not alone in his failure to analyze Simmel's model; indeed, none of the most prominent figures in modern exchange theory acknowledges, or seems aware of, Simmel's formulation.

One reason for the failure to appreciate Simmel's approach to motivation is that it is found in a more philosophical work where the explicit goal is to critique Karl Marx's "labor theory of value" and, at the same time, to analyze the consequences of money in human affairs. Yet, as he develops his argument, Simmel proposes two models that are relevant for us and that certainly would have been important for Parsons. One is a general model of human action, very similar to Mead's (1938); the other is a model of social exchange that anticipates modern exchange theory. In Fig. 3.3 I have merged the two models in a manner that is consistent with Simmel's argument.[1]

The middle portions of the model, moving from left to right, summarize

[1] Obviously, I have taken some conceptual liberties in presenting Simmel's ideas in this model, but I believe that Fig. 3.3 summarizes his argument accurately. What has always amazed me is contemporary theorists' apparent unwillingness to appreciate the power in Simmel's ideas with respect to motivational issues.

Simmel's general view of human action. The motivation for action is an "impulse" that reflects either biological or social needs. Impulses lead humans to establish goals or ends that they perceive will consummate an impulse. To realize the goals, individuals select relevant "tools"; Simmel's view of tools is very broad and includes all those resources—material and symbolic—that people can mobilize to realize goals. Actors then manipulate the environment with their tools or resources and, depending on their success, may consummate their impulses. If the environment presents barriers to the satisfaction of impulses, then manipulations become more covert as actors rehearse and think about ways to realize their goals. Moreover, it is in this blockage of goals that "value" inheres, for those ends and objects that cannot be easily attained increase in value for the actor. Indeed, since the actor will now need to use more "tools" or resources and engage in more complex and costly manipulations, these ends or objects come to have more value. Thus far, the model in Fig. 3.3 is similar to Mead's model, which is presented in Fig. 3.4, although in many ways it is less sophisticated.

Yet it is the blending of this model of action with exchange concepts that marks Simmel's contribution. When Simmel addresses the question of exchange per se, he adds the top and bottom portions presented in Fig. 3.3. He does not himself do this diagrammatically, as I have done, but his intent is reasonably clear with a careful reading of the discursive text (Simmel, 1907: 66–98). Those objects and ends that are not easily attained, that are scarce, or that are controlled by others will be valuable to an actor, especially if their attainment is necessary to realize goals established to consummate strong impulses. Thus, value inheres in one's needs or impulses, as well as in the scarcity of objects necessary to consummate these impulses. Such valued objects become a principal criterion for the establishment of goals and for the selection of tools, which involves the mobilization of resources—both material and symbolic—for exchange.

As actors enter the manipulation phase of the act in an exchange, they engage in impression management in order to conceal their need for the resources (objects) of others and to highlight the value of their own resources. Such impression management, Simmel argued, creates an inevitable tension in interaction, which, when impression management becomes outright misrepresentation, can erupt into conflict. Still, impression management represents an offer of resources to another in exchange for their resources, and if others accept, then exchange occurs. Yet, because actors often conceal the actual nature of resources, consummation does not always result; if manipulation does not lead to an exchange of resources, or if the exchange does not yield what was bargained for, then the scarcity of objects increases, as does their value. As a result, their pursuit will become ever more salient in an actor's establishment of goals, selection of tools, and manipulations of relations with others.

Simmel also recognized that exchange relations involve a power dimension. His basic argument is that the more one actor values the resources of another, the greater the latter's potential power over the former. Moreover, the more an actor possesses "liquid" resources, such as money, which have generalized exchange value, the greater will be the potential power of that actor in exchange relations (Simmel, 1907: 98).

For Simmel, then, action becomes *inter*action through the exchange of resources. The dynamics of interaction revolve around the respective value of actors' resources, their capacity to mobilize symbolic and material resources, their abilities at impression management, and the resulting ability to gain power by making other actors value one's resources. In this line of argument are all the basic elements of modern exchange theory, as we will see in the next chapter.

In sum, by the end of the first decade in this century, the utilitarian tradition had already been transformed into an exchange theory of motivation. The further merger of behaviorism into exchange theory was decades away, but for all who would look closely, the affinity of the three models was readily apparent. Yet, as Parsons (1937) approached the topic of social action, he missed this affinity, as did all scholars until recent decades. And, as I will argue in the next chapter, it is in the further merging of exchange theory with interactionist theory that a more adequate theory of motivation is to be found.

One very evident avenue of convergence was in Simmel's and Mead's respective models of action (compare Figs. 3.3 and 3.4); and since Simmel superimposed an exchange theory over this model of action as he moved to the analysis of *inter*action, it is even more surprising that no one in these early decades picked up this potential fit between the emerging interactionism inspired by Mead and the exchange theory developed by Simmel. Another avenue of convergence was Mead's behaviorism and the affinities of behaviorism with utilitarianism (on which Mead himself remarked). Mead's (1934) most important work on interaction represented a critique of Watson's (1913) extreme methodological position, leading Mead to term his approach "*social* behaviorism." Such social behaviorism reintroduced "thought and reflection," thereby making it highly compatible with utilitarianism, and potentially, with Simmel's exchange approach.

There were, then, these several lines of convergence, which Parsons and others ignored. For Parsons, this is a rather remarkable oversight—as an American he should have been more aware of Mead; and as a German-

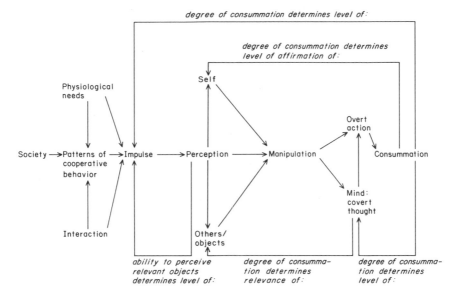

Fig. 3.4. Mead's social behavior model of motivation.

speaking scholar who earned advanced degrees in Germany, he should have been more familiar with Simmel.

Mead's Social Behaviorism

Mead is sometimes accused of not developing a theory of motivation. This conclusion is not entirely fair, although he did tend to concentrate more on the process of interaction per se than on those processes motivating such interaction. Yet, in *The Philosophy of the Act* and in various portions of *Mind, Self, and Society*, he did provide an outline of a general theory of motivation. In Fig. 3.4, I have synthesized his ideas from these two works. Mead's explicit model of motivation comes from his analysis of the phases of "the act" (Mead, 1938): impulse, perception, manipulation, and consummation. These phases are placed in the middle portions of the model in Fig. 3.4. The more peripheral elements in the model represent my superimposition of concepts from *Mind, Self, and Society*, where emphasis is on the process of *inter*action as opposed to "acts" or "action."

The editors of *The Philosophy of the Act* imposed, incorrectly I think, the notion of discrete "stages" in Mead's conceptualization of the act. Mead's actual analysis envisions configurations of acts, with an individual at any given point in time being typified by a complex of acts at varying phases of consummation. For any one impulse, however, there is a sequencing of phases, although feedback loops are an important dynamic in Mead's model.

An "impulse" is a state of disequilibrium with the environment, or a lack of adjustment and adaptation to one's surroundings. This emphasis on adjustment follows from Mead's "pragmatism"; although he never specified the nature of the environment or the types of potential disequilibrium, these can be inferred from other works. Hence, as the left hand portions of the model in Fig. 3.4 delineate, cooperation with others is the most rewarding activity for humans; and so the inability to adjust and adapt to others will represent the most important class of impulses, especially for sociological analysis. The behavioral tendencies of an individual will, to a large extent, reflect a configuration of adjustments to all the social settings in which this individual participates. Individuals will, of course, be most concerned with adjustment and adaptation to immediate interaction situations in which they find themselves. Impulses emerge, however, *only if* adjustment is not proceeding smoothly.

In a vein similar to Freud, Mead (1938) argued that impulses increase in intensity if they are blocked. Such blockage can occur at any phase of the act: if one cannot perceive relevant objects to eliminate the impulse; if one cannot think of a line of conduct to consummate the impulse; or if overt behaviors do not lead to consummation. Thus, unconsummated impulses, especially those revolving around adjustment and adaptation to others, will build in intensity the longer they go unconsummated.

Impulses create selective perception of objects relevant to the elimination of an impulse. One's perceptual field will reflect the configuration of one's impulses at any given time. Moreover, long-standing impulses will, as they grow in intensity, increasingly circumscribe an individual's perceptual field, including their perceptions of themselves as objects.

The "perception" phase of the act revolves around images of oneself as an object in a situation (what Mead termed the "me") as well as the perception of "others" and "objects" relevant to the consummation of an impulse. For Mead (1934: 113–44) self is conceptualized in two ways: as a more stable self-conception, or structured set of meanings that individuals have about themselves in all situations; and as transitory "images" of themselves in a concrete interaction setting. How individuals perceive and behave in a situation will thus be circumscribed by their more stable self-conception as well as by their more immediate images of themselves. For Mead, "others" in a situation are also conceptualized in two basic ways: as specific people and as "generalized others" or "communities of atti-

tudes" that people use as a perspective or framework for evaluating themselves as objects and for orientating their potential responses. Thus, perceptions of interaction are circumscribed by generalized others (norms,
values, beliefs, and other cultural codes) and by the existence of specific
individuals with whom actors "role-take" (Mead, 1934: 78–83). Conversely, just which generalized other is invoked and which others are perceived as relevant are influenced by the nature and intensity of impulses,
as well as by one's more stable self-conception.

The "manipulation" phase of the act consists of overt behavior and/or
the covert "imaginative rehearsal" of alternative lines of conduct. Mead's
basic generalization on these processes is that, when impulses are blocked,
covert thought will precede further efforts at overt behavior. Thus, once
unreflective behavior does not consummate an impulse, this blockage
stimulates a process of covert reflection made possible by the human capacity for "mind" (Mead, 1934: 76–133). Such "minded deliberations" always involve an effort to reconcile the impulse with one's self-conception
as well as with the others and objects perceived to exist in the situation.
An act can cycle at this manipulation stage for a time, as imaginative rehearsal and the emission of behavior fail to consummate an impulse. Indeed, the longer this blockage persists, Mead argued, then the greater the
strength of the impulse, the more perception of oneself, others, and objects
revolves around this impulse, the more thought processes become domi-
nated by efforts to map out a successful line of adjustment, and the more
overt behavior is guided by the effort to consummate the impulse.[2]

"Consummation" is the elimination of the source of disequilibrium, or
impulse. Consummation also confirms one's conception of oneself, especially if the source of the impulse involves disequilibrium with others.
Moreover, consummation also affirms the appropriateness and relevance
of those generalized others, and to a lesser extent, other persons and objects, invoked in a situation to resolve an impulse. Conversely, blockage of
consummation creates doubts about self-definitions, questions about the
appropriateness of generalized others, and suspicions of persons and objects as relevant to elimination of the impulse.

Such is Mead's model of motivation. I will come back to Mead in later
chapters when discussing the other two elements of interaction, the interactional and the structuring processes, but for the present, my concern is

[2] My sense is that Mead and Freud converge here. Mead appears to have argued that unconsummated impulses increase in intensity with blockage; and as a result, they come to increasingly dominate perception, thought, and action as they grow in intensity. Freud adds, of
course, the notions of unconscious processes and defense mechanisms, such as repression, to
Mead's formulation. But those who claim that Mead does not provide a theory of motivation
have not fully appreciated the implications of his analysis in *The Philosophy of the Act*.

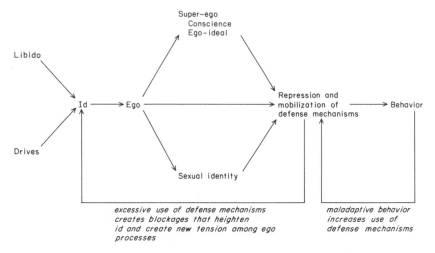

Fig. 3.5. Freud's model of motivation.

with his ideas on what mobilizes and energizes people during interaction. As is evident, Mead presents us with a highly sophisticated model, which, surprisingly, Parsons never incorporated into his early or later efforts. Even more remarkable is the fact that so few scholars (one exception is Shibutani, 1968) have employed Mead's model of motivation, even those working within the interactionist tradition.

The Freudian Psychoanalytic Model

I would be remiss if I did not discuss, if only briefly, Freud's model of motivation, especially since Parsons was later to adopt elements from this model more than any other and since other important theorists who are analyzed in the next chapter have used more sociological adaptations of Freud's analysis. Freud's conceptualizations shifted a bit over time, but in many ways, his early ideas are the most interesting (Freud, 1900). In Fig. 3.5 I present my interpretation of Freud's basic model of motivation.

Contrary to many popular accounts of Freud's ideas, the "id," "ego," and "super-ego" are not entities but processes. In fact, I have arrayed these concepts in a way that emphasizes that they are subprocesses within a more encompassing set of phases. I have also arranged the diagram in a manner that invites comparison with Mead's model in Fig. 3.4, since I see the two as convergent. Before examining each element in the model, let me comment briefly on some general points of convergence. First, like Mead's model, Freud's is cybernetic and involves crucial feedback loops for each phase of action. Second, as noted, "blockage" is a critical element in both models, since the inability to consummate impulses tends to increase their intensity, and thereby their salience, in conscious perceptual processes or in unconscious dreams. Third, both Mead and Freud saw humans' efforts at consummating impulses as mediated by reflective capacities, especially as people seek to reconcile impulses with their sense of identity ("self" for Mead; "sexual identity" for Freud) and with more generalized societal expectations ("generalized other" for Mead; "super-ego" and "ego-ideal" for Freud). Overt behavior thus reflects the conscious—and, for Freud, the often unconscious—mental manipulation of potential lines of conduct, as ego reconciles impulses, self, and societal expectations.

In these general terms, then, Mead's and Freud's models are similar. The major differences between the two thinkers revolve around Freud's emphasis on unconscious processes and the mobilization of defense mechanisms. And in this sense, Freud's ideas represent an important supplement to Mead's and other sociological models, which tend to underemphasize these dynamics.

Turning to the model itself in Fig. 3.5, libido, or sexual drives conceptualized in their broadest sense (sex, love, affection, approval), and other organic and social drives are channeled through "id" processes into a series of impulses that mobilize individuals in their efforts to achieve "cathexis" or consummation. The "ego" reconciles these impulses with "reality" through a series of processes. First, although id processes force ego to heighten perception of relevant ways to consummate an impulse, these impulses must be channeled and controlled by the ego's perception of realities in the external environment, both social and physical. Second, impulses are assessed in terms of general values, standards, and norms of social groupings. This assessment is achieved through the "super-ego," which revolves around two subprocesses: the internalized prohibitions of group standards, or "conscience" in Freud's words; and the internalized "ideals" of social groups, or "ego-ideal" in Freud's terminology. And third, impulses are reconciled with a person's "sexual identity," which, for Freud, involved more than a narrow definition of one's sex.

In order to reconcile id impulses with group standards, self-definitions, and objects in the external world, ego mobilizes defense mechanisms that, in turn, circumscribe overt behavior. Since Freud's data consisted primarily of people exhibiting maladaptive behavior, he probably overemphasized repression and other defense mechanisms. Yet, sociologists have tended to underemphasize these processes; for indeed, behavior and interaction always involve elements of repression (of hurt, anger, frustration, shame, etc.) and the use of multiple defense mechanisms (displacement, projection, reaction-formation, etc.).[3] Of particular importance is Freud's recognition that behavioral maladjustments stemming from repression and use of defense mechanisms feed back upon id and ego processes and, as a consequence, they can become problematic cycles. One cycle revolves around defensive behavior creating further maladjustments, which, in turn, create renewed efforts at readjustment through escalated reliance on defense mechanisms. Another set of cycles concerns the use of repression that leaves powerful id impulses unconsummated, thereby burdening ego processes with the task of reconciling escalating id impulses with self, group standards, and external environmental constraints. Such burdens cause further repression and reliance on defense mechanisms, with the result that id impulses can be further intensified.

If we qualify Freud's analysis with Mead's insight that people are "pragmatic" and that they often achieve successful adjustment to their social environment, then these cycles need not constantly escalate people's energies in pathological directions. Conversely, we need to qualify most sociological theories, which tend to underemphasize the fact that people oftentimes do not adjust well to situations and that such maladjustments set into motion powerful motivating forces. Any effort at developing a general theory of motivation cannot, therefore, ignore this basic insight of Freudian and psychoanalytic theory.

Durkheim's Social Solidarity Model

Emile Durkheim is typically not associated with discussions of motivation, even in sociological circles. Even Parsons's (1937) analysis of Durkheim's contribution to conceptualizing "action" is devoid of much reference to motivating forces, except the general assertion that Durkheim stressed the constraint of ideas. More recent use of Durkheim's approach (e.g., Collins, 1975: 153–55), however, sees him as developing a theory of motivation. Here, the emphasis is on Durkheim's later work (Durkheim, 1912) and the significance of ritual for sustaining an interaction, with the result that as such diverse scholars as Durkheim and Goffman are seen as kindred intellects (Collins, 1975, 1984). My view is that this argument goes a bit too far, but Collins and others are correct in their assertion that an important contribution to motivational analysis is found in Durkheim's analysis in *Elementary Forms of the Religious Life*: humans are motivated

---

[3] This deficiency in sociological theory is, I believe, being increasingly recognized, as the recent resurgence of interest in "the sociology of emotion" appears to document. Let us hope this interest will expand in the future.

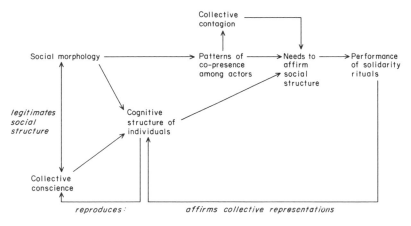

Fig. 3.6. Durkheim's model of motivation.

to affirm the social order, and the vehicle for this affirmation is the use of rituals.

Parsons (1937) did not make use of this insight, but if we combine Durkheim's early works (Durkheim, 1893, 1895) and his later works (Durkheim, 1912; Durkheim and Mauss, 1903), the model presented in Fig. 3.6 emerges. In his earlier works, Durkheim did not seek to specify the social psychological linkage between what he termed "social morphology," or the number of people and their organization into structures, and the "collective conscience," or the "volume," "intensity," "determinateness," and "content" of the symbol systems shared by people in such structures. But if we read between the lines of several works, beginning around 1903 and culminating in the 1912 treatise on religion, the model in Fig. 3.6 summarizes this shift in emphasis from a dogmatically sociologistic to a more social-psychological perspective. The left portion of the model is the early Durkheim, whereas the causal sequence that moves to the right and then feeds back to the left is the later Durkheim. Let me review briefly this set of causal processes.

By the time Durkheim and Marcel Mauss published *Primitive Classification* (1903), Durkheim argued that an individual's cognitive structure with respect to such fundamental notions as time, space, and juxtaposition mirrors the structural organization of society. In turn, such basic cognitive structures feed back, via the collective conscience, to legitimate and sustain the very social structure or morphological arrangements that generate them in the first place. It is, of course, this line of argument that early structural linguists, such as Ferdinand de Saussure (1915), used to initiate what increasingly became known as "structuralism," although latter-day structuralists like Claude Lévi-Strauss (1963) turned Durkheim on his head.[4] Nonetheless, this message is repeated in *Elementary Forms of the Religious Life*, but here Durkheim added a model of ritual. As actors find themselves in co-presence, they feel a need to affirm their solidarity and the social structure that determines their co-presence.[5] This need is intensified by collective contagion, or what Durkheim termed "effervescence." The result is the practice of rituals (and, of course, in the context of religious life, the worship of totems). Such performances of rituals reinforce and affirm the collective conscience and the structure of the society. Thus, the cycles outlined in Fig. 3.6 represent Durkheim's best effort to explain how actors in the course of interaction go about maintaining social structures.

If we generalize beyond the question of religious rituals and seek the motivational mechanism in Durkheim's model, then it is the "need" of individuals to affirm their solidarity in groups and their use of interaction rituals to do so. For Durkheim, then, the ultimate motivating force in human interaction is the need to affirm group membership and a sense of solidarity with others, leading actors to initiate and sustain interaction rituals.

Extending Durkheim this way, one can see how Collins (1975, 1985, 1986) and others have blended Durkheim with Goffman's (1967, 1959) dramaturgy and other interactionist traditions, including more phenomenological variants like ethnomethodology (Garfinkel, 1967). For Durkheim implicitly argues that much of what actors actually do in interaction is to emit rituals that sustain their sense—often a very fragile sense—of group involvement and "facticity" in the social order. They engage in such behaviors because the paramount motivating force behind all interaction is the need for individuals to feel attached to groups.

Thus, in contrast to Parsons's (1937) portrayal of Durkheim's thought, this interpretation has actors actually doing something—emitting rituals to meet their most basic needs and, at the same time, sustaining social structures. As we will come to see in the next chapter, this model of motivation is often implicit in many contemporary analyses of motivation; and thus, I think it fair to conclude that Durkheim provided an important

[4] Indeed, if structuralism had remained true to its Durkheimian heritage, it would be a far more interesting and less mystical perspective.

[5] My colleague Randall Collins takes exception to my interpretation of Durkheim on this point. Here is what he said, in a private communication: "I question the way you state that co-presence and contagion lead to 'need to affirm solidarity.' It's not so much a need [or] desire for solidarity, but just a mechanical result of being in a certain configuration. It's only after symbols are created that people feel a need to come back to recreate the group, and to protect it—i.e., this happens only after they have become attached to certain membership symbols. They also get the experience of emotional effervescences randomly and accidentally, depending on what group of configurations they happen to pass through during the course of the day."

lead in developing a general conceptualization of motivational processes in human interaction.

Conclusion

At the time that Talcott Parsons wrote *The Structure of Social Action*, then, there was a wide range of theories about motivation. He ignored most of these theories, and as a result, postulated no "force"—save for cultural values and organic/material needs—that drives actors. Parsons was, of course, to expand upon the question of motivation, but in these later works, his views do not visualize motivation as an element of *inter*action. Instead, motivation becomes buried in action systems, primarily the behavioral and psychological, as "energy" in a grand cybernetic hierarchy (Parsons, 1978). True, he insightfully used Freudian concepts in the analysis of psychodynamics (Parsons, 1958), but even in this essay, there is a deemphasis on *inter*action in favor of action.

My point is not to flog Parsonian action theory, because what is true of Parsons has also been true of most sociological theory in this century. Rather, the selective review in this chapter is intended to bring motivation back into sociological analysis. These conceptualizations represent the range of views that have become incorporated, often implicitly, into more contemporary analyses of motivational dynamics. Indeed, more recent approaches have synthesized in creative ways the models presented in this chapter, and thus, they often represent an improvement over these older models. Yet there is great insight in these initial formulations, and as I move toward a more composite model of motivational dynamics, these models will be a crucial intellectual tool—but first I need to qualify and supplement them with a variety of contemporary formulations.

4

Contemporary Models of Motivation

IN THE LAST TWO DECADES, theorists have adopted elements of the models presented in the last chapter and combined them in ways that provide a better view of the dynamics of motivation. One line of synthesis has been the repackaging of behaviorism and utilitarianism into explicit exchange-theoretic models. Such models have, as I mentioned in Chapter 3, rediscovered Simmel's basic insights, although they have added important refinements. Another creative line of synthesis has been the continuing effort to extend Mead's interactionist ideas into explanations of human action. Here, particular emphasis has been on "self" as an underlying force in human motivation. Yet another creative effort is represented in Anthony Giddens's "structuration theory," where the ideas of Freud, as mediated by interactionist-oriented psychiatrists have been combined with more modern traditions, such as dramaturgy, phenomenology, and time-space geography, to produce a highly original approach to motivation. Another breakthrough has come from Harold Garfinkel and his ethnomethodological colleagues, who, as we will see, implicitly combine Durkheim's solidarity theory with phenomenology and symbolic interactionism. And finally, there is Randall Collins's highly eclectic effort to merge Durkheim's emphasis on ritual with concepts from dramaturgy, exchange theory, and ethnomethodology.

As is evident, these modern efforts are eclectic and synthesizing, although none is explicitly a theory of motivation. Rather, each is concerned primarily with human interaction and organization, but in approaching these broader concerns, all develop an implicit model of motivation. My goal in this chapter is to make these models explicit, with an eye toward what they can offer the synthetic model of motivation to be developed in Chapter 5. In selecting these research traditions, I have not, of course, exhausted all of the important theories. Yet in its wide range of approaches, this group represents a good place to begin developing a composite model and some abstract laws on motivational processes.[1]

[1] The following discussion of these models is a greatly expanded version of J. Turner, 1987.

The Exchange-Theoretic Model of Motivational Processes

Although Simmel's early efforts do not appear to have inspired contemporary exchange theories, the utilitarian and behaviorist traditions have nonetheless been merged into a variety of such theories. These vary primarily in their language, with some leaning toward a behaviorist vocabulary and others toward an economist's terminology. But whatever the conceptual language, they are all very similar.

Exchange theories correct for the failure of both utilitarianism and behaviorism to conceptualize interaction. For utilitarians, interaction is viewed as action in an impersonal, amorphous, and competitive market, whereas for behaviorism, responses are analyzed only in relation to a stimulus situation. It is not surprising, therefore, that as concerns with interaction have increased, these two traditions have converged. Yet I do not see the resulting exchange theories as adequate conceptualizations of interaction. They rarely discuss in any detail the process of interaction; instead, they analyze what motivates people to interact and what patterns of structure are likely to emerge out of such motivational dynamics. In terms of Fig. 2.1, exchange theory is most useful as a model of motivational and structuring dynamics, least interesting as a conceptualization of interactional dynamics. That is, exchange theories inform us of what drives people to interact by emphasizing assessments of potential rewards (gratifications) in terms of actors' values (preferences), and they tell us what patterns of structured relations are likely to result from actors' respective payoffs (profits) in exchanges of rewards. But the process of interaction itself is simply seen as a negotiation and exchange of resources and rewards. Thus, it is perhaps ironic that the very issue that encouraged the convergence of utilitarianism and behaviorism—that is, interaction—is the most inadequately conceptualized dynamic in exchange theories.

This conclusion is illustrated in Fig. 4.1, where the basic elements of exchange-theoretic models of motivation are delineated. Since individuals find some kinds of resources more rewarding or gratifying than others, all exchange theories operate with a presumption of value domains (Emerson, 1986) or hierarchies of value. Such preferences are sometimes seen as hierarchical or rank ordered; I suspect, however, that values are not well ordered but instead constitute overlapping fields or domains of preferences. In addition, most exchange theories—though not all—emphasize three general classes of rewards as particularly important in human affairs—

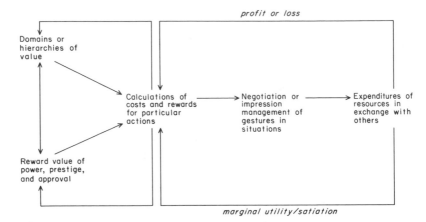

Fig. 4.1. The exchange-theoretic model of motivation.

power, prestige, and approval. Power, or the capacity to control the actions of others by virtue of possessing highly valued resources, is typically viewed as the most preferred reward (Blau, 1964); prestige, or the capacity to extract honor and esteem for one's resources, is the next most valued reward; and finally, approval, or simple acceptance as a peer, is the least valued (Homans, 1974).

In terms of these three classes of rewards and the domains of value, actors make calculations, often implicit, about the costs and benefits of particular actions. Costs for any line of action involve the resources that are "spent" to get rewards from others and the alternative rewards that must be foregone to pursue a given line of conduct. In order to realize "profit" (costs will be less than the value of rewards) in an exchange, actors engage in a process of "negotiation," again often implicitly, to impress others with their own resources and perhaps to de-emphasize the value of the others' resources. Out of such mutual impression management come expenditure and exchange of resources. As is shown in Fig. 4.1, there are two crucial feedback processes in these exchanges, one revolving around a sense of profit or loss (rewards minus costs) and another around satiation, or marginal utility. These feedback processes influence the salience of values and rewards as well as subsequent calculations and negotiations.

Unlike utilitarianism, there is no presumption in exchange theories that actors seek to maximize rewards or utilities; rather, it is only assumed that they try to make some profit. Moreover, it is not assumed that calculations are rational and logical; indeed, they are often implicit and/or constrained by external cultural and social forces. And, because of these constraints, as well as the inherent distortions in the negotiating process, actors rarely have complete information about their alternatives. Thus, interaction is motivated by actors' implicit domains of preferences, as these are influenced by satiation and past profits or losses, while revolving around a process of nonrational, nonlogical, nonmaximizing, and, at times, nonconscious calculations and negotiations over what resources must be given up to receive valued resources from others. One's payoffs (profit/loss as conditioned by marginal utilities) will determine the flow and structure of the interaction over time.

Such is the basic argument of exchange theory, but in closing, I should note again that except for notions of "negotiation," "calculations," and "impression management," these exchange theories provide little detail of interactional processes—that is, what actors actually do when they negotiate. Yet, as we will see in Chapter 5, the core ideas from exchange theory offer important elements to a more synthetic model of motivational processes.

The Interactionist Model

Modern interactionist theory has built upon the conceptual legacy of George Herbert Mead (1934), but curiously, it has ignored Mead's (1938) concerns about motivation. There are, of course, exceptions (Shibutani, 1968; Gecas, 1986; Miyamoto, 1970; Miyamoto and Dornbusch, 1956) to this conclusion, but in general, interactionist theory has focused on signaling and gesturing rather than on the motivational processes behind these interactional processes. Interactionist theories do converge, however, on one important motive force: self-conceptions.

The importance of self-conceptions as central to human motivation was first given clear expression by William James (1890), especially in his analysis of self-esteem or self-estimation. And while Charles Horton Cooley (1902) and Mead (1934) visualized self as a central process in all human behavior and interaction, its place as a motivating dynamic is somewhat ambiguous in their work. Recent interactionist thinking has translated Mead's ideas into a more coherent view of self and motivation (e.g., Shibutani, 1968, 1961; Stryker, 1980; and Rosenberg, 1979). In general, two dimensions of self-conception are emphasized as critical motives: self-esteem, or the level of self-worth evident in attitudes about oneself; and self-consistency, or the degree of coherence and compatibility in attitudes about oneself (see, in particular, Rosenberg, 1979: 53–62). Similar points of emphasis can be found in more classic efforts in psychology (e.g., Allport, 1943) and in various psychoanalytic works (see, for example, Sullivan, 1953; Erikson, 1950).

Unfortunately, the concepts of self-esteem and self-consistency have been underemphasized in more purely sociological analyses of interaction, although Erving Goffman's (1959) early dramaturgical work and Ralph Turner's (1978) role theory both view self as a force guiding the course of an individual's interactions with others. There has been instead an over-emphasis on the processes of constructing definitions (Blumer, 1969), on developing a sense of reality (Garfinkel, 1967), and on analyzing the course of interaction (Knorr-Cetina and Cicourel, 1981) rather than on the social-psychological motives behind such interaction. In my view, much of what energizes interaction is the need to maintain a given level of self-esteem and to sustain consistency among attitudes about oneself. As to which of these two is the more important, I believe that consistency is the more primary motive force, in turn causally influencing self-esteem.

In this context, I should at least mention another arena of controversy in the analysis of self. More recent works have tended to stress that self is transitory, situational, and easily altered. From this perspective, people are seen as having multiple selves in different situations. Indeed, notions of a "true" or "real" self are viewed as cultural fictions (Collins, 1975).[2] This orientation runs counter to earlier analyses of self, which emphasize a "core self" that is stable and trans-situational (Kuhn and McPartland, 1954). My view is that people have both "core" and "situational" selves. Furthermore, I believe that they are highly motivated to sustain consistency between core-self feelings and situational-self definitions. At the same time, and partly as a result of their success in achieving consistency, they attempt to maintain their level of self-esteem for both core and situational selves. Even if one does not accept my argument on this matter, the general theoretical point is unaltered: people are motivated to sustain esteem and consistency in their sense of self, whether situational and changeable or trans-situational and stable.

Fig. 4.2 outlines the underlying model of motivation in most interactionist theories. For interactionists, self-conceptions are constructed from configurations of core attitudes about oneself as a certain kind of person. Such self-conceptions motivate interaction in that they generate efforts to maintain self-esteem and self-consistency. Presentations of oneself in situations through such interrelated processes as staging (Goffman, 1959), role-making (R. Turner, 1968, 1962), claim-making (Habermas, 1984), accounting (Garfinkel, 1967), and other interpersonal mechanisms (Cicourel, 1973) are both energized and circumscribed by one's self-

[2] I would conclude that, of all the issues over which my friend and colleague Randall Collins and I do battle, it is this one: no matter what the situation or place, he is consistent in the position that there is no core or unified self, a fact which is countered by his own consistent presentation of self in our long-standing debate.

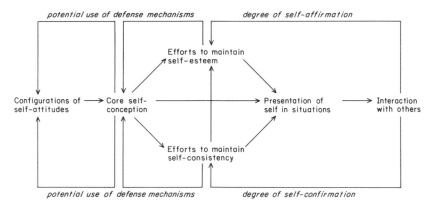

Fig. 4.2. The interactionist model of motivation.

conception, particularly needs to sustain consistency among, and hence positive esteem for, elements of one's self-conception.[3] Through role-taking (Mead, 1934) and other procedures for seeing oneself in "the looking glass" (Cooley, 1902), one derives a degree of self-affirmation of esteem and self-confirmation of consistency. Failure to achieve affirmation and/or confirmation escalates needs for maintaining esteem and/or consistency, which, from an interactionist perspective, can lead to re-presentation of self or, from a psychoanalytic interpretation of these dynamics, can activate defense mechanisms (rationalization, selective interpretation, repression, projection, etc.) to sustain a given configuration of self-attitudes.

Both the re-presentation of self and the use of defense mechanisms probably operate simultaneously, although most interactionist theories stress the interpersonal processes of self-presentation. Indeed, I am probably imposing the psychoanalytic notion of defense mechanisms on the interactionist model, although interactionists often talk in these terms when they address such issues of "selective perception," "reflexivity," and efforts to "sustain identity" (Shibutani, 1961: 214–41; Strauss, 1959). My goal in invoking the notion of defense mechanisms is to make explicit what is often left implicit in more purely interactionist analyses: if people fail to have their sense of self confirmed in a situation, they are highly mobilized to "do something about it." If they cannot exit the situation or change the responses of others, they will seek to repress information from others that

[3] I would argue that the underlying motivational force for sustaining consistency is to be found in "dissonance" (Festinger, 1957), "congruity" (e.g., Osgood and Tannenbaum, 1955), and related Gestalt-inspired theories. Indeed, I think that this theoretical tradition has much to offer motivational theory, especially that developed by symbolic interactionists.

contradicts their self-conception. In addition to sheer repression, they may also use other defense mechanisms. For example, they may employ a combination of repression and selective perception, filtering through "cognitive rose-colored glasses" only that information that confirms self; or they may seek to rationalize away contradictory messages by impugning the character of those who are the source of these messages; and so on. The central issue here is this: actors will work very hard to maintain a given configuration of self attitudes, especially those of their core self; and if they cannot change the responses of others, they will reinterpret them, at least to the point where this is no longer possible or where severe behavioral pathologies set in.

Thus, people's configurations of self-attitudes are sustained by powerful motives for self-consistency and self-esteem, even to the point of activating defense mechanisms. These considerations suggest the utility of examining more psychoanalytic models of motivation as a supplement to the interactionist model in Fig. 4.2.

Giddens's Psychoanalytic Model

Among contemporary sociological theorists, Anthony Giddens (1984) has been the most willing to criticize and then selectively borrow from the works of Freud and his more sociologically inclined revisionists, such as Erik Erikson and Harry Stack Sullivan. He has combined psychoanalytic ideas with recent analyses of language and interaction, but unfortunately, he has ignored the interactionist-inspired portions of some psychoanalytic theories, especially those involving the analysis of self-consistency and self-esteem (Sullivan, 1953) as important motivating forces. Nonetheless, there is a creative mix of ideas in Giddens's theory, although it is just that—a mix—rather than a formal theory or model. I cannot do full justice to the subtle blend of diverse traditions in his general theoretic approach, but the insertion of a psychoanalytic dynamic is, I feel, the most important aspect of his analysis of motivation.

Unlike many sociologists, Giddens is willing to discuss *un*conscious motives, but he does so by rejecting Freud's earlier assumption that day-to-day activities are unconsciously motivated. In contrast, Giddens (1984: 50) stresses, "the unconscious only rarely impinges upon the reflexive monitoring of conduct." Rather, a great deal of daily activity involves "reflexive monitoring"—that is, paying attention to one's own and others' actions—in social situations of co-presence. Borrowing from Alfred Schutz (1932) as well as other phenomenologists and ethnomethodologists, Giddens sees such reflexive monitoring as connected to two levels of consciousness.

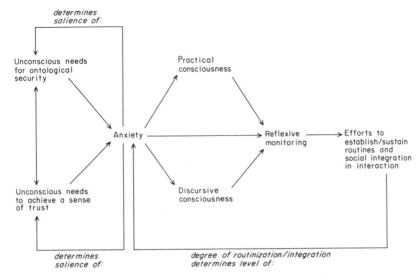

Fig. 4.3. Giddens's psychoanalytic model of motivation.

First, there is "discursive consciousness," which involves the capacity to give reasons for and talk about what one does. Second, there is "practical consciousness," which, in Schutz's term, is the "stocks of knowledge" that actors possess or, in Giddens's term, the implicit knowledge that actors have about social conditions. The elements of such practical consciousness remain implicit; actors are seldom able to express them verbally through their capacity for discursive consciousness. Yet, unlike the division between the unconscious, on one hand, and these processes of practical and discursive consciousness, on the other, there is no bar or barrier of repression. Actors regularly draw from practical consciousness in their discursive moments and in their interpretations of events that they reflexively monitor. Conversely, they easily place into their stocks of practical consciousness new knowledge as they monitor and interact with others.

Much of what actors do, then, revolves around using and replenishing stocks of knowledge in interaction, monitoring these interactions, and giving reasons for one's own acts and those of others. What, then, motivates the interactions in which these factors operate? As can be seen in Fig. 4.3, Giddens emphasizes the unconscious, but he abandons strict adherence to Freud in favor of the more sociological models in psychoanalysis, such as Erikson's (1950). Adapting Erikson's concepts for his purpose, Giddens sees the drive to achieve a "sense of trust" with others as central to motivation. A related drive is the need for a kind of ultimate "ontological security," where one feels that matters in the social world are as they appear to be. Achieving trust and ontological security are mutually reinforcing; and in Giddens's model, they are the unconscious "force" behind the conscious activities of individuals in interaction. The mediator of this force appears to be "anxiety," although Giddens (1984) does not include it in his formal models and glossary of definitions. It is, however, discussed as the consequence of social relations that are not "routinized" (made predictable) and/or "integrated" (conducted in terms of crucial interpersonal techniques, such as "tact," "turn-taking," "bodily positioning," etc.).

Unconscious motivation thus exerts only a diffuse pressure on consciousness and interaction. Yet it is still the ultimate driving force behind people's efforts to establish interactive routines and to draw upon stocks of practical consciousness and, when necessary, to give discursive reasons for their conduct as they engage in a variety of interpersonal practices to sustain their sense of an integrated social setting. Thus, Freudian analysis becomes linked to interactionist concerns about the use of presentations to organize one's place in an interaction setting and to produce a common definition or interpretation of the situation. This linkage is performed by the intervening processes of anxiety and practical consciousness. Anxiety in social interaction will escalate motives for ontological security and trust, at least up to a point. As long as interactions are routinized and integrated, however, these unconscious motives reveal low salience. Practical consciousness provides the stores or stocks of implicit knowledge that actors use to routinize and integrate interaction.

As is evident in Fig. 4.3, then, Giddens sees motivation as an unconscious process that is activated when efforts to establish routines and social integration through interpersonal practices are disrupted. These unconscious needs for ontological security and trust operate as a diffuse pressure on consciousness by virtue of their capacity to activate anxiety. Such anxiety, or feelings of uncertainty and disequilibrium, increases when conscious processes fail to routinize and integrate social interactions. Thus, interaction is driven by an unconscious foreboding that anxiety will escalate when interaction fails to be routinized and integrated.

While this is not a very precise model, it makes several important contributions. First, unlike so much sociological theory, the model introduces unconscious forces, which must, I believe, be a part of a sociological theory of motivation. Second, the model connects unconscious forces to interaction processes, especially those revolving around people's efforts to establish routines and social integration. Thus, for Giddens, social interaction is driven by deep-seated and unconscious fears about a failure to achieve trust and security in situations.

Such arguments are in one sense psychoanalytic, but they are also very Durkheimian, as a cursory comparison of Fig. 3.6 with Fig. 4.3 will reveal.

There is, I think, a convergence here of what are often seen as very different traditions—psychoanalysis, interactionism, and Durkheimian functionalism. That is, people are driven in interaction by typically unconscious needs to create a sense of trust, security, or solidarity; and in order to do so, they use ritual and other interpersonal techniques to affirm their sense of attachment to social structures. But Durkheim's model extends even further. In addition to interactionist emphasis on interpersonal techniques and Freudian concerns with trust and security, it also can be seen to constitute the underlying model of an intellectual tradition that is often hostile to both psychoanalysis and interactionism: ethnomethodology.

The Ethnomethodological Model

One of the great revolutions in sociological theorizing over the last two decades is the detailed analysis of interaction processes, especially of talk and conversation (Heritage, 1984). The early arguments of ethnomethodologists, such as Harold Garfinkel (1967), Harvey Sacks (1972), and Sacks, Emmanuel Schegloff, and Gail Jefferson (1974), as well as kindred spirits like Aaron Cicourel (1973), are that individuals employ a series of implicit "folk" practices, or "ethnomethods," to create a presumption that they share a common world. For each interaction, actors attempt to generate a sense that there is an external, factual order "out there" as well as a universe of shared intersubjective experiences. Early polemics (e.g., Mehan and Wood, 1975) about these practices as the *only* reality have fortunately receded, with the result that, even though its practitioners still would protest, "ethnomethodology," "cognitive sociology," and "conversational analysis" can be viewed as an important supplement to more traditional sociological approaches to interaction.

Ethnomethodological analysis leaves unsaid what motivates people to use ethnomethods to convince each other that they share external and intersubjective worlds. Yet I think that the implicit views of ethnomethodologists on this question are Durkheimian. That is, humans need to feel that they are part of a larger solidarity, or to adopt a more ethnomethodological style of jargon, that there is "facticity" to social encounters. Interaction is thus constrained by actors' need to feel—even if this is somewhat of an illusionary sense—that they share a common factual and fixed world.

But unlike Durkheim, who emphasized ritual performances as the mechanism for creating group solidarity, ethnomethodologists have stressed the much more subtle processes that are used in conversations to promote the sense that actors share a common world. This shift in emphasis represents an important supplement to sociological analyses of interaction because prior to ethnomethodology, theoretical concern had been on the more obvious forces of social order—values, norms, beliefs, negotiated definitions of situations, and the like. In contrast, ethnomethodology argues that there are very important procedures that actors use to create a deep, underlying presumption of a factual social order. Garfinkel's (1967) original "breaching experiments" documented the extent to which people rely upon an implicit sense of a factual, external, and shared world; for when this sense was disrupted, emotional reactions were disproportionate to the surface significance of the disruption. In fact, one might argue that interaction cannot proceed smoothly with respect to other issues, such as exchanges of resources, establishment of routines, and affirmations of self, without this underlying sense of "facticity."

Most ethnomethodologists would be unwilling to draw these conclusions, but if their analyses of conversations are to represent more than a shrill critique of "normal sociology," then this must be the way that we incorporate ethnomethodologists into mainstream sociological theory. Fig. 4.4 delineates how I think ethnomethodology can be represented as a sociological theory of motivation.

As is outlined in Fig. 4.4, implicit and perhaps unconscious needs for a "sense of facticity"—that is, a presumption that individuals in interaction share common external and internal worlds—motivate actors to use folk practices, or ethnomethods.[4] I see such ethnomethods as being of three basic types: those that are invoked to repair breached interactions (or interactions where the sense of facticity has been broken); those that provide documentary interpretations for conduct (why actors are doing what they are); and those that are used to sustain the flow of ongoing interactions by encouraging actors to "gloss," "let pass," or "not question" certain statements of others.

Thus, the gesturing activities of individuals, primarily in their conversational exchanges, revolve around procedures for repairing conversations by providing new documentary information (statements of form and background materials, for example) or by initiating new sequences of glosses for potentially unclear information; for providing information about the "normal form" and "background materials" necessary to interpret statements in a conversation; and for filling in, waiting, or glossing over information in a conversation in order to promote the sense or illusion that

---

[4] An anonymous reviewer suggested that perhaps the underlying need is actually one revolving around creating "cognitive order and understanding," which would make the approach highly compatible with the Gestalt tradition. Whether my Durkheimian approach or this suggested one is more correct, the essential thing is the effort to bring ethnomethodological ideas into the corpus of mainstream sociological and social-psychological theorizing.

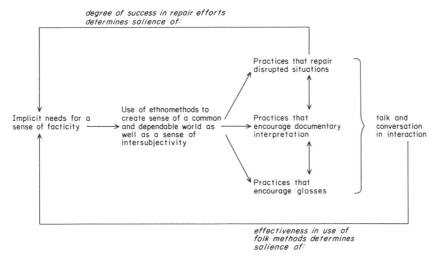

Fig. 4.4. The implicit model of motivation in ethnomethodology.

these actors share a common world. Such "repair work" escalates needs for facticity, at least up to a point; and when these efforts at repair prove unsuccessful, interaction will involve the extensive use of ethnomethods to reestablish a sense of intersubjectivity and the presumption of a common factual order. And, depending on their success, other interpersonal practices in situations also feed back to raise or lower the need for facticity, as indicated by the arrow at bottom of Fig. 4.4.

Such a model adds, I think, an important dimension to theories of motivation. It makes a topic—indeed, a central dynamic—of talk and conversation. It links the implicit procedures by which talk is performed—pauses, assertions, turn-taking, glosses, interruptions, etc.—to the motives of individuals and to what sustains the smooth flow of interaction. Yet ethnomethodological analysis either ignores or grossly underemphasizes other motivating processes—efforts at self-confirmation, desires to realize profits, needs to feel trust, impulses to affirm group solidarity, and the like—which we find in the models presented in Figs. 4.1, 4.2, and 4.3. But before moving to an effort to blend these models together, we should examine another effort at synthesis, Randall Collins's theory of interaction rituals.

Collins's Interaction Ritual Model

Over the last decade, Randall Collins has sought to blend a variety of theoretical traditions into a synthetic version of "conflict sociology." In this effort can be found the ethnomethodologist's emphasis on talk and conversation, Durkheim's (1912) ideas on rituals and solidarity, exchange theory's concern with payoffs, and even Weber's vision of inequality, power, and conflict. Collins's work spans both micro and macro sociology, but I concentrate primarily on his more recent attempts at analyzing interaction ritual chains (Collins, 1986), for it is here that he expands upon his earlier theory motivation (Collins, 1975). The basic argument is that actors use their resources to their advantage in social situations, seeking to extract a profit in exchanges with others. The two most generic resources in such exchanges are "emotional energy" (positive feelings and sentiments about oneself in a situation) and "cultural capital" (stores of symbols that people can talk about, especially with respect to approval, prestige, authority, group membership, and control of material conditions). People thus "use" emotional energy and cultural capital in an effort to increase them, and because conversation and talk are the principal vehicles for such exchanges, much conversation involves attempts by participants to increase their levels of emotional energy and cultural capital through "talk."

Collins argues that actors monitor a situation in order to determine if its basic nature is work/practical, ceremonial, or social. The nature as well as the degree of energy and capital expended varies in terms of which of these three types prevails or dominates a situation. Work/practical situations involve the expenditure of conversational energy and capital to establish one's place in the group and its authority hierarchy, division of labor, and ranking system. Ceremonial situations revolve around the deployment of conversational energy and capital to emit appropriate rituals that can increase one's sense of group involvement and membership. And social situations evidence the use of resources to enhance standing in groups, to promote authority as well as prestige, and to secure favorable coalitions. When actors "feel good" (that is, augment their levels of emotional energy) and increase their cultural capital (affirm their sense of group membership and perhaps a favored position in the group), then they are likely to develop needs to keep a conversation going and/or to repeat conversational encounters. Out of such "chains" of conversations social structures are produced and reproduced, but my concern is not with this more macro portion of Collins's argument. Rather, it is with the implicit theory of motivation, which I have modeled in Fig. 4.5.

At the core of Collins's theory is the Durkheimian presumption that group membership is the prime driving force behind needs to initiate conversational encounters and to use energy and cultural capital in such encounters. The mechanics of interaction revolve around the monitoring of situations to determine the nature of the conversational resources required

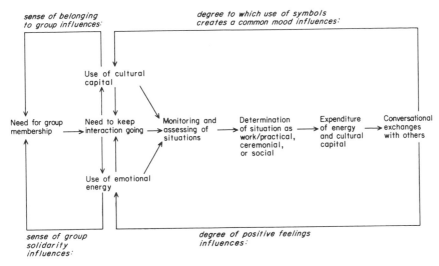

Fig. 4.5. Collins's theory of motives in interaction chains.

and then the spending of emotional energy as well as cultural capital in an effort to extract an emotional and cultural profit. If such profits are not forthcoming, then motivational energy may initially increase in an effort to recover one's losses, but if profits are still not forthcoming, then motivational energy will decrease. As a result, actors will seek to avoid such situations; if this is not possible, then their talk and conversation will be perfunctory, highly ritualized, and involve little "investment" of energy or capital. Conversely, when profits are high, energy levels will increase and the willingness of actors to use cultural resources will be high, resulting in animated talk and conversation, since such talk enhances their sense of belonging to, and solidarity with, the members of a group.

Such a model supplements the exchange-theoretic perspective by emphasizing the importance of needs for group membership as the ultimate reward and by recognizing the significance of conversation/talk in exchange relations. It also supplements the ethnomethodological perspective by classifying situations in terms of the types of conversational resources employed and by specifying in more detail why actors seek a sense of facticity (i.e., because of needs for group membership, for positive emotions, and for augmented cultural capital) and why they use conversational practices to achieve this. Collins draws these conclusions implicitly, for they are never articulated in a separate model of motivational processes. Yet his approach reveals the potential of a more synthetic approach, especially one that incorporates what Collins ignores.

Conclusion

This completes my review of various sociological models of motivation. In these two chapters, I have sought to explicate the basic variables and their causal connections in a wide variety of past and present theories. Though each theory has something to offer, no one theory by itself is adequate. The next step, then, is to synthesize the useful elements of various models into a composite or synthetic model—such is my goal in the next chapter. Yet, as the strategy outlined in Chapter 2 argues, more than a complex model is necessary. The model must be translated into testable propositions; and so, as I move toward synthesis, I must also attempt to develop some elementary laws or principles of motivation.

5

Toward a Synthetic
Model of Motivation

EACH OF THE MODELS presented in the last two chapters captures important dynamics of motivational processes; yet, by themselves, none completely delineates these processes. In this chapter, I will begin by assessing what each can potentially contribute to a more synthetic portrait of motivation. Then I will attempt to pull these useful elements together into a composite model that, in turn, can be used to develop some elementary propositions on human motivation. Such an exercise can overcome the deficiencies in Talcott Parsons's (1937) early effort to understand action as well as those of many present-day approaches to interaction where the motivation of actors seems to be ignored.

Elements in a Theory of Motivation

Let me begin with utilitarianism, behaviorism, and exchange theory. Behaviorism and utilitarianism provide a theory of motivation with a crucial insight: people do things in order to receive gratifications or utilities. Hence, interaction among individuals is, to some degree, energized by people's efforts to realize rewards or utilities and avoid punishments or costs. Exchange theory pulls these useful portions of behaviorism and utilitarianism together into an explicitly interactional theory. It emphasizes the importance of approval, prestige, and power as sources of gratification in social relations and adds conceptualizations of covert calculations of profits and interpersonal tactics of impression management as actors negotiate over the exchange of utilities or reinforcers.

People are not simple computers or psychic cash registers calculating profits, however. Far more important than simple considerations of profit are other motivating processes that circumscribe people's use of resources in interaction. In fact, it might be reasonable to argue that hierarchies of value for individuals are determined by the strength of these other motivating forces and that calculations of profit revolve around meeting the need states generated by other motive forces.

One of the other motivating forces is "self," the major focus of Mead's and modern interactionists' theories. The resources used in an exchange are shaped by people's efforts to sustain a conception of themselves as a certain kind of person and, at the same time, to cooperate with others. Impression management in exchange situations is, in essence, a "presentation of self" in an effort to confirm the substantive content of self, affirm a given level of self-esteem, and create or maintain a place in an ongoing cooperative context.

Many of the processes that influence exchange dynamics and efforts at self-affirmation and confirmation are unconscious, especially people's efforts at reducing anxiety. This emphasis is, of course, Freud's great contribution to sociological theory, although sociologists typically do not want to talk about unconscious processes. The reasons for this reluctance are diverse, ranging from problems of measurement to doubts about the mysticism often associated with conceptualizations of the unconscious. But, if we can specify what these unconscious processes are, then much of the imprecision in some formulations is eliminated.

Durkheim (1912) provided us with one force that unconsciously drives human behavior, especially ritual activity. Humans need, Durkheim asserted, to interact in ways that affirm the emergent structure of social relations. In Collins's (1975, 1986) more contemporary theory, this dynamic revolves around needs to create a sense of group membership and inclusion in social relations. For Collins, exchange relations involving the expenditure of cultural capital and emotional energy are, in the end, designed to assert one's membership in a group and, if possible, to enhance one's position in the group. More generally, we can hypothesize that people's efforts to affirm self and to realize a profit in exchange negotiations are shaped by typically unconscious needs to sustain a sense of group inclusion. Thus, the presentation of self in exchange relations and the effort to extract a profit during interaction are deeply based in typically unconscious motives for being part of the ongoing flow of cooperative interaction. When stated in this way, Durkheim's argument and Collins's elaboration converge with Mead's emphasis on the capacity of adjustment and cooperation with others in order to provide reinforcement and gratification.

Group inclusion is also related to what Giddens (1984) has conceptualized as a "sense of trust" in others. Borrowing from Erik Erikson's (1950) model of socialization, Giddens has isolated, I think, an important property of motivation. People need to "trust" others in the sense that, for the purposes of a given interaction, others are "reliable" and their responses "predictable." When people achieve a sense of group inclusion, I suspect that their feelings of trust are heightened. Moreover, much of what motivates exchange relations and efforts at self-affirmation/confirmation is a need to perceive, if only implicitly, reliability and predictability in others.

Conversely, the level of profits in exchanges and the degree of self-reinforcement are shaped by people's success in routinizing relations and achieving this perception of trust. In addition to trust, Giddens's formulation draws our attention to "ontological security" as a motivating force. People have a mostly unconscious need to believe that things are as they appear and that an interaction sequence is what it seems to be.

Giddens's formulation of ontological security is, I believe, related to ethnomethodological concerns about meeting needs for "facticity." Hence, much of the need for ontological security is mediated by successful use of ethnomethods to create background "accounts." Such methods are often unconsciously used and interpreted; it is only when social relations require repair, creating an escalated sense of ontological *in*security, that the importance of these accounting practices penetrates consciousness. It can be argued that exchange negotiations and presentations of self cannot proceed smoothly until actors have created an implicit "account" of what is real and sense that they share a common, factual world. For without this sense of "facticity," it becomes difficult to achieve the sense of ontological security and trust that are so essential to self presentations and exchange relations.

Such, then, is my cursory review of what I see as the most useful elements of the various sociological models of motivation outlined in the last two chapters. The next task is to use these elements to construct a dynamic model of motivational processes.[1]

A Dynamic Model of Motivational Processes

A dynamic model views motivation as a process among interrelated elements that mutually influence each other. As a dynamic process, motivation is directional, unfolding over time and involving numerous causal effects among its elements. In particular, motivation reveals many feedback processes that can alter or sustain the direction of the process. Yet, there is also a simultaneity among some motivational processes. Motivation is not a simple linear feedback system; it involves multiple causal processes, many of which operate simultaneously and in parallel fashion. Moreover, motivation operates at varying levels of an individual's conscious awareness. Sometimes actors become highly conscious of their efforts to engage in a particular course of action, but in general, motivational processes are implicit, operating beneath the surface of explicit awareness and reflection. As Mead (1938) emphasized, it is when "impulses" are blocked that conscious awareness and thought ensue. And so, in my view, motivational pro-

---

[1] An earlier and somewhat different version of this model appears in J. Turner, 1987.

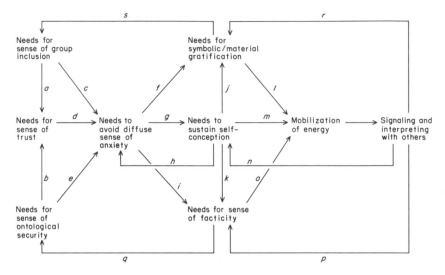

Fig. 5.1 A composite model of motivation.

cesses become conscious only when interactions are not proceeding smoothly; even here, conscious attention is selective, rarely reflecting on all of the operative motivational processes.

With these considerations in mind, Fig. 5.1 presents a provisional model of motivation. This model pulls together the dynamic processes evident in other approaches, although I should emphasize that it is hardly definitive. At best, it represents only a tentative effort to synthesize a sample of existing approaches to motivation. And, as I emphasized at the outset, the model in Fig. 5.1 is not a general theory of motivation per se, but only a model of motivation *during interaction*.

Let me begin by outlining the general contours of the model. First, its elements are all variables whose values can change. Second, the variables are causally connected in the sense that the values for one can, either directly or indirectly, affect the values of the others. Third, the direct causal processes move from left to right and the feedback process from right to left. Fourth, variables stacked in the same vertical column in the model are viewed as operating simultaneously at that point in the process. Fifth, the closer variables are to each other *and* the more they are connected by causal paths, then the greater is the degree of effect on each other. And sixth, as one moves from left to right in the model, I see the motivational processes as becoming increasingly conscious; that is, elements at the far left tend to operate at a more unconscious level than those at the right

The variables in the model are all labeled with discursive text and the causal connections are lettered (*a*, *b*, *c*, etc.). The term "need(s)" appears frequently in the discursive labels of variables, and perhaps I should first explain why I am using such an ambiguous word. In a sense, the term "need(s)" must be viewed as a primitive; it is difficult to define, but my usage is intended to denote the fact that people have certain fundamental states of being that create feelings of deprivation and that mobilize them to act on their environment in ways to eliminate this sense of deprivation. In Fig. 5.1, then, a need is a perpetual condition of potential or actual deprivation that sets into motion behavioral activity. Hence, to take one example from the model, a "need for a sense of group inclusion" denotes the fact that humans will be perpetually mobilized to avoid the feelings of deprivation that come from not achieving a sense of being part of, and being implicated in, ongoing group activity. Granted, the concept of "need" is still problematic and vague, but it nonetheless connotes what I see as a crucial dynamic of human affairs.

Moreover, by using the term "need," I can link these other motivational processes to the question of "value" in exchange theories. Utilitarianism and behaviorism, as well as their elaboration into exchange theory, have difficulty in specifying hierarchies or domains of values for individuals during interaction. My formulation of "needs" represents one way to clarify this question: the major "value domains" for actors during interaction are needs for group inclusion, trust, ontological security, maintenance of self, and facticity. That is, what actors find symbolically or materially gratifying in an interaction are those physical props and symbols that can meet these needs. At the very least, this is a hypothesis worthy of further consideration, because it does help resolve the problem of value so prominent in exchange theories.

Turning now to the model in more detail, the far left side lists three basic needs, "group inclusion," "trust," and "ontological security." Such needs are typically unconscious in the sense that most individuals are unaware of their operation during interaction *until* one or more of these fundamental sources of deprivation is not adequately met. And even under this condition, the sense of deprivation is generally experienced as diffuse anxiety, at least initially. As a result, it will be difficult for the individual to pinpoint precisely the underlying cause of that anxiety. However, I should not move too far to the right in the model before discussing these variables at the left in more detail.

As I mentioned above, a "need for a sense of group inclusion" is the potential deprivation associated with a failure to feel "involved in" and "part of" ongoing social relations. This variable comes from Durkheim (1912) and perhaps Mead (1934), although my more direct and immediate source is Collins (1975, 1986). I use the term "group" in a loose sense to refer to ongoing interactions among mutually aware actors; and the term "inclusion" to indicate that people want to see themselves as part of this inter-action context. The need to sense inclusion does not necessarily require corresponding feelings of high solidarity, however. Many interaction sit-uations are temporary and emotionally uninvolving, with the result that one does not need to feel emotionally close to others but only a part of the interactive flow in a situation. Of course, some interactions are part of more permanent relations, and in these types of interactions, individuals must develop a more intense sense of solidarity in order to feel included. Just what "inclusion" involves, then, is situational, but actors tend to "know" implicitly the criteria for assessing whether or not they are ex-cluded from a group context. And when they perceive or sense exclusion, they experience diffuse anxiety, as indicated by causal arrow c.

The second needs variable is "need for a sense of trust," taken from Gid-dens's (1984) adaptation of Erikson's (1950) analysis of the stages of so-cialization. As causal arrow a indicates, feelings about group inclusion in-fluence the degree to which an actor has interpersonal trust or the implicit belief that the responses of others are predictable and reliable. When one does not feel part of an interaction context, then having trust in the pre-dictability of others is difficult. In other words, the basic idea behind this "trust" variable is that people must feel that there is a rhythm to interac-tions and that the responses of others will be predictable and patterned. Again, the nature of the rhythm varies in terms of the situational circum-stances. For example, the kind of predictability one requires in a grocery store checkout line is very different from what is necessary in a close friend-ship; but in both, people act so as to promote predictability in the inter-action. And as with the inclusion variable, people's stocks of knowledge (Schutz, 1932) provide them with an implicit sense of what constitutes pre-dictable rhythms in varying types of situations. When this sense of implicit trust and predictability in interaction is disrupted, individuals experience diffuse anxiety, as is denoted by causal arrow d.

The third variable on the far left of Fig. 5.1 is also from Giddens's (1984) analysis. People need to feel "ontological security" or the sense that things are as they appear. That is, in order to avoid diffuse anxiety (causal arrow e) individuals seek to create a feeling that they understand "what is" and "what exists" in a situation, that there are no hidden dimensions that could disrupt this implicit interpretation. We need, therefore, to feel that the world around us has a fixed and dependable character. And, as causal ar-row b indicates, achieving such security in one's personal ontology is cru-cial for achieving trust or the sense of predictability in the responses of others.

All of these variables, as they influence each other, and as they are in turn influenced by feedback processes to be discussed later, affect people's ongoing level of anxiety in an interaction situation. I see anxiety, or a sense of diffuse discomfort and disequilibrium with the environment, as a mediating emotional state between less conscious needs for inclusion, trust, and security, on the one hand, and increasingly more conscious motives, on the other. When early theorists, such as Mead (1938) and Simmel (1907) discussed "impulses" as states of maladjustment that promote action (see Figs. 3.3. and 3.4), I think they were denoting with the concept of "impulse" what I have labeled "anxiety" here. However, in their formulations, impulses can be very short-term, mild, situational, and revolve around non-interpersonal issues. On this score, then, our formulations differ, because Fig. 5.1 emphasizes that diffuse anxiety arises from four axes of interpersonal maladjustment—that is, a failure at achieving a sense of group inclusion, interpersonal trust, ontological security, and the yet-to-be-discussed need to sustain self (causal arrow h).

At any rate, the model in Fig. 5.1 views diffuse anxiety, or a generalized and unspecified sense of disequilibrium, as an important source of interpersonal energy (in this emphasis, I am probably closer to Freud than are most sociologists). Until one can achieve a sense of trust, security, and inclusion in interaction, behavioral responses will cycle around efforts to deal with the anxiety associated with these three needs. Furthermore, because these needs tend to remain unarticulated, creating nonspecific anxiety, individuals often have great difficulty pinpointing the source of their disequilibrium, with the result that considerable interpersonal energy can be devoted to meeting these needs as individuals grope around for a solution to their often vague feelings of discomfort.

Just how people seek to resolve their anxiety is, however, greatly circumscribed by the other motivational processes delineated in Fig. 5.1. The most central of these is the need to sustain a self-conception. The dynamics of sustaining self are complex and involve a number of unresolved issues.

One of these is the issue of the "dispositional" versus the "situational" self or "core self" versus "peripheral self." My view is that both are critical motivating dynamics. On the one hand, people have more permanent configurations of attitudes about themselves that they seek to sustain in *all* interaction situations; on the other hand, people have more contextually based self-attitudes that they seek to confirm in certain types or classes of situations.[2] As causal arrow g denotes, diffuse anxiety will increase needs for sustaining self-conception as both more permanent and situational attitudes; and as arrow h emphasizes, one's level of diffuse anxiety is either

[2] Even if one takes the extreme situational view, as Collins (1975) and Goffman (1959) appear to do, the place of self in the model is unchanged. People will experience anxiety when their situational self is unconfirmed. Moreover, when needs for trust, inclusion, and security produce anxiety, they will be especially concerned about situational self-confirmation.

raised or lowered by the degree of success in doing so. I would hypothesize that the failure to sustain core self-attitudes generates more intense, diffuse, and long-term anxiety than do failures to confirm situational self-definitions. Yet it is probably the failure to confirm situational attitudes that will be the most "noticed" by an individual. Individuals are also more likely to feel immediately mobilized to "do something" about a failure to sustain a situationally based view of themselves (as denoted by causal arrow *m*). In contrast, problems in reinforcing core self may be submerged by defense mechanisms, creating more diffuse levels of anxiety (arrow *h*) that are not easily labeled by an individual and that do not suggest immediate courses of action. (Again, I think that Freudian analysis has much to offer interactionist interpretations of self.)

Another unresolved question is whether efforts to sustain self revolve around needs to maintain consistency among potentially alterable self-attitudes (Gergen and Morse, 1967) or around needs to preserve intact a given self-concept (Lecky, 1945). That is, do people seek to sustain a given conception of themselves or do they simply try to keep in harmony the potentially changeable elements of their self-conception? Again, my answer is that people do both. My sense is that as individuals mature, they seek to preserve a given self-conception, even to the point of employing defense mechanisms to do so (and thereby escalating their level of diffuse anxiety). But at the same time, normal individuals are also realists; when a self-concept cannot be preserved, people develop new self-definitions, but they do so in gradual ways that are consistent with, and in harmony with, older self-definitions (Swann, 1983). It is reasonable to hypothesize, I think, that situational definitions are more easily changed and reconciled with other situationally based elements of self than are elements of one's core self. But even when individuals can no longer sustain all of their core self-definitions, they usually shift these definitions in a manner that promotes consistency. If this shift cannot occur and/or cannot be done in ways that promote self-consistency, then levels of diffuse anxiety increase (arrow *h*). And, as a consequence, the mobilization of energy, as well as signaling and interpreting, in an interaction can become potentially pathological.

Another issue is whether individuals' needs for consistency/stability in self-definitions are more critical than needs for maintaining or enhancing self-evaluations, or self-esteem. Once again, both processes are important (Gecas, 1986, 1982). Efforts to sustain self-conceptions reveal behaviors designed to secure responses of self-*affirm*ation from others (i.e., to maintain self-esteem and perhaps a sense of efficacy) and, at the same time, to prompt responses of self-*confirm*ation from others (i.e., to keep substantive elements of self intact and consistent). The results of such efforts are denoted by feedback path *n-h*. To some extent, self-affirmation depends upon self-confirmation; that is, people's level of esteem is greatly affected by their capacity to sustain a core self whose definitional elements are consistent; the converse is less true. But these dimensions of self—esteem and consistency—are also independent sources of motivation. When one's positive evaluations of self are not affirmed by others, one experiences anxiety and is highly mobilized to "do something" about such failures of self-affirmation (path *g-m*). Part of the reason for such mobilization is, of course, that failure to affirm self-evaluations creates inconsistency among self-definitions; but equally important, efforts to sustain esteem per se are powerful motivating forces. In fact, I would hypothesize that such efforts are more salient to an individual than consistency questions and will produce more anxiety (arrow *h*) as well as more intense efforts at resolution (causal path *g-m*).

Thus, when conceptualizing as a motivational dynamic the "need to sustain a self-conception," I am subsuming a number of more complex dynamics. But a synthetic model like that in Fig. 5.1 requires this kind of collapsing of processes. Moreover, the dynamics of self-related processes are amenable to this synthesis, for in the end, individuals attempt to sustain a self-conception by affirming and confirming both its core and situational elements.

Operating simultaneously with efforts to sustain self are activities designed to meet needs for symbolic and material gratifications. Just what symbols and material props are gratifying is, to some degree, determined by the context of an interaction. For example, a situation of authority would define the symbols and materials of power as gratifying (the right to give orders, to control space, to demand deference, to make money, etc.), whereas a friendship relationship would involve symbols of mutual approval and material arrangements facilitating interaction. Equally important as the context of an interaction are other motivational processes. These also define what is gratifying, and while their variability is also context-dependent, they evidence independent effects on people's perceptions of what is rewarding. Let me explore some of the ways that these other motivational processes circumscribe needs for gratification.

First, as causal path *c-f* indicates, needs for group inclusion influence what is defined as gratifying as well as the intensity of needs for gratification. Needs for inclusion dictate that symbols and material props signifying group inclusion are likely to be highly gratifying, especially when inclusion needs are high and escalate levels of diffuse anxiety. Second, needs for trust or predictability of interactions, as demarked by causal path *d-f*, are also relevant to needs for gratification, if less so than needs for inclusion. That is, symbols and material props that provide interactants with a sense of predictable rhythms will be rewarding, but not as rewarding as those marking group membership. Third, as causal path *e-f* indicates, needs for ontological security will also influence what is gratifying, but less so than either needs for trust or group inclusion. Fourth, and as important as needs for group inclusion, needs to sustain self exert powerful constraints on needs for gratification, as is denoted by causal arrow *j*. Individuals find particularly gratifying those symbols and material arrangements that confirm the substantive content of their core and more peripheral self, especially with respect to issues of esteem and consistency. Fifth, previous outcomes of signaling and interpreting with others, as marked by feedback loops *r* and *s*, will condition what individuals find gratifying. Those symbols and material props that have in the past created a sense of emotional enhancement by virtue of their capacity to confirm/affirm self, that have denoted a favorable place in group processes, and that have provided a sense of trust as well as security will be a cause of an actor's expenditure of energy (as denoted by causal loop *r-l*).

Although needs for sustaining self can operate via causal path *j-l* on the mobilization of interpersonal energy (that is, through their influence on needs for gratification), they also exert more direct effects following causal arrow *m*. Indeed, independently of needs for material or symbolic gratification, people negotiate over ways to sustain their respective self-conceptions; or, in Goffman's (1959) terminology, much interaction involves "presentations of self" as actors seek to construct "lines" of conduct that save and preserve "face" (Goffman, 1967).

An equally important causal force is denoted by the path emanating from needs for facticity. People mobilize considerable energy in order to construct an implicit "account" of a situation. That is, through the use of ethnomethods (Garfinkel, 1967), they create a sense of a shared and factual world. One could hypothesize that this implicit "account" of what is real becomes a critical background feature of the given situation, which in turn, facilitates actors' ability to meet other interpersonal needs.

The process of mobilizing energy thus occurs at multiple levels and phases. In terms of phases, I think needs for facticity and the consequent use of ethnomethods are typically initiated before efforts at self-confirmation and exchanges of resources. With respect to levels, these are displayed as vertical columns across Fig. 5.1. In the middle column, the more explicit motivational levels of interaction—needs for gratification, self-confirmation, and facticity—are shown. On the far left are the deeper and typically unconscious needs for ontological security, trust, and group inclusion. Thus, what one can actually observe in interaction—the expen-

diture of energy through signaling and gesturing—is motivated and energized by a more complex set of processes. Most sociological theory has, I
think, concentrated far too much on the levels of motivation depicted in
the middle and on the right side of Fig. 5.1. The forces on the left side are
equally important, perhaps even more significant for the smooth flow of
interaction and ultimately for the maintenance of patterns of social organization.

This conclusion becomes even more evident when certain feedback processes in the model are examined in more detail. At the bottom of Fig. 5.1
are two crucial feedback loops, denoted by causal arrows p and q. As
people employ ethnomethods in their signaling and interpreting (causal arrow o), they seek to convince each other that they share, for the purposes
at hand, a common factual world. As signals are sent and interpreted, the
feedback process denoted by arrow p is critical. For if interactants do not
create a sense of a common world, then needs for facticity will increase
and set into motion increased use of ethnomethods to assert an account,
to repair a damaged one, or to gloss over potentially discordant elements
of an account. I would hypothesize that interaction will cycle around this
causal path until an account is constructed, creating a situation where the
expenditure of energy to meet other needs will be held in partial suspension.

If an interaction continues to cycle around problems of creating an account, then feedback arrow q indicates that deeper needs for ontological
security will escalate, creating a sense of diffuse anxiety (arrow e). In turn,
this anxiety will increase further needs for facticity (arrow i) as well as
needs for sustaining self (arrow g) and gratification (arrow f), but these
latter two needs will not be activated to the extent of the need for facticity.
As arrow b indicates, the increased salience of needs for ontological security will raise needs for trust, which will also increase anxiety and, to a
greater extent than do needs for security, needs for self-maintenance and
gratification (causal paths d-g, d-f). As is evident, then, these complex and
indirect feedback processes can escalate exponentially needs for facticity
as well as other motivational processes. This exponential escalation can
also help explain why Garfinkel's (1963, 1967) early "breaching experiments" generated such seemingly disproportionate emotional reactions
from subjects. The explanation resides, I think, in the refracted effects of
interpretive problems in feedback arrows p and q. Conversely, when the
use of ethnomethods is successful in creating an account, then more than
just needs for facticity are reduced in salience, thereby allowing other interpersonal negotiations to proceed.

Feedback loop n similarly sets into motion a series of complex reactions.

When presentations of self do not lead to confirmation and affirmation of either core or situational selves, then presentational activities will increase as a proportion of signaling and interpreting, but not unless some background accounts are constructed. If some aspect of self is not confirmed or affirmed after repeated efforts, then feedback loop h would indicate that anxiety will increase and set off even more escalated efforts at sustaining self (via causal path h-g-m). Moreover, since the anxiety is likely to be diffuse and nonspecific, needs for gratification (path h-f) and facticity (path h-i) will also increase, though not to the degree of needs for sustaining self. Moreover, if these needs for facticity and gratification increase too much, then feedback arrows s and q indicate that needs for inclusion, trust, and security would also increase, as would the level of diffuse anxiety fueling needs for self, gratification, and facticity. And conversely, if self-presentations are successful, then these same causal paths will reduce not only the salience of needs for self but also those for facticity and gratification (and indirectly those for inclusion, trust, and security).

Feedback arrow r denotes the rewards that people receive in their exchanges with others. If they receive a level of symbolic and material rewards that is proportionate to their expectations and that allows them a profit, then interaction will proceed smoothly, but it will be influenced by the effects of marginal utility or satiation. If people do not receive a profit, then needs for symbolic and material gratification increase, setting into motion renewed efforts to achieve relevant symbolic and material resources. But if needs for gratification are not met, then needs for a sense of group inclusion increase, as is indicated by feedback arrow s. The activation of this latter need escalates diffuse anxiety, which operates to raise exponentially needs for symbols and material arrangements that signal group membership (causal path s-c-f) and, to a lesser extent, needs for self-confirmation (s-c-g) and facticity (s-c-i). Thus, if exchange relations prove consistently unprofitable, I would hypothesize that actors will find the symbols and props of group inclusion increasingly rewarding and that presentations of self will revolve ever more around confirming and affirming self as a group participant. Moreover, if needs for group inclusion increase to a very high level, then needs for facticity can also rise, although to a lesser extent than needs for sustaining self and gratification. If such needs for group inclusion jump to extremely high levels, then the use of ethnomethods will revolve increasingly around creating a shared sense of common group structure. And finally, as needs for group inclusion increase, then needs for a sense of trust will rise (arrow a), setting into motion, via causal arrow d, escalated anxiety as it influences other motivational processes, as described earlier.

Conclusion

The analytical model in Fig. 5.1 summarizes my best estimation of the motivational processes behind social interaction. As an analytical model, it simplifies; and in the spirit of Parsons's (1937) strategy for "analytical realism," it highlights at an abstract level phenomena that are embedded in each other and in the more general flow of human organization. Unlike Parsons's analytical realism, my model emphasizes processes and conceptualizes elements in the model as variables whose values can change. But much like Parsons's approach, all analytical models are too complex to test as a whole, despite the fact that they obviously represent simplifications of empirical processes. And thus, a model such as this one is most useful when it can be translated into a series of propositions.

The models presented in this and subsequent chapters are intended to facilitate such conversion. In making this conversion, additional theorizing is involved. For as one creates statements of covariance among variables, some causal connections are given more emphasis than others. Yet we are not ready for a full propositional analysis, since the values of the variables in the model will be influenced by interactional and structuring processes to be denoted in later chapters. As will be recalled from Fig. 2.1, motivational, interactional, and structuring processes are interconnected. These relationships will become increasingly evident as composite models are developed for interactional and structuring processes.

Yet even at this point, it is possible to offer some propositions from the model in Fig. 5.1. We will want to rewrite these as more variables become available from models on interactional and structuring variables, but as a preliminary summary, it might be useful to list some of the key relationships from the model.

1. The overall level of motivational energy of an individual during interaction is a steep s-function of the level of diffuse anxiety experienced by that individual.

2. The overall level of diffuse anxiety of an individual during interaction is an inverse and additive function of the extent to which needs for group inclusion, trust, ontological security, and confirmation/affirmation of self are being met.

   a. The intensity of needs for group inclusion is an inverse function of the extent to which efforts at signaling and interpreting yield symbolic and material gratifications that mark group membership.

   b. The intensity of needs for ontological security is an inverse function of the degree to which the use of ethnomethods during signaling and interpreting creates an implicit account of "what is real" in a situation, and hence, a sense of facticity.

c. The intensity of needs for trust is an inverse and multiplicative function of the degree to which signaling and interpreting meet needs for ontological security and group inclusion through, respectively, the use of ethnomethods and the profitable exchange of symbols and props marking group membership.

d. The intensity of needs for self-affirmation/confirmation is an inverse function of the degree to which presentations and interpretations of self are successful in sustaining the content and consistency of core and peripheral self-definitions.

3. The degree to which an individual will seek to maintain an interaction, or to renew and reproduce it at subsequent points in time, is an additive function of the extent to which needs for group inclusion, trust, ontological security, self-confirmation/affirmation, gratification, and facticity are being met.

In reading this short list of propositions, several lines of emphasis become evident. First, I see an individual's overall level of motivational energy as directly caused by the diffuse anxiety that results from a failure to meet needs for group inclusion, ontological security, trust, and self-affirmation/confirmation. Among these motivational forces, only the self variable is typically subject to high levels of conscious reflection; and thus, I am arguing that much motivational energy is ultimately tied to more unconscious forces.[3] Indeed, if we take Freud's view of "libido" in its broadest sense, then the conceptualization of group inclusion, trust, and ontological security as the mainsprings of motivation is very similar to Freud's argument. In this emphasis, there is an implied critique of much sociological theory, which has tended to ignore the topic of motivation in general or, when it has addressed the topic, has tended to stress self-presentation, exchange calculations, and use of interpersonal techniques. These may be the most visible aspects of motivation, but I believe it is their feedback effects

[3] I am also taking a position that appears to emphasize the dark side of motivational energy. That is, humans are motivated by the fear of anxiety that comes with a failure to meet certain fundamental need states. I must confess that this conclusion bothers me in my humanistic moments, but it is somewhat mitigated by my third proposition, where things are seen in a more positive light. People will try to sustain and repeat those relations that meet basic needs, but there is, I argue, always a fear of not having them met, which keeps their energy up. Thus, my theory mixes two somewhat different traditions: interpersonal energy is related to the anxiety that comes with not meeting ends or the fear of not meeting them; a willingness to participate in social relations is related to the fact that they do not produce this anxiety. Thus, a desire to avoid the anxiety that would ensue if reinforcing social relations ceased meeting basic needs is what ultimately generates interpersonal energy.

on deeper levels of motivation that generate the most motivational energy in people. In essence, then, sociological theory has not given sufficient attention to those unconscious processes that fuel anxiety.

Second, I suspect that many of the relations specified in these propositions are nonlinear, although I have emphasized this conclusion only with the first proposition. Since apathy and withdrawal eventually occur if needs go unconsummated, especially for the more visible motivating forces such as self-presentation, profit seeking, and use of ethnomethods, it is likely that the reactions among these motive states are nonlinear. However, withdrawal and apathy are, in essence, two of many defense mechanisms that simply repress or leave unconsummated more fundamental motive forces. As these go unconsummated, they build in intensity and create diffuse anxiety, which, in a pathological cycle, can encourage even more extensive use of defense mechanisms—a dynamic that will also reveal a nonlinear profile. And, as Freud would have argued, such defensive cycles create enormous motivational energy that will, in the end, become manifest. Given the complexity of these dynamics, I found it difficult to specify the exact form of the relationships; though I have stated most of them as linear, it is quite probable that they are nonlinear.

Finally, let me stress again that this list of propositions is only provisional and selective. It does not examine all of the causal processes outlined in Fig. 5.1; rather, it represents what I see as the most crucial set of motivational forces. But to the extent that we seek to break the model down into a more manageable and testable form, this list of propositions—as well as the various hypotheses offered during my discussion of the model—can serve as a starting point for using the model to understand specific empirical situations.

III

Interactional Processes

6

Mead's and Schutz's Early Models of Interaction

A NUMBER OF SCHOLARS have viewed Talcott Parsons's *The Structure of Social Action* as a "promising beginning" that was regrettably abandoned in favor of a macro functionalism (e.g., Scott, 1963; Coleman, 1986). Though Parsons's early theory of motivation is applauded by even his most severe critics, my view is less enthusiastic in two senses. First, his early work is, in reality, an expanded and elaborated version of utilitarian approaches, as a comparison of Figs. 1.2 and 3.1 will reveal. Second, his abandonment of his theory of motivation is less of a problem than his failure to take the next theoretical step and develop a model of interaction. For the great flaw in Parsons's action theory is that actors can potentially "act" but not "*inter*act." Indeed, as I emphasized in Chapter 1, Parsons followed Weber's lead and moved rather quickly into a macrostructural interpretation of reality, in which actors increasingly became cogs in the status roles of the social system. All this has, of course, been said before and need not be elaborated upon. The more interesting point in such criticisms is that Parsons appears to have been unaware of Alfred Schutz's (1932) early analysis of Weber's rather static, typological, and classificatory approach to social action and interaction. Even more amazing is his failure to examine, at least during this early phase of his writing, the relevant work of George Herbert Mead (1934). In the thought of these two scholars we find the basic elements of all contemporary approaches to what Parsonian and Weberian action theory has always lacked: a model of interaction.

Mead and Schutz came from very different intellectual traditions—American pragmatism and behaviorism for Mead, German phenomenology for Schutz. But these respective analyses converged and, at the same time, complemented each other. For this to occur, Mead had to take behaviorism away from the methodological straitjacket imposed by John B. Watson (1913)[1] and delve into the processes of thought and meaning, whereas Schutz had to liberate phenomenology from the solipsism of Ed-

---

[1] I have been told that Watson was in Mead's famous course on social psychology at the University of Chicago; if this is so, then Mead was attacking his former student, who apparently had missed the central point of Mead's lectures.

mund Husserl's (1913) phenomenological project and "*un*bracket" the external world of other people. Taken together, these early works of Mead and Schutz made behaviorism and phenomenology the conceptual cornerstones for a theory of interactional processes.

Thus, in moving to the second basic process in the analysis of micro dynamics—that is, interactional processes—the best place to begin is with what Parsons ignored: the ideas of Mead and Schutz. As will be recalled from the discussion in Chapter 2, interactional processes involve what people actually do when they influence each other's behavior. The last three chapters have analyzed what energizes or motivates behavior during the course of interaction; the next three chapters will explore how motivated individuals respond to one another. As is perhaps obvious, but nonetheless fundamental, interactional processes revolve around individuals' capacity to signal their course of behavior with gestures, to interpret each other's gestures, and to adjust their responses. Elsewhere, I have called this process "the mechanics of interaction" (J. Turner, 1986a), but the label is less important than a detailed analysis of the processes of signaling and interpreting. Mead and Schutz provided the conceptual canopy for understanding these interrelated processes, and modern theorists have been filling in the details. Let me begin with Mead and then turn to Schutz, saving for the next chapter a review of the more modern supplements to these early thinkers.

Mead on Interactional Processes

G. H. Mead (1934) sometimes employed the concept of "triadic matrix" to describe the essential dynamics in all interaction. First, an organism gestures as it moves in the environment, and in so doing, it sends out signals to other organisms. Second, another organism perceives this movement by becoming aware of gestures, and then responds to these gestures by altering its movements in the environment, thereby sending out its own signals. Third, the original organism perceives these latter signals and responds to them by altering its course of behavior. When these three events have occurred, the triad is complete, and interaction has taken place.

Mead argued that although human interaction contains the basic elements of this triad, it is qualitatively different from nonhuman interaction. This qualitative difference stems from what Mead believed (perhaps incorrectly) to be certain unique behavioral capacities of humans. First, humans use "conventional" or "significant" gestures, in that the signs communicated among humans "mean" the same thing to both the sending and the receiving organism (that is, they call forth similar responses, whether covert or overt). Second, humans have the capacity to "role-take," or to interpret the conventional gestures of others and mentally "take" or assume the perspective and likely course of action of others. Third, humans possess a capacity for "self," in that they can view themselves as objects in a situation by reading their own gestures as well as those of others; and they can use this sense of self as a guideline to organizing their responses to others. Fourth, humans reveal a capacity for "mind" in the sense that they can "imaginatively rehearse" alternative lines of conduct, foresee varying outcomes, inhibit what are seen as inappropriate responses, and select an appropriate line of conduct. Fifth, by virtue of their capacities for "role-taking" and "mind," humans can assume the perspective of "generalized others" or "communities of attitudes" and use this perspective as a framework for self-evaluation and choosing an appropriate line of conduct.

I do not believe that these behavioral capacities are unique to humans, although we no doubt possess them to the greatest degree.[2] In any case they do make human interaction highly complex, allowing us to engage in multiple behaviors simultaneously or in very rapid sequence. If these behavioral capacities are combined with those in Mead's analysis of motivation (see Fig. 3.4), a model somewhat like that in Fig. 6.1 emerges.

As discussed in Chapter 3, Mead's (1938) analysis of "the act" emphasized four phases: (1) "impulses," or states of disequilibrium with the environment; (2) heightened and selective "perception" where objects, including oneself, others, and generalized others, are viewed in regard to their relevance for restoring equilibrium; (3) "manipulation" of the external environment through overt behavior and/or the internal, mental environment through the covert behavioral capacities for "mind," or the capacity to "imaginatively rehearse" alternatives; and (4) "consummation," or elimination of the impulse. Blockage of impulses escalates their intensity, heightens perception, and encourages minded deliberations as well as overt efforts at environmental manipulation. Thus, interaction is, in Mead's view, always circumscribed by the configurations of impulses, as these influence perception and thought. Of course, both past and present interactions with others are the primary source of impulses; configurations of impulses are changed as old impulses are consummated or frustrated and perhaps new ones initiated.

As Fig. 6.1 emphasizes, the most critical processes in such motivated in-

---

[2] I think Mead was incorrect in his assumption that animals cannot do many of these things. Anyone who owns a dog recognizes the canine's rudimentary capacity for using significant gestures and role-taking. More importantly, some mammals, such as higher primates and perhaps some marine mammals, evidence considerable capacity to use conventional gestures, to role-take, and to think. What Mead saw as a basic dichotomy is a continuum involving degrees of behavioral capacities.

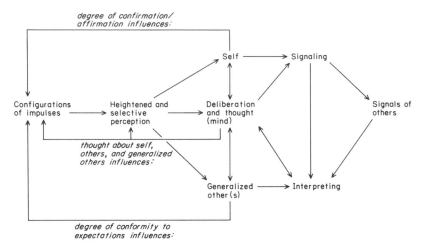

Fig. 6.1. Mead's model of interaction.

teraction are (1) perceptions of "self" as an object; (2) perceptions of relevant "generalized others"; (3) covert manipulation, or reflective and deliberative thought involving assessment of alternatives, self, and generalized other(s); (4) overt manipulation, or signaling through the emission of gestures; and (5) interpretation of others', as well as one's own, gestures in terms of generalized others and conceptions of self.[3] All of these five processes have, directly or indirectly, an impact on the configurations of an individual's impulses as they circumscribe the flow of an interaction.

One critical variable in this model is self as a primary constraint on how

[3] One reviewer of this model asked where Mead's analysis of the "I" and "me" was. These concepts have been, I think, rather overemphasized in commentaries on Mead. The actual passages where they appear (Mead, 1934: 125, 145–46, 173–78, 192–213, 273–81, 371–73) are some of the most abstruse in his work. Hence, I prefer not to use the concepts, but this is how I interpret them: "me" is an actor's self-image in a situation; as such, it reflects, in order of importance, one's deliberations over, and perceptions of, what one has just done; the "looking-glass" reactions of others as reflected in their gestures; the evaluation of behavior from the perspective of the generalized other; and the assessment of one's more enduring self-conception. "I" is simply behavior. As Mead says, "the 'I' can only be known in experience"; that is, the "I" is only seen through "me" or self-images. Thus, behavior consists of "I"-"me"-"I"-"me" bundles, in which actors behave ("I") and then see their behavior ("me"). This process need not always be overt, of course. Actors can weigh a behavioral option ("me"), emit the behavior "in their mind" ("I"), and then think about the consequences of such emission ("me"). All of these ideas are found in Fig. 6.1 and have in fact been described as processes (1) through (5)—thus, (1) represents "me" images, (2) more complex "me" images, (3) "I"-"me"-"I"-"me" bundles, (4) "I," and (5) complexes of "me" images. This presentation avoids the controversy over whether Mead used the term "I" to denote indeterminacy in human behavior, though I think he did in this sense: even if you think about what you are going to do ("me"), you cannot be sure just what you have done until after you have actually acted ("I"), and then observed your behavior ("me").

individuals signal, or emit gestures. For Mead, an individual's self-conception mediates between configurations of impulses, generalized others, and assessment of alternatives, on the one hand, and signaling through gestures, on the other hand. It is for this reason that self is placed closest to signaling in the model in Fig. 6.1.[4] For although thought or covert deliberation has direct effects on how people signal, such reflective thought is influenced by people's self-conception. Moreover, perceptions of self have a direct causal effect on signaling, independent of conscious thought. That is, people's signals are often unconsciously influenced by their conception of themselves as a particular kind of individual.[5] Moreover, Mead implicitly hypothesized that the degree to which one's sense of self is confirmed and affirmed by the signals of others (via the causal paths through interpreting and deliberation in the figure) has dramatic effects on configurations of impulses (as is denoted by the feedback arrow at the top left portion of the figure). When one's self-conception in a situation is not confirmed and affirmed, impulses to secure such affirmation/confirmation are heightened, with the result that perception, thought, and signaling are increasingly oriented to considerations of self.

The other critical causal variable in interaction is the "generalized other." Unfortunately, Mead's discussion of this variable is brief, but with some reasonable inferences it is possible to draw out the full implications of his analysis (Turner, 1982). His ideas converge with Durkheim's (1893) analysis of the "collective conscience," in that the importance of shared cognitions on interaction is emphasized. Mead appears to have borrowed the concept of generalized other from Wilhelm Wundt's (1916) notion of "mental communities," in which actors are seen to share certain attitudes. Mead makes the generalized other more sociological by emphasizing that "communities of attitudes" are attached to ongoing patterns of coordinated interaction. Such communities of attitudes represent a cognitive perspective or framework that informs individuals of the appropriate ways of responding to a situation. In particular, the generalized other provides the criteria for self-assessment, for reflective thought, for signaling, and for interpreting the signals of others. It says, in effect, that only these kinds of self-assessment are to be invoked, only these parameters of thought are rel-

---

[4]There is, of course, considerable disagreement over Mead's conceptualization of self. Mead uses the term "self" in three different ways: (1) as a synonym for "actor" or "individual," (2) as a concept denoting the process of self-control on the part of individuals, and (3) as a concept denoting actors' cognitions about themselves as objects. I am emphasizing (3) here, with implications for (2) in the sense that one's self-conception represents ordered cognitions that delimit and control the gestures that people emit. See Turner and Beeghley (1981: 502–3) for my more detailed modeling of the relation between Mead's various uses of the concept "self."

[5]Here, I may be reaching a bit, but I think that Mead would agree with this interpretation.

evant, only this range of signaling is appropriate, and only these patterns of interpretation are useful.

The generalized other thus places parameters on how people see themselves, think, interpret, and signal; and at the same time, it can provide more detailed instructions about how to proceed during interaction. In fact, Mead appears to conceptualize several levels of generalized others. There can be a very general perspective or set of attitudes as well as more detailed instructions about how individuals should respond in a situation. The important point in Mead's analysis is that as people interact, they develop shared cognitive perspectives and frameworks for ordering their responses, especially with regard to how one thinks, interprets, signals, and views self. Moreover, once such perspectives are created and used, they become attached to the situation and circumscribe subsequent interactions. And so, as individuals develop relatively stable patterns of coordinated activity ("society" in Mead's terms), they also develop shared attitudes and orientations that further structure the situation. Thus, for most interactions, there exists a relevant configuration of both abstract and specific generalized others for mediating interaction.

The placement of the generalized other in Fig. 6.1 marks its relative causal effects on the other variables. The most direct effect is on how people think, which, in turn, has indirect effects on how individuals define self, signal, and interpret. The other direct causal path connects the generalized other(s) with the process of interpretation: the generalized other provides the mental set or framework for interpreting the gestures of others.[6] In turn, the degree of conformity of others' gestures, and indirectly one's own, to the dictates of the generalized other has consequences for an individual's configuration of impulses, as is denoted by the feedback arrow at the bottom left portion of Fig. 6.1.

In sum, then, Mead conceptualizes self and generalized other(s) as the primary variables determining how people think, signal, and interpret. Moreover, the values for these variables have important causal effects, via feedback loops, on people's impulses, or sense of equilibrium. Signaling is most directly influenced by self, whereas interpreting is most directly determined by the generalized other. And while reflective thought, as stimulated by impulses, heightened perception, and perhaps blockage, or unconsummated impulses (see Fig. 3.4), also influences how individuals signal and interpret, the process of thinking is highly circumscribed by people's self-conception and their invocation of generalized others. How-

[6] Hence, "me" images are typically filtered through the "generalized other." I should also note that there is a clear convergence between Mead's conceptualization of the "generalized other" and Freud's view of the "super-ego." They are both pointing to the internalization and use of group standards to evaluate actions.

ever, if blockage of impulses occurs, especially with respect to confirmation of self and conformity to the expectations of generalized others, then people become increasingly conscious of themselves as objects in the situation and of the dictates of the generalized other—thereby underscoring that "mind," or reflective thought, has important effects on both self and generalized other. Yet, even here, this increased awareness of self and generalized others feeds back and constrains further conscious thought as well as the processes of signaling and interpreting during interaction. As the feedback arrow in the middle left portion of Fig. 6.1 underscores, such thought about oneself and generalized others also has important direct effects on an individual's impulses.

These seminal ideas, as modeled in Fig. 6.1, represent the conceptual canopy for most modern theorizing on interaction. As I document in the next chapter, most contemporary theory has simply sought to specify in more detail how self and cognitive frames influence thinking, signaling, and interpreting among individuals. These details are not trivial, for Mead's formulation is skeletal and often vague.[7] Contemporary analyses have added considerably more detail to a conceptualization of interactional processes.

Mead's ideas are not the only early source of inspiration for modern theorizing about interaction. In recent decades, what is often viewed as an alternative to traditional interactionist analysis has emerged in sociological theory, drawing its inspiration from phenomenology, especially as revised by Alfred Schutz. Yet, as will become evident, Schutz's approach and those contemporary perspectives it has influenced represent not an "alternative" to Mead, but rather a supplement to the general model portrayed in Fig. 6.1.

Schutz's Contribution to Mead's Conceptual Canopy

In Fig. 6.2, I have modeled Schutz's analysis of interaction in ways that emphasize convergence with Mead's ideas. There are important differences in their approaches, but first let me stress their similarities. Schutz never really developed a coherent theory of motivation; and in his early work (Schutz, 1932), this is most evident. He implies that actors' "interests" motivate them to interrupt their ongoing "stream of consciousness," creating "acts of attention," or what he also termed "the act" and "activity." Such acts of attention can also be generated by the "pure ego," which, presum-

---

[7] This is the reason, I believe, that Mead's ideas are often taken in different directions. For example, Blumer's (1969) interpretation is very different than mine, although it too fits Fig. 6.1.

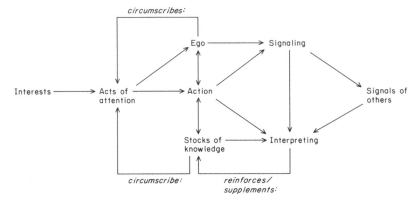

Fig. 6.2. Schutz's model of intersubjectivity.

ably, is the desire of an individual to call attention to itself as an object in a given situation. In a sense, "acts of attention" correspond to the "perception" phase of the act in Mead's motivational scheme. The essential point is that, for whatever motivational reasons, actors become selectively attuned to aspects of their environment.

Such selective perception determines how they see themselves as objects ("ego"), how they think ("action"), and how they frame, or put into perspective, a situation ("stocks of knowledge"). Schutz's conceptualization of "ego" is very imprecise, although it appears to correspond roughly to Mead's view of self. The concept of "action" more closely parallels Mead's conception of "mind" as imaginative rehearsal or, in Schutz's words, the "projection of the act into the future." And "stock of knowledge" is similar to Mead's formulation of the "generalized other" in at least this sense: it represents a cognitive structure that orders past experiences and makes them available for interpreting the gestures of others, thinking about alternatives, seeing oneself as an object, and signaling with "significant-signs" a course of behavior.

Interaction thus consists of signaling and interpreting gestures in terms of stocks of knowledge that order past experiences and provide a perspective or framework for interaction with others. In this general sense, Schutz's scheme converges with Mead's, but as I mentioned above, there are important shifts in emphasis.

Perhaps the most obvious difference is that "the other" is far less central in Schutz's analysis than in Mead's (Perinbanayagam, 1975). As a phenomenologist, Schutz was more interested in consciousness per se, than Mead, who was primarily concerned with how coordinated activity ("society") was possible. Indeed, Schutz phrases the question of interaction in terms of "intersubjectivity." That is, how do individuals gain access to each other's subjective states? His answer to this question is the signaling and interpreting of gestures in terms of the framework provided by stocks of knowledge. But in this answer, which on the surface resembles Mead's, additional differences between the two emerge.

Unlike Mead, who tended to see interaction as a very active process of signaling, interpreting, and constructing lines of coordinated activity,[8] Schutz argues that individuals generally "take for granted" a "reciprocity of perspectives" and that interaction typically involves signaling and interpreting in ways that avoid questioning this implicit presumption. Thus, in contrast to Mead's actor, who actively signals, role-takes, and rehearses alternatives, Schutz's actor assumes intersubjectivity unless shown otherwise. But at the same time that actors avoid questioning their presumption of intersubjectivity, they are not passive; they do actively signal and interpret in an effort to fine-tune and enhance their feelings of intersubjectivity. Here again, we can see how Schutz's model deviates from Mead's analysis in several important respects.

First, Schutz's conceptualization of "stocks of knowledge" is more precise than Mead's analysis of the "generalized other." For Schutz, humans' "past experiences are present as *ordered*, as knowledge or as awareness of what to expect, just as the whole external world is present . . . as ordered. Ordinarily and unless [humans are] forced to solve a special kind of problem, [they] do not ask questions about how this ordered world was constituted" (Schutz, 1932: 81). Thus, though stocks of knowledge are implicit, they frame and order situations in terms of past experiences.[9] Such stocks of knowledge give experience a sense of continuity in such fundamental dimensions of reality as time, space, relations, rules of inference, rules for using significant signs, categorizing others and situations, and providing contextual meanings for signs. In other words, interaction is possible because humans presume that they have common stocks of knowledge and because they use these stocks to orient themselves in time and space, determine the contextual meaning of gestures ("indexicality," in modern jargon), categorize objects and people, and determine the appropriate "rules" or "procedures" for making inferences about the gestures of others and for emitting their own signals.

Second, Schutz's analysis stresses what, in Mead's vocabulary, might be termed "levels of role-taking." As people implicitly use stocks of knowl-

[8] It is this aspect of Mead that Blumer (1969) emphasizes—indeed, *over*emphasizes.

[9] Yet Schutz misses what Durkheim, Freud, and Mead emphasized, respectively, with their concepts of the "collective conscience," the "super-ego," and the "generalized other." For all of these theorists, action is not just cognitively framed, it is "constrained" by internalized moral standards (that is, of course, Parsons's concern also).

edge to interpret the gestures of others, they do so with varying degrees of penetration into each other's consciousness. Whether a great deal or only a little penetration can or should occur is determined by stocks of knowledge that provide guidelines on what is possible and appropriate in a situation. At the more surface level of role-taking, actors mutually "typify," or place each other into stereotypical categories, and then proceed to interact without great effort to achieve more intimate intersubjectivity. A somewhat more complex role-taking occurs when actors read gestures to determine the "in-order-to" motives of others, to understand where an observed behavior falls in the context of a more extended project. A deeper level of understanding comes when the gestures of others can be read to provide information about "because-of" motives, or the past experiences of others that have led up to their current behavior. And there is a level of role-taking involving "sympathetic penetration," where actors feel as though they intimately share each other's subjective experiences.

Third, Schutz emphasizes that signaling and interpreting are highly contextual. Just what a gesture "means" depends upon the larger context in which it appears. Stocks of knowledge usually provide the necessary information for making accurate interpretations in several senses. They contain linguistic rules of inference for determining what a word or phrase means in a given linguistic context. They also enable interpretation of what nonverbal gestures mean in different situations. Thus, much signaling and interpreting involves understanding the context-dependency of gestures; and the "meaning" of a gesture can, to a very great extent, only be determined by implicit knowledge of what can occur in varying types of situations.

In sum, then, Schutz's model of intersubjectivity adds a number of important insights: a more robust conceptualization of the processes by which individuals employ generalized perspectives or frameworks to interpret the gestures of others; a recognition that much interaction involves creating a sense of common intersubjective experience by tacit agreement not to question potentially discordant information; a conceptualization of "role-taking," to use Mead's label, that involves varying levels of penetration into subjectivity; and a view of signaling and interpreting that emphasizes the contextual basis for determining the meaning of gestures. Although many of those who have drawn out the implications of Schutz's thought in recent decades tend to consider their analysis antithetical to those who have followed Mead (e.g., Garfinkel, 1967), my sense is that the modern traditions emerging from Mead's pragmatism/behaviorism and Schutz's adaptation of phenomenology are highly complementary. This is best seen by synthesizing their respective models.

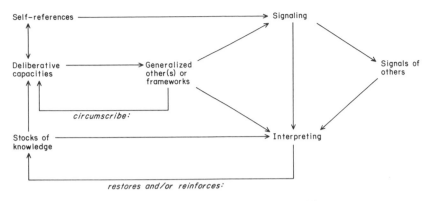

Fig. 6.3. A skeletal composite of Mead's and Schutz's models.

Conclusion: A Synthesized Model

In Fig. 6.3, I have combined Mead's and Schutz's models into a composite that provides a skeletal outline of the current theoretical work on interactional processes. As the model underscores, the processes of mutually signaling and interpreting are the vehicle by which actors influence each others' responses. For unless the signals of actors are mutually interpreted and used to organize subsequent signaling, interaction does not occur. A theoretical analysis of interaction must, therefore, explain the dynamics of signaling and interpreting of gestures.

As is portrayed in the composite model, actors use their stocks of knowledge as deep-background configurations of experiences to frame, in broad strokes, their deliberations about themselves, their emission of signals, and their interpretation of the signals emitted by others. Moreover, individuals in interaction must focus their stocks of knowledge through the invocation of the relevant generalized other(s), which provide(s) a more precise framework for interpreting gestures, thinking about alternatives, viewing oneself, and signaling a course of behavior. The generalized other thus makes more specific how actors are to orient themselves in a particular interaction. It provides more clear-cut standards and criteria by which one weighs potential alternatives, conceives of self, signals intentions, and interprets the responses of others.

In approaching more contemporary theories of interaction, then, our goal should be to develop a more detailed analysis of how people signal and interpret through their behavioral capacities for using implicit stocks of knowledge, focusing these stocks through shared cognitive frameworks, deliberating on potential responses, and seeing themselves as objects. As the composite model communicates by the juxtaposition of these variables, an individual's self-conception, as broadly framed by stocks of knowledge and more clearly defined by the criteria of the generalized other, circumscribes how an individual signals in an interaction, whereas stocks of knowledge, as concretized by the cognitive ability to invoke more specific frameworks, are most directly critical in interpreting the gestures of others. All of these dynamics presuppose, of course, the ability to think reflectively, for it is through this capacity that stocks of knowledge are accumulated and brought to bear in a situation, that conceptions of self are possible, and that generalized frameworks can be invoked. Moreover, as the causal arrows in the model stress, reflective thinking is more than a mediator between stocks of knowledge, self, and generalized others, on the one hand, and signaling and interpreting, on the other. While thought and reflection are clearly constrained by self, stocks of knowledge, and generalized frameworks, these "mind" processes also exert direct and, to some extent, independent effects on signaling and interpreting.

Such is my view of the early theoretical legacy as Talcott Parsons confronted it in 1937 with the publication of *The Structure of Social Action*. Parsons did not use this legacy, but most contemporary theorists have employed the skeletal outline in Fig. 6.3, usually emphasizing only some dimensions of signaling and interpreting, while ignoring others. Theorists have also tended to assert that the variables in their own theories are the *only* critical processes. In contrast, I suggest that only when these theories are combined under the guidance of the composite model in Fig. 6.3 will an adequate conceptualization of signaling and interpreting emerge.

7

Contemporary Models of Interaction

AS CONTEMPORARY THEORISTS have implicitly worked with the skeletal model provided by Mead and Schutz, they have emphasized some signaling and interpreting processes at the expense of others. The result is a series of discrete models that, though full of insight, ignore many important dimensions of social interaction. In this chapter, I present the underlying models in the work of diverse theorists, with a special eye to how their ideas can be reconciled for the synthesis presented in Chapter 8.

In selecting the theorists to be examined here, I have chosen for detailed review the most visible representatives of particular theoretical traditions. I open with an examination of Ralph Turner's role-theory perspective, then explore the dramaturgical analysis of Erving Goffman, especially as his early work on dramaturgy was modified by his conceptualization of ritual and framing. Next, I present Harold Garfinkel's ethnomethodological "alternative" in a way that encourages reconciliation with mainstream theorizing about interaction; and finally, I extract elements from Jürgen Habermas's critical theoretic project, particularly his formulation of "validity claims" in the "ideal speech act."

Turner's Role Theory

Over the last 25 years, Ralph Turner has used Mead's model of interaction to develop a strategy for the analysis of roles (1979, 1978, 1968, 1962). In so doing, he has blended contemporary symbolic interactionism (e.g., Stryker, 1980; Manis and Meltzer, 1978; Blumer, 1969; Strauss, 1959) with role theory (e.g., Heiss, 1981; Biddle and Thomas, 1966) in ways that maintain the emphasis of symbolic interactionism on process and, at the same time, revitalize the more structural concept of "role." Too often, I feel, the notion of "role" is abandoned in micro analysis; contrary to perhaps a majority of current micro theorists, I see the dynamics of "roles" as fundamental in human relations.[1]

---

[1] Yet I will not use it to denote normatively regulated behavior associated with a "status position," which was Parsons's (1951) use in his conceptualization of the "status-role."

Turner has developed his approach partly in response to the problems of role theory (R. Turner, 1962), which include an excessively structured view of interaction,[2] too great a concern with deviant roles, and a failure to extend the central concept in Mead's approach—role-taking—in creative directions. As a result of addressing these problems, Turner implicitly employs a model of interaction that emphasizes the process of role-taking and, as will become evident, its conceptual companion, "role-making."

Turner views role-taking in much the same terms as Mead—reading and interpreting the gestures of others so as to assume their perspective, disposition, and likely line of conduct. But Turner adds an important element to this conceptualization: humans operate with the "folk assumption" that behavior is organized into *identifiable* roles. That is, people assume that the gestures of others constitute a syndrome or system of signals.[3] This syndrome of signals constitutes a role that, according to Turner, involves stereotypical sequences of behavior that are part of the knowledge base of competent actors. Indeed, in Turner's view, humans tacitly employ a "folk norm of consistency" that predisposes an assessment of behaviors in terms of their internal consistency and their capacity to signal *what* role others are playing. Until shown otherwise, people assume that gestures are consistent and mark an underlying role. Hence, the process of role-taking involves interpreting the behavior of others as a syndrome of gestures that reveals a role. For at the heart of role-taking "is the tendency to shape the phenomenal world into roles" (R. Turner, 1962: 21).

Turner (1962: 23) recognizes, however, that "interaction is always a tentative process, a process of continuously testing the conception one has of the role of the other." Role-taking is thus both active and provisional because additional gestures will be assessed in terms of how they fit with the role marked by previous gestures. This set of processes is termed by Turner "validation" or "verification." Actors read new gestures to see if they are consistent with those emitted earlier; and so they verify, or fail to verify, the imputed role. Verification depends upon the capacity of the imputed role to maintain the flow of interaction and/or to correspond to external criteria, such as relevant group norms and contextual features of the situation. Should gestures fail to be verified, a reassessment is in order, but this reevaluation will still involve the use of the "folk norm of consistency" in an effort to discover and verify a new role.

While Turner argues that actors typically possess only "loose cultural frameworks" of norms, beliefs, values, and contexts for interpreting gestures and imputing roles, I advocate a more extreme position: competent

---

[2] Turner critiques not only Parsons but also most "role theorists" who assume that "structure" is simply a system of complementary roles.

[3] This line of argument derives more from Schutz than Mead, although I'm not sure if Turner is directly borrowing from Schutz here.

actors possess relatively fine-tuned conceptions of roles and they use these as guidelines in role-taking, imputation, and verification.[4] In contrast, Turner would assert that, to some degree, imputation and verification involve a more creative and situational interpretation of another's role. Although this is the case under some conditions, I argue that, in most circumstances, role-taking begins with the use of shared role-conceptions as the basis for imputing a role. Only when the gestures of others do not seem to correspond to these more shared and standardized conceptions do actors begin to construct a situationally unique role for others.

Moreover, as Schutz (1932) stressed, role-taking occurs at varying levels—from mutual typification to deeper insight into another's subjective states. This point can be used to extend Turner's argument into a simple hypothesis: long-term interactions, especially those involving strong emotional feelings, will increasingly move from imputation in terms of culturally shared role-conceptions to more idiosyncratic constructions and imputations of another's role. Yet, even here, these idiosyncratic roles are constructed within the parameters of culturally shared role-conceptions (for example, in any culture, actors evidence common conceptions of what "friendship" involves or what "long-term" interaction should produce).

Thus, Turner's analysis of role-taking extends Mead's, and more implicitly Schutz's, ideas in creative ways. The left and bottom portions of Fig. 7.1 outline this critical process in ways that encourage comparison with the skeletal model presented in Fig. 6.3. Actors possess "loose cultural frameworks," which I see as similar to Schutz's conceptualization of "stocks of knowledge." A critical aspect of these cultural stocks is the "folk norm of consistency," in which individuals assume, until it is clearly demonstrated otherwise, that the gestures of others constitute a syndrome marking a role. These cultural frameworks, ordered by folk norms of consistency, lead actors to develop (through socialization and experience) an inventory of role-conceptions, which represent clusters or syndromes of behaviors denoting both general classes and more specific types of roles— for example, mother, father, son, daughter, good worker, close friend, acquaintance, serious student, etc. By virtue of humans' capacity for "mind," or deliberation, actors "run through" this inventory of conceptions as they role-take with others. They seek to determine which roles the gestures of others signal, make preliminary imputations, and then on the basis of sub-

[4] In saying this, however, I am *not* arguing that one's position in a system automatically dictates the role to be played. Rather, people know the syndromes of gestures associated with an enormous number of roles and can use this knowledge to interpret what others are doing. Moreover, actors may be unconscious of all their gestures and the role that they imply for others; yet these others will generally be able to assign a role—say, "sullen and depressed student-intellectual"—to an individual, and when confronted with a given set of gestures, most people will come up with the same role-designation.

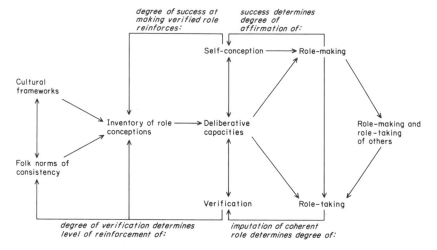

Fig. 7.1. A modified model of Turner's role theory.

sequent interpretation of gestures, verify and reverify these imputations. If verification occurs, then the role-conception involved as well as the folk norm of consistency are reinforced, thereby increasing their salience in the behavioral repertoire of an individual.

The top portions of Fig. 7.1. outline another creative extension of Mead's (1934) ideas. The converse of role-taking is role-making: individuals consciously and unconsciously orchestrate their emission of gestures in order to "make," or assert, a role for themselves in situations.[5] The same cultural frameworks, folk norms of consistency, and inventory of role-conceptions used to interpret the gestures of others are also employed to role-make.

A critical causal force in these role-making efforts is a person's self-conception(s). The particular roles that individuals select from their inventory of role-conceptions and the way that they signal during role-making are influenced by their conceptions of themselves as certain kinds of individuals deserving of particular responses from others. Although Turner is somewhat unclear as to whether people possess multiple selves for different situations or a trans-situational self cutting across all inter-actions, the critical point remains the same: actors' conceptions of themselves determine what roles they seek to play and how they will play them. Even when the macrostructure dictates the formal position of a person

[5] Unconscious motives often operate to make a person's role somewhat different than he or she perceives (this is why, I think, watching ourselves on videotape in explicit role-making situations is always somewhat bothersome; seeing ourselves as others do, we recognize how our "role" may not be what we intended).

(e.g., worker in a bureaucracy), an individual's self will dictate the more fine-tuned role that is asserted (e.g., "competent and ambitious worker on the way up"). This role exists in the shared inventory of role-conceptions of all competent actors in this situation; and the individual will orchestrate gestures in a manner that evokes this role in the role-taking activities of others. Thus, the signaling side of interaction involves a process of making a role for oneself that confirms and affirms one's self-conception; individuals seek to avoid situations where they cannot make for themselves a role which affirms their sense of self. Or, if such situations cannot be avoided, then role-making will communicate "distance," "disdain," or "alienation" from a role that is viewed as "beneath one's dignity."

While Turner does not explore all of the causal paths outlined in Fig. 7.1, several supplement his analysis. The processes of role-making and role-taking constitute a cycle that reinforces (or fails to do so) self-conceptions, inventories of role-conceptions, cultural frameworks, and folk norms. That is, when reading the gestures of others, one not only imputes roles that, when verified, reinforce frameworks, norms, and inventories; one also confirms and affirms self, via a process first adequately conceptualized by Cooley's (1902) analysis of "the looking-glass self." In turn, the degree of reinforcement of self influences an individual's role-making, for if the interaction is to proceed smoothly and without tension, self must be reinforced. Otherwise, interaction will be short term, or, if it cannot be kept short, it will be filled with tension. If an individual's self has been chronically unreinforced by others, then role-making and role-taking will involve such overlays of anxiety and use of defense mechanisms that normal interaction becomes exceedingly difficult. Thus, as emphasized by the double arrows and feedback loops in Fig. 7.1 connecting self-conception, deliberation, verification, and role-taking, self-conception influences how the gestures of others are interpreted; when self is pathological, dramatic distortion in role-taking and verification will be evident.

A related cyclical process revolves around verification, as influenced by the dynamics outlined above. In order for actors to be "normal" or "competent," a high degree of reinforcement in their inventories of roles, their application of folk norms of consistency, and their use of cultural frameworks is necessary. Actors who seem incapable of successful role-making or role-taking are not simply the victims of pathologies in self-conception; their past interactions will have involved a failure to develop those culturally shared concepts. There is, I believe, a very subtle and complex process of "knowledgeability" over when and how to use these frameworks, norms, and inventories in "appropriate" ways in varying "types" of situations. Such implicit knowledgeability requires high degrees of past reinforcement in role-making and role-taking. If this has not happened—and if self has also been unreinforced, as is likely in such cases—then severe behavioral pathology is likely.

In sum, then, Turner's analysis, as I have represented it in Fig. 7.1, adds new insight into the conceptual skeleton provided by Mead and Schutz. Any analysis of interactional processes must now view role-taking and role-making as complementary dynamics of interpreting and signaling.[6] Also, in developing a more refined view of Schutz's "stocks of knowledge," we must recognize that these inventories of implicit understandings contain broad cultural frameworks, folk norms of consistency, and extensive inventories of role conceptions. And we can begin to supplement Mead's view of self by recognizing that signaling and interpreting processes are highly circumscribed by the degree to which self-conceptions have been reinforced in past interactions. In my view, then, all of the dynamics outlined in Fig. 7.1 are fundamental to a conceptualization of interactional processes. Yet, as we proceed in this chapter, it will become evident that they still need to be supplemented by other theoretical formulations.

Goffman's Analysis of Rituals, Frames, and Stages

Erving Goffman's approach to the study of micro social processes is probably the most widely read and cited of contemporary theorists (e.g., Goffman, 1974, 1967, 1959). Yet, despite his fame as an analyst of everyday life and social interaction, his overall theoretical framework remains implicit, and even somewhat obscure. Without doubt, his works are filled with creative conceptual insights into how people interact, but his underlying theoretical model has never been articulated. The reason for this resides, I think, in his critical view of alternative micro approaches. For though he was trained within the Chicago School, he rarely mentions Mead and his more contemporary followers, thereby leaving the lineage of his ideas unclear. And as Collins (1985: 216–17) has noted, he was often critical of those who extended Schutz's ideas, especially those who emphasized ethnomethodology and language analysis (see later discussion, as well as pp. 49–51 in Chapter 4). Seemingly, he viewed modern symbolic interactionism, role theory, ethnomethodology, and European structuralism as deficient alternatives to his mode of micro analysis. Coupled with his deliberate inattention to Mead and symbolic interactionism, this critical stance creates additional confusion about the source for his ideas.

---

[6] Role-taking and role-making are part of the gesturing process; they are *not* the dictates of social structure, which, at best, provide only general guidelines for the range of roles that can be made in a situation. Thus, in contrast to Turner, I believe social structures provide the "loose framework" within which actors use their fine-tuned and extensively stocked inventory of role-conceptions to make roles for themselves and to interpret the roles signaled by others.

This confusion is further compounded by what Collins (1975, 1984) sees as Goffman's affinity with Durkheim, a taboo topic for most interactionists.[7] For Goffman has recognized that macrostructures and collective orientations circumscribe what actors do in concrete interaction. This willingness to recognize the significance of Durkheim's (1893, 1912) insights into the importance of shared collective orientations and ritual has placed him at odds with most micro theorists, who reject structural and functional modes of theory. In turn, Goffman has viewed with apparent suspicion the overconcern of contemporary symbolic interactionists with self-conceptions as well as the tendency of ethnomethodologists, critical theorists, and European structuralists to reduce social structure to the dynamics of speech, language, and linguistics. Indeed, for Goffman, language, speech, gestures, and other interpersonal processes are circumscribed by, if not derivative of, macrostructural processes that determine not only the co-presence of actors, but also their orientations and their sense of what they can and should do in concrete situations. Surprisingly, however, this line of argument never prompted Goffman to develop a macrostructural theory. Indeed, his work is decidedly micro, emphasizing by example and illustration what actors do in interactive contexts structured by a macro universe standing paramount but unexpressed. This lack of a clear macrostructural conceptualization coupled with his critical attitude toward much micro theory makes the origins as well as the basic substance of his theory difficult to discern, especially since he often argues by empirical example rather than precise logic.

The difficulty of making a formal analysis of Goffman's theory is compounded by his tendency to develop and then abandon concepts. Yet few would argue with the assertion that there is an underlying theoretical model in the corpus of his work as it evolved over several decades. But what is this model? In Fig. 7.2 I have sought to delineate its broad contours. The model was in flux over the years, especially as Goffman became disenchanted with the direction of micro sociology, but I have presented it as a unified whole. Obviously, considerable inference is involved in presenting this model, but such inferences are inevitable if we seek to formalize Goffman's work.

In Goffman's view—and here he borrows from Schutz as well as from Durkheim—individuals possess a large inventory of shared understand-

[7] I have never understood this. I suspect that Blumer (1969) is largely responsible, for despite Alexander's (1987) interpretation of his work, I sense that Blumer was addressing Durkheim more than Parsons. But as I have noted, Mead and Durkheim clearly converge in their notions of, respectively, the "generalized other" and the "collective conscious." Thus, though contemporary interactionists might be horrified by Goffman's use of Durkheim, I doubt if Mead is turning over in his grave on the matter; indeed, I believe that he would approve of Goffman's approach.

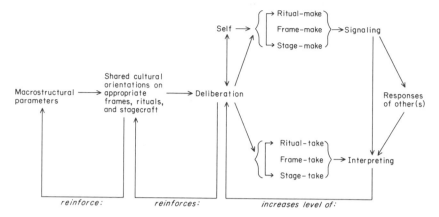

Fig. 7.2. Goffman's implicit model of rituals, frames, and stages.

ings and orientations. Interaction involves using these in the process of calculating and negotiating with others; and as these shared cultural orientations are employed, they are reinforced, especially through the emission of rituals. Goffman is very Durkheimian in his recognition that ritual activities reinforce the "collective conscience" and the structure of socal relations in a society (Durkheim, 1912). But Goffman's (1967) great contribution is his recognition that ritual permeates every aspect of daily life, including the most mundane interactions. Indeed, every interaction is punctuated with opening and closing rituals; and it is such routine rituals that signal actors' involvement in a context, smooth the sequencing of interaction in this context, and reinforce the larger cultural and structural context. Thus, for Goffman, a great deal of signaling in interaction revolves around "ritual-making," if I can create a term, in which actors mutually emit rituals, or stereotyped sequences of gestures that call forth stereotyped sequences from others. In this process, actors affirm their mutual involvement in, as well as dictate the sequencing of, the interaction. Such rituals mark an interaction at critical junctures, particularly openings and closings, but also at crucial turning points in between. In this way, the flow of an interaction is greatly facilitated, allowing people to enter, proceed, and exit unambiguously.[8]

For various types of interaction situations, particular rituals are appropriate; and actors carry a knowledge of this as part of their cultural orientations. As they use rituals appropriately, interaction is facilitated, and

_____

[8] Moreover, I would argue that rituals are very important in efforts at role-making and at interpreting the roles that others are attempting to make for themselves. In this sense, there is no great incompatibility between Turner's and Goffman's respective approaches.

the macrostructural forces that create types of situations are reinforced.

Goffman's (1974) last major work emphasized that, as individuals gesture and emit rituals, they "frame" an interaction. The basic—if analytically somewhat vague—analogy is to a "picture frame" that encloses a subject matter and marks the boundaries of what can and cannot occur. In emitting gestures, then, individuals "frame-make" and thereby enclose what is acceptable and exclude what is "out of bounds." However, humans' deliberative capacities allow them to shift frames rather easily, broadening, narrowing, or even changing their substantive content. To some degree rituals are the vehicle by which this occurs, but rituals that actually signal movement to a new frame are often very subtle. This facility for framing and reframing interaction allows for interpersonal flexibility and, at the same time, circumscribes the range of responses, thereby avoiding what Durkheim (1893) termed *anomie*.[9]

As with rituals, actors possess stores of frames, knowledge about the gestural procedures for shifting frames, and understanding about the interactive contexts in which varying frames and their transformations are appropriate. And, as with rituals, when interaction proceeds smoothly through the use of frames, cultural orientations are reinforced, as is the broader macrostructure.

In addition to signaling frames and rituals, actors also use the physical props of a situation, including their capacity to juxtapose themselves in varying proximity to each other, as yet another vehicle for signaling. Goffman's (1959) early work emphasized this staging and "dramaturgical" or "stagecraft" dimension of interaction. In this analysis, he argued that interaction is like a stage, with actors entering and exiting "front" and "backstage" regions where different demeanors are possible, emitting gestures to create a "performance" in terms of the script dictated by the macrostructure and shared cultural orientations, using the physical props of the stage to enhance a performance, and juxtaposing themselves to others and to various props in order to further augment a performance. Thus, interaction often revolves around people's use of relative positioning of bodies, movement back and forth between "backstage" and "frontstage" regions, and employment of physical props to signal a course of action. Such "stage-making" tells others what to expect from an individual and what is expected in return for a particular performance. Stage-making thus

---

[9] Durkheim's (1893, 1897) conceptualization of anomie has, at times, been misinterpreted. For Durkheim anomie means a "lack of regulation" in two senses: a failure to regulate aspirations and desires and a failure to provide coordinating institutions. Goffman's notion of frames embraces both of these ideas, without the assumption of "functional pathology" in Durkheim's analysis. Moreover, Durkheim (1912) could never delineate the interactive processes by which anomie is avoided; Goffman's concept of framing provides one such mechanism.

facilitates the framing of a situation by creating an "interpersonal ecology" that limits what can occur; in turn, such "geographical" frames dictate what rituals are appropriate in signaling one's entrance, exit, and performance on the interpersonal stage. And once again, as actors interpret the reaction of their audiences to successful performances, cultural stocks of stagecraft are reinforced, as is the macrostructure that determines the stages, props, and people available for any given performance.

The importance of people's self-conception, or identity, for these processes of stage-making, frame-making, and ritual-making is unclear in Goffman's analysis. The title of Goffman's first major work—*The Presentation of Self in Everyday Life*—would seem to indicate that people's conception of themselves as a certain kind of person has a powerful causal effect on how they present themselves "on stage," and presumably how they frame and emit rituals. Yet, to some analysts, Goffman seems highly critical of symbolic interactionists' heavy emphasis on self as a causal force in organizing how individuals signal and interpret. For as Collins (1985: 215) remarks, "even his theory of the presentation of self is essentially a model of the self as a modern-day myth that people are forced to enact rather than a subjective entity that people privately possess." I think this goes too far; my reading of Goffman is that people do possess a sense of self in situations and that, far from being a "cultural myth," self exerts considerable influence on both signaling and interpreting. At the least, if there is no stable "core self," individuals reveal multiple and contextual selves that they seek to affirm through stage-making, frame-making, and ritual-making.[10] Moreover, there are dozens of passages in Goffman's work that suggest he sees self as exerting great influence on how individuals interpret the gestures of others. In other words, to adopt Mead's concept of "role-taking" to Goffman's analysis, how individuals interpret the staging, framing, and ritual activities of others is, to some degree, influenced by self.

Thus, as is indicated in Fig. 7.2, actors interpret their own gestures and those of others by "ritual-taking," "frame-taking," and "stage-taking"; and the conception of themselves as certain types of individuals greatly circumscribes how they interpret a situation. Otherwise, there would be no "motive force" in Goffman's analysis. Without self, actors are like Parsons's "cultural dupes," doing what the macrostructure and cultural orientations tell them; or, alternatively, if one does not accept Collins's (1975, 1984) Durkheimian interpretation of Goffman, actors would be like interpersonal chameleons, changing their behavior at will and without apparent fear of the psychological consequences. Thus, self must be part of Goff-

---

[10] Goffman's unwillingness to conceptualize a "core self" represents, in my view, a weakness in his scheme, making his "actor" too interpersonally glib and facile.

man's model, despite his failure to clarify how it operates in interpersonal dynamics.

In sum, then, I see Goffman as having made three important contributions to the study of interaction. First, his work was the first to recognize that everyday life is punctuated with rituals that mark group membership and that structure the sequencing of everyday interaction. Second, his earliest works were instrumental in conceptualizing the ecology and geography of interaction as crucial signaling processes. And third, his last major work transformed rather static notions like "definition of the situation" into a more active process of framing and reframing interaction settings. As will become evident, these three aspects of Goffman's work are fundamental to my synthesis of various theories in Chapter 8.

Garfinkel's Ethnomethodological Alternative to Micro Analysis

I have already examined ethnomethodology in Chapter 4. There, I emphasized that ethnomethodology appears to view actors as motivated by a need to sense or presume that they share a common factual world, with the result that individuals employ "ethnomethods," or "folk methods," for creating, sustaining, or repairing a sense of "facticity."

This perspective comes right out of German phenomenology, especially via Edmund Husserl (1913) and Alfred Schutz (1932). But it is Harold Garfinkel who provided an interesting conceptual twist that, to say the least, has generated considerable controversy. The controversy revolves around the assertion that what traditional sociologists study does not really exist and that sociologists are much like lay actors in creating a perception— indeed, an illusion—that what they see is "real." I think that the ensuing philosophical debate over this issue, like many such debates, has not been very productive. What has been useful is a model of interaction that, despite the claims of Garfinkel and his followers, is not so much an "alternative paradigm" but an important supplement and complement to other micro approaches.[11] This model is delineated in Fig. 7.3.

As is evident from this model, the process of "accounting" is the central signaling and interpreting dynamic in ethnomethodological analyses of human interaction (Heritage, 1984). As the model in Fig. 4.4 underscored, the use of ethnomethods is central to the accounting process, but the model

---

[11] Indeed, I think that ethnomethodologists mounted such an extreme critique of "normal sociology" that they lost considerable credibility and, as a result, were forced into a kind of cult fringe within sociology. This situation is to be regretted, although it is largely the ethnomethodologists' own fault. The truly regrettable result, however, is that the importance of ethnomethodological ideas has often gone unappreciated.

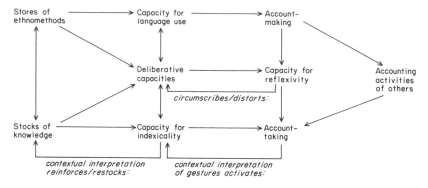

Fig. 7.3. Garfinkel's implicit model of accounting.

of interaction in Fig. 7.3 is far more robust than that earlier one of motivation. Before outlining more precisely just what accounting involves, let me first examine the other variables in the model.

While Garfinkel (1967) is somewhat vague on the point, he appears to assume that actors have a certain "knowledgeability" about contexts of interaction. But what does he mean here? My sense is that he implicitly employs Schutz's notion of "stocks of knowledge," or tacit understandings about the social world, that can be invoked and combined by virtue of humans' capacity for deliberation. Stocks of knowledge are like tools in a tool chest; they can be used to create, or "make," varying types of accounts. Stores of ethnomethods (e.g., knowledge of how and when to gloss, let pass, question, sequence, turn-take, search for normal forms, etc.) are a crucial part of such stocks of knowledge, for, as I indicated in Chapter 4, they structure the gesturing procedures that actors employ to assert, sustain, and repair an account of "what's real." Thus, without the use of ethnomethods, the organization of stocks of knowledge into an account would prove difficult. The principal vehicle by which stocks of knowledge and stores of ethnomethods are used to make an account is talk and language. Language allows individuals to "sign objects," or designate what exists in an environment, and, when accompanied by ethnomethods, to convince others to accept the account produced by language use.

Once an account is offered (what I am terming "account-making"), it influences the accounts made by others. The gestures, primarily talk and language, of these others are then interpreted through what I am terming "account-taking." This process of interpretation involves using general stocks of knowledge and stores of ethnomethods to understand what others are communicating. Garfinkel has stressed two important dimensions of this process: "indexicality" and "reflexivity." In taking the account of another, actors interpret gestures, especially talk, in light of the context—both linguistic and situational. Stocks of knowledge are used by actors to discover the contextual meaning or indexicality of words and other gestures, whereas stores of ethnomethods enable actors to determine what portions of such talk and gesturing are critical to the reality being asserted by an account. Yet there is a reflexiveness to all interpreting processes, for to some degree, actors interpret the accounts of others in terms of their own accounts and try to see in the gestures of others what they want to observe. They also try to ignore any discordant information in these gestures of others.

It is out of these processes, then, that individuals account-make and account-take. But what precisely is an account? Adopting Schutz's (1932) ideas, Garfinkel views actors as approaching situations with a presumption that they share common internal and external worlds, until it is proven otherwise. This presumption, often implicit and unacknowledged, is an "account" because it attempts to account for—to make sense of and to explain implicitly—what is real. Such accounts are thus built upon a base of presumed commonality and reluctance to question potentially discrepant gestures. In addition, actors share knowledge about classes of objects, types of utterances, varying interpersonal contexts, and procedures for connecting these in rendering or interpreting accounts. This knowledge is not fixed in the form of norms about how to behave; rather it is generative, offering individuals considerable flexibility in how to combine and recombine these elements of knowledge in constructing, or interpreting, an account.

To "make" or "take" an account involves the capacity to "sign" objects with talk, thereby documenting "what's real." Such signing is performed not only in terms of the grammar of language, but also by the use of implicit ethnomethods—pauses, assertions, patterns of turn-taking, insertions of verbal fillers, etc. This use of ethnomethods helps connect signed objects and tie them together in a way that informs others of how to interpret the account being offered. Moreover, the use of ethnomethods signals to others where they should suspend doubt and accept without questioning the account. Hence, ethnomethods help organize and attach objects, utterances, contexts, and other elements of actors' implicit knowledgeability to the here and now of an interaction, while at the same time, signaling those points in the organization of an account where assumptions about a shared world should not be questioned.

Such ethnomethods thus operate to order the elements of an account and sustain the sense that actors really understand each other and the character of the situation. And, should these mutual accounting processes fail, then ethnomethods are used in an effort to reconstruct, or remake, the account.

Garfinkel's (1967, 1963) famous "breaching experiments" demonstrate the process by which actors reassert via the use of ethnomethods the account of a situation or what should go unquestioned.

Garfinkel and other ethnomethodologists have been rather strident in their assertion that such accounts are all that is real. From their perspective, "reality" is illusionary, always contextually constructed through mutual account-making and account-taking of individuals in concrete settings. My view, to be polite about it, is that this is an overstatement, but there is still a profound insight here. Much of what actors do in interaction is to subtly signal and implicitly interpret mutually intelligible accounts of "what's real." Of course, this is not all that they do, but it greatly facilitates other interpersonal processes—such as role-making and role-taking, framing, ritualizing, and staging. Accounts thus provide a deep background of suspended doubt and presumed trust that enables other interactional processes to proceed without excessive interpersonal work.

Habermas's Conceptualization of the Ideal Speech Act

Jürgen Habermas has been one of the foremost critical theorists and philosophers of recent decades. Much of his approach, I must confess, is too mired in protracted dialogue with the early masters and in concern with the great philosophical issues to be of interest to the strategy of theory building that I advocate. Moreover, while I share Habermas's ideological concerns with eliminating forms of domination, I find his approach hopelessly naive about the invariant dynamics of inequality, domination, and power in human societies. Even where I think his work makes a significant theoretical contribution, especially with respect to the process of interaction, it is difficult to separate ideology, formulas for the "good society," and theoretical analysis. Of course, Habermas and other critical theorists would not view this blending of theory, practice, and ideology as regrettable. On the contrary, they would see it as inevitable and desirable.

My concern here is not so much with Habermas's larger intellectual project (e.g., 1970c, 1976a, 1979), but only with that portion of his analysis concerned with the processes of communication, speech, and interaction (for a more detailed review of Habermas's work, see J. Turner, 1986b: 184–212). For in the 1970's, Habermas turned to consideration of "the ideal speech act," in which communication among individuals is not distorted by forms of inequality and domination (Habermas 1970a, 1970b). He listed several features of such undistorted communication: gestures are noncontradictory; communication is public and conforms to cultural standards; actors can distinguish between language per se and what language denotes and describes; communication leads to intersubjectivity and the ability to create shared collective meanings. In extending this concern with actors achieving intersubjectivity through undistorted communcation, Habermas (1976b) formulated what I see as an important idea: communication involves more than words, grammar, and syntax; it also involves what he termed "validity claims." And increasingly, his conceptualization of interaction has come to revolve around this process of asserting, and responding to, validity claims in the gestures of others, especially their speech acts (Habermas, 1984).

What, then, is a validity claim? Habermas argues that during the course of interaction, actors emit and interpret claims along three lines: claims asserting that a course of action as indicated through speech is the most effective and efficient means for attaining an end; claims indicating that behavior is correct and proper in accordance with relevant norms and cultural standards; and claims maintaining that the subjective experiences as expressed in speech acts are sincere, authentic, and revealing of real subjective states. Thus, as actors gesture and talk, they make claims about the means-end, correctness, and sincerity of their actions. Moreover, others implicated in such communications accept or challenge these claims, leading to a process of "rational discourse" where actors mutually negotiate over their respective validity claims. To do so, they must share certain common stocks of knowledge about what constitutes means-ends effectiveness, sincerity, and normative conformity in a wide variety of interaction contexts.

These core ideas in Habermas's work are, of course, embellished in a rather large intellectual context, most of which is irrelevant to my purpose. But the idea that interaction involves what I would term "claim-making" and "claim-taking" is highly insightful. That is, as individuals emit signals and interpret those emitted by others, they are making and interpreting claims about means-ends, sincerity, and appropriateness.

In Fig. 7.4, I have selectively taken from Habermas's much more elaborate analysis what I see as the critical elements in an implicit model of interactional processes. Habermas often employs Husserl's term "lifeworld" and Schutz's notion of "stocks of knowledge" in a similar manner, although he might consider "stocks of knowledge" only a portion of a more encompassing "lifeworld." I use these terms interchangeably in discussing Fig. 7.4, because they denote similar processes. For Habermas the lifeworld is a "culturally transmitted and linguistically organized stock of interpretative patterns" (1984: 302) on which individuals draw during the course of interaction. There are, in his view, three basic types of interpretative patterns, or stocks of knowledge: those pertaining to cultural traditions, values, and beliefs and to linguistic structures and their use in in-

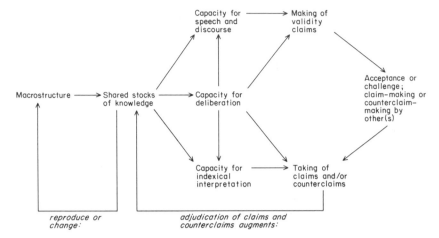

Fig. 7.4. Habermas's implicit model of claiming, discourse, and interaction.

teraction; those about how to organize social relations and what patterns of interaction are proper and appropriate; and those concerning what normal people are like and how they should act. As is evident, much of the Weberian and Parsonian tradition is reinserted into the process of interaction with this adoption and adaptation of Husserl's and Schutz's ideas.

Such stocks of knowledge represent criteria shared among individuals, who use them, in their capacity for deliberation, speech, discourse, and indexicality, to assert or "make" validity claims for themselves and to interpret or "take" claims of others, sometimes consciously and after deliberation, but often unconsciously and without prior thought (hence the direct causal path in Fig. 7.4 from stocks of knowledge to speech and discourse). Others respond to such claims in their own speech acts, accepting, revising, or challenging these claims; at the same time, of course, they make their own validity claims or counterclaims. If the claims of one actor are challenged by another, then "discourse" ensues and the interaction will, in a sense, cycle around claims and counterclaims until actors perceive each other's speech and gestures to exhibit means-ends effectiveness, normative appropriateness, and sincerity as measured against the implicit yardstick of their three types of "stocks of knowledge at hand."

In my view, this process is extremely subtle, complex, and often implicit, in several respects. First, the claims and counterclaims are typically unrecognized by the individuals involved; nonetheless, speech is filled with assertions about means-ends, appropriateness, and sincerity (for example, in American jargon, "How can you say that?"; "Well, if you ask me"; "I'm trying to be straight with you"; "Come on!"; "Who you trying to kid?"; "I wouldn't kid you, would I?"; and so on). Second, interactions are difficult to sustain, I think, unless actors implicitly adjudicate and reconcile their respective claims (for example, "Oh, now I see what you mean"; "Yeah, from that point of view it makes sense"; "Well, under the circumstances, I guess that's all you could do"; "Oh, I misunderstood"; and so on). Third, the application of stocks of knowledge is highly indexical, in that the situation or context dictates, to some degree, just what would constitute means-ends effectiveness, sincerity, and appropriateness. Individuals can thus use stocks of knowledge in highly flexible and fine-tuned ways, assessing claims and contexts simultaneously. And fourth, as actors acquire experience in the process of making, taking, adjudicating, and reconciling claims, they increase their stocks of shared knowledge and their capacity for interactive discourse, as is indicated by the feedback arrows in Fig. 7.4. Hence, the use, reinforcement, and augmentation of stocks of knowledge not only facilitate interaction; these interactive processes are also what maintain those stocks of shared interpretive patterns so essential to the production and reproduction of macrostructures (as denoted by the far left feedback arrow in Fig. 7.4).

These ideas from Habermas's larger critical project are, I think, quite profound and add considerably to our understanding of social interaction. Stripped of their ideological slant (e.g., free and open discourse is "good"; distorted communication is "bad"; the "good" macrostructure is built upon a foundation of "rational discourse"; and so on), Habermas has isolated a central dynamic in human interaction (though not the only dynamic, as my discussion in previous sections should emphasize). He has provided a creative adaptation of Schutz's and Husserl's phenomenological projects that reconciles phenomenology with Mead's, Weber's and Parsons's varying approaches.

Conclusion

This chapter completes my review of contemporary theories of interactional processes. In this and the preceding chapter, I have presented discursive theoretical projects in rather formal terms so that synthesis and reconciliation can be more readily performed. We began with Mead's and Schutz's ideas as the conceptual core of all modern theorizing on interactional processes and have discussed what I see as the most representative and creative examples of theory in what are often viewed as antagonistic approaches. We are now ready to pull the critical ideas of these diverse contemporary theorists together in a composite model that, like all other efforts in this area, owes its inspiration to the genius of Mead and Schutz.

8

Toward a Synthetic Model of Interaction

THE NEXT STEP in developing a model and series of propositions on interactional processes is to extract the critical insights of the theorists examined in the previous chapter and then to merge them together under the conceptual canopy provided by Mead and Schutz. In this way, we can do what Parsons never did: conceptualize how motivated actors signal and interpret during the course of their *inter*action. A synthetic model can give us a sense for the structure of such signaling and interpreting, while a selective translation of causal paths into propositions can make the model more amenable to empirical assessment. Let me begin by reviewing and, in some cases, elaborating upon the concepts of the theorists discussed in the last two chapters. In this way, the variables to be presented in the composite model on interactional processes can be more precisely defined.

Elements in a Theory of Interactional Processes

As a cursory comparison of Fig. 6.1 and the composite model to be presented in Fig. 8.1 would indicate, I have taken much from George Herbert Mead (1934). In particular, his conceptualization of "mind," "self," "role-taking," and "generalized other(s)" provides several central concepts for a theory of interactional processes. Mead conceptualized "mind" as the ability to perceive alternative lines of conduct, imagine and rehearse the future consequences of various alternatives, and understand the meanings of gestures. This set of interrelated processes will be labeled "deliberative capacities"; as will become evident, this capacity for thought and deliberation has important causal effects on other interactional processes.

Like "mind," Mead conceptualized "self" as behavior revolving around the facility for seeing oneself as an object in situations. But he was somewhat ambiguous over the question of whether self is a structure that transcends specific situations or merely a series of transitory images peculiar to each interaction setting. My view is that self is both, with the more permanent exerting considerable influence over the situational. That is, self will be conceptualized as a relatively enduring configuration of attitudes, dispositions, definitions, and feelings about oneself that selectively filters the self-image in concrete situations. While self is built up over the years from such transitory images, I argue that it increasingly becomes structured and that it reveals a highly reflexive character, in several senses. First, self will cause selective perception of others' reactions in ways that reinforce a person's existing configuration of self-references. Second, through the motivational dynamics outlined in Chapter 5 (see Fig. 5.1), self will cause selective interaction by encouraging individuals to avoid those situations where self-images are discordant with their more enduring self-conception. Third, self will cause the mobilization of defense mechanisms, particularly denial and repression, in order to avoid incorporation of images inconsistent with the self-conception. Fourth, self will cause the use of interpersonal practices to signal to others, as well as to oneself, distance and disdain from those situations that do not reinforce an existing conception.

I am not asserting that self-conceptions do not change. But, unlike so much contemporary micro theory (e.g., Collins, 1975) that makes people into interpersonal chameleons, I believe that self is structured and resistant to change, especially in the short term. I am thus siding with those who assert that there is a "core" set of attitudes, dispositions, definitions, and meanings about one's self that are organized into a sense of identity (McCall and Simmons, 1966; Kuhn and McPartland, 1954; Weigert, Teitge, and Teitge, 1986).

Part of this core self, however, involves situational definitions (Stryker, 1980; Strauss, 1959). Self is not simply an inflexible structure that is invariant across situations; on the contrary, part of its structure includes varying definitions, dispositions, and attitudes in different types of situations.[1] People tend to classify situations into a relatively small number of types (as part of the framing process outlined by Goffman); and as they do so, they implicitly (and sometimes explicitly) see themselves in a somewhat different light from situation to situation. But there is a structure to this process, since there is a finite number of situations and a relatively clear

---

[1] In fact, we are probably more conscious of these situational and variable self-definitions than we are of trans-situational and more permanent core self-feelings. At least we can give them more articulate expression. In contrast, our core definitions are sometimes only marginally conscious and are frequently the victims of defense mechanisms. This is why highly verbal tests of "self," such as the "twenty statements test," do not always work very well; some individuals offer only peripheral self-definitions, some a combination of core and peripheral self, and others their core self-feelings. I would trust more psychoanalytic procedures to measure core self than a pencil and paper questionnaire or an interview. Thus, I do not agree with many interactionists in their assertion that self is solely a "linguistic construct"; its most core elements are related to feelings and emotions that can be given linguistic expression, but this expression is *not* the same as their emotional structure.

configuration of self-references tied to each of these general classes of situations. Moreover, there tends to be a consistency among self-referencing processes in different contexts; for while people can hold and sustain discordant cognitions, they nonetheless seek consonance and relative consistency among their cognitions, particularly those about themselves as objects.

Thus, as Mead (1934) emphasized, self is a central dynamic in human interaction. And, as will become evident, I see it as particularly critical in the process of signaling. People try to sustain their self-conception of themselves in all situations,[2] and thus, their signaling is directly caused or, at the very least, highly circumscribed by relatively stable configurations of self-referencing attitudes, dispositions, definitions, feelings, and meanings. Mead did not emphasize this presentational aspect of self through signaling, but rather, the process of interpretation through role-taking.

Mead's (1934) concept of role-taking is essential to any theory of interaction. For without the capacity to read the "conventional" or "significant" gestures of others (that is, those with common meaning), interpret their significance for the likely course of overt behavior emitted by others, and sense the covert dispositions and attitudes behind overt behavior, interaction would not be possible. Thus, I will use Mead's view of role-taking as embodying these three capacities, although we should remain attuned to Schutz's insight that role-taking occurs at varying levels of intersubjective penetration.

As I indicated in the previous chapters, Mead's conceptualization of the "generalized other" is not only brief but somewhat ambiguous. My use of this concept will, therefore, involve considerable inference and redefinition. In general terms, I will follow Goffman's (1974) lead and visualize the generalized other as a set of attitudes, or a perspective, that frames a situation. A generalized other is thus a framework that is both imposed upon, and at the same time, emergent from interaction. My sense is that, on the one hand, people carry in their cognitive structure an inventory of generalized frameworks for basic types or classes of situations, and, on the other hand, they alter and refine these frameworks during the course of interaction, especially as interactions are repeated over time. Moreover, people can encounter situations where no "ready-made" perspective seems relevant, thereby forcing them to do considerable interpersonal work in order to develop an overarching frame for the situation.

Generalized others also vary in terms of their level of abstraction. Some

[2] They often do so unconsciously, but more typically, they are consciously aware of some efforts to sustain their most conscious (and typically situational) self, while being only dimly aware of other efforts and completely unaware of still other efforts to sustain (typically core) self.

are highly abstract and pertain to basic classes of situations encountered by all actors in a culture. As individuals encounter a situation, they implicitly invoke these more generic and general frames in order to orient themselves to the relevant dispositions, feelings, meanings, and attitudes to be displayed in that situation. Yet people also supplement these more abstract and standardized frameworks with their own experiences in situations. Thus, interactions will, over time and when repeated, develop their own frameworks that are unique to the setting where the interaction occurs. Rarely does this more concrete framework contradict the more abstract and culturally shared frames; instead, it elaborates and fine tunes it.

In sum, then, Mead's model of interaction provides, in somewhat elaborated form, the central concepts for a synthetic model of interactional processes. A model of signaling and gesturing must, therefore, include as critical variables the processes of deliberating, self-referencing and presenting, role-taking, and invoking generalized perspective, or in Goffman's terms, frames and frameworks.

These processes cannot occur, however, unless individuals reveal a certain common "knowledgeability." Alfred Schutz's (1932) early adaptation of Edmund Husserl's (1913) phenomenology introduces the concept of "stocks of knowledge at hand" to describe such mutual knowledge and represents a reformulation of Husserl's notion of "lifeworld" in a more sociologically interesting direction. For Schutz, stocks of knowledge consist of "ordered experiences" that actors implicitly use to interpret the gestures of others and to organize their own responses. Schutz's early work on this topic was later supplemented and completed by Thomas Luckman (Schutz and Luckman, 1974); unfortunately, this more detailed analysis of the "lifeworld" is rather philosophical and imprecise. But the essential idea is crucial: people acquire sets of cognitions that implicitly structure their perceptions of, and orientations to, the world. These cognitions provide a tacit sense of order and continuity with respect to such fundamental dimensions of experience as time, space, relations, categories of objects, contextual meanings of signs, and rules for using symbols. Actors thus have a fund of shared cognitions about the world that greatly facilitates interaction; for without this shared knowledgeability, emitting "proper" signals and understanding those offered by others becomes extremely difficult.

Schutz's conceptualization of stocks of knowledge can be extended in ways that are consistent, I believe, with his formulation. For the process of signaling and interpreting, I think that certain kinds of knowledge stores are more critical than others. First, actors must possess a complex set of cognitions about indexicality, or context. These cognitions involve knowledge about what gestures "mean" in varying types of situations and what implicit rules and procedures are to be used in order to create meanings in different contexts. Second, actors must possess rather detailed knowledge about the behavioral sequences and configurations that can potentially be used in varying types of situations and the implicit generative rules by which such behavioral sequences are combined, recombined, and organized in "normal" interaction. Third, and related to the above, actors must reveal knowledge about diverse kinds of rituals and the contexts in which they can be employed. Fourth, individuals must be able to understand the classes of frames that can be imposed upon situations and the unarticulated procedures for shifting frames during interaction. Fifth, actors must understand stagecraft, or the meanings that the physical props, the divisions of space, and the relative positioning of varying numbers of actors have in specific contexts. Sixth, actors must evidence stores of knowledge about what is "normal," "sincere," "deviant," "authentic," and "appropriate" in a wide variety of contexts.

The most remarkable aspect of these six classes of stocks of implicit knowledge is the ease and facility with which actors draw upon them during the course of interaction.[3] One must both possess the stock in one's "cognitive warehouse" and understand the rules and procedures by which these stocks are combined and recombined in order to create or interpret meanings in a particular context. The details of these processes are not well understood, but they are nonetheless fundamental to interaction.

I have obviously reformulated Schutz's conceptualization of stocks of knowledge in a manner that follows from my discussion of various contemporary theories in the last chapter. In a sense, these theories have informed us about the dimensions along which actors stock their knowledge warehouse during the course of their lives. And so, as they signal and interpret, they draw upon these accumulated stores of knowledge about contexts, behavioral sequences, rituals, frames, normality, authenticity, appropriateness, staging, ethnomethods, and the generative rules of their combination and recombination.

The processes of signaling and interpreting thus revolve around these six dimensions of "knowledgeability" as filtered through people's mental deliberations and efforts to confirm their self-conception. Ralph Turner's (1979, 1978, 1968, 1962) extension of Mead's analysis of role-taking with

[3] My colleague Randall Collins notes that people could not just go through a "laundry list" and come up with the right mix of items in these six classes of stocks of implicit knowledge. In his view, there must be a more "fundamental set of generative elements." I think that he is correct here, but what are these generative elements? The great promise of "structuralism" was that it supposedly sought to understand such processes; and, in my view, the great failing of structuralist theory is that it has told us virtually nothing about them. For the present, then, the "six classes" is the best that I can do, I encourage others to help me specify in more detail the cognitive dynamics involved. Fig. 8.1 represents one effort to do so; and I will take a further stab at articulating some generative processes for various cognitive dynamics in later chapters.

the concept of role-making provides an important conceptual link between stocks of knowledge and self, on the one hand, and the processes of signaling and interpreting, on the other. My view is that as people role-take with others, they read their gestures through the cognitive prism of their own knowledge stores and self-conception. This is particularly evident in Turner's (1962) assertion that actors implicitly invoke a "folk norm of consistency" (what I would see as one of the generative rules in actors' knowledgeability) to interpret the gestures of others as constituting an identifiable role. This cognitive search for the role of the other circumscribes just what frames become relevant, what accounts can be imputed, what claims can be accepted, what rituals mean, and what staging can occur. Of course, the converse is also true: role-taking is influenced by these other interpretative processes. Yet much role-taking occurs before the gestures of others are actually read, as actors draw from their knowledge stocks and invoke generalized frameworks to orient themselves to the potential range of roles that others can play in a particular situation.

Turner's analysis of role-making can also be viewed in this manner, except for the fact that self-conceptions exert considerably more direct influence than do stocks of knowledge and generalized frameworks on the roles that people attempt to make for themselves. Nonetheless, efforts at role-making circumscribe the frames, stages, rituals, claims, and accounts that people signal to others during interaction. Of course, just what roles can be asserted in a given situation is delimited by the context of an interaction, as it is interpreted through the prism of stocks of knowledge possessed by an actor.[4]

Goffman's (1974, 1967, 1959) analysis of framing, ritual, and staging further specifies how role-taking and role-making occur. In order to "make" or "take" a role successfully, actors must also ritualize, frame, and stage a situation. Again, to review and to elaborate in my own terms, ritual

[4]I have long felt that there is a conceptual affinity between Turner's role theory and what has been termed "expectations states theory" or "the theory of status organizing processes" (see, for example, Berger, Conner, and Fisek, 1974; Berger, Cohen, and Zelditch, 1972; Berger and Zelditch, 1985; Webster and Driskell, 1978). As Turner has emphasized, people use "cues" to assert roles for themselves, and once such roles are successfully made, they tend to endure. Expectation states theory places these dynamics in a broader theoretical context: actors' external status positions and the cues that mark these (speech, dress, titles, etc.) create "expectations" about what kind of role a person can and should play; and once this role is played, it becomes an expectation for subsequent interactions. Thus, people often do not have to actively "work at" making a role; it just emerges by virtue of these status-organizing processes. But when people do actively try to make a role that conforms to a self-conception, they must have the resources (external status, relevant abilities, etc.) "to bring it off." Thus, role-making is, I think, a sub-dynamic of status-organizing processes; as a result, it might be viewed as one way for theorists to reconcile conceptualizations of position (status) in macrostructural analysis with the role-making micro dynamics of individuals in face-to-face interaction.

refers to the use of stereotyped sequences of gestures to open, organize, and close an interaction.[5] Framing denotes the process of cognitively delimiting the range of acceptable behaviors in a situation. And staging denotes the use of physical props, the division of space, and the relative positioning of actors. These activities involve drawing the relevant rituals, frames, and staging procedures from stocks of knowledge, circumscribed by a person's self and the role being asserted. Similarly, role-taking is facilitated by interpreting the frames, staging, and rituals emitted by others. Such interpretation involves a simultaneous process of drawing from stores of knowledge, reading the gestures of others with respect to the frames, rituals, and staging being asserted, and reconciling as well as adjudicating these two in order to interpret the other's gestures in a particular context.

The concept of framing is perhaps the most difficult to define, especially since Goffman's (1974) presentation of his ideas on this matter is rather turgid. I am adapting his metaphor of a "picture frame," which, by virtue of the signaling and interpreting activities of actors, imposes a boundary on a setting, but I view the process of framing and reframing as more structural than did Goffman. For he tended to see actors as shifting and altering frames—ranging from ego-centered frames to those of the whole society—in a situation, whereas my view is that there is a limited number of frames that are typically used by actors in most interactions. Moreover, because reframing is interconnected with other interactional processes that establish a certain inertia, it can often prove difficult to change frames. Yet, since frames are not always pre-made and culturally given, framing remains a complex and subtle process in which individuals use implicit understandings and generative rules in their shared stocks of knowledge to construct an appropriate frame.

My own sense is that people's stocks of knowledge reveal information about four basic types of frames: physical, demographic, sociocultural, and personal. Furthermore, competent actors understand the "meaning" of these frames in varying types of contexts;[6] and on the basis of mutual interpretations of this meaning, they can delimit the range of their re-

---

[5] Collins's objection to my use of the concept of ritual provides a good definition of his use, which had previously been vague to me. He said, in a private communication, my definition in the text above "is part of it, but it misses the dynamics of rituals—mutual focus of attention, build-up of common mood, resulting charging of objects or gestures with symbolic significance representing membership in the group. Your treatment of rituals makes it only a matter of cultural memory." My sense is that his definition is much more than ritual; it is the production of social solidarity, which makes Collins's theory about "interaction-solidarity chains" rather than "interaction-ritual chains."

[6] Table 8.1 specifies the elements of framing, but the generative rules or procedures that create meaning are unknown. Here is a challenge to structuralists: tell me the generative rules. Anyone who can achieve this will have gone further than any other structuralist working in the social sciences.

TABLE 8.1
An Extension of Goffman's Analysis of Frames

Physical frames:	Demographic frames:
Use of props	Number of persons
Use of stages	Density of persons
Use of ecology	Migration of persons
Sociocultural frames:	Personal frames:
Institutional	Friendship
Organizational	Biographic
Interpersonal	Intimate

sponses. For each of these basic types of frames, there are several general classes of activity that are used to impose the frame. In Table 8.1, I have listed these, and each is discussed in more detail below.

Physical frames involve gestures that invoke aspects of the physical setting to delimit what can occur in an interaction. One way to impose a physical frame is to use physical props (desks, chairs, clothing, etc.) to signal the enclosure of an interaction within certain bounded limits. Another way is to use various stages, especially frontstages or backstages, to signal what can occur (for example, pulling someone aside to a less publicly visible space, or backstage area, dictates that a certain kind of interaction is now going to occur). A third class of physical signals involves using the ecology of a setting (walls, offices, corridors, etc.) to signal what is to occur. These kinds of physical frames can be used singularly or in concert. When used together in highly visible signaling, they dramatically circumscribe the range of responses (for example, pulling someone aside and away from others to a vacant office, closing the door, and pulling chairs together closely limits the potential range of responses and signals the likely direction of the interaction).

Demographic frames involve gesturing in ways that determine the population of actors involved in an interaction. One class of signals revolves around increasing or decreasing the number of people available for interaction (for example, stepping aside from a larger crowd, turning backs on others, or moving away to a new stage all signal a change in interpersonal demography). Another form of demographic signaling is to alter densities of actors co-present (for instance, calling people together into a smaller space or moving into or out of a crowded area signals a particular frame for subsequent interaction). A third class of signals influences the movement of interactants to and from a setting (for example, looking intimately into another's eyes limits access to the interaction by others and changes the exit demeanors of participants).

Sociocultural frames involve the use of signals to call attention to relevant norms in a situation. Institutional frames are gestures that invoke the general norms for the basic arenas of social life—work, play, family, religion, politics, and the like (for example, sets of signals like "As your supervisor . . . ," "Speaking as a teacher . . . ," "Knowing you as a son . . ." all frame situations within, respectively, institutional norms for work, education, and family). Organizational frames are signals that increase the salience of those more specific norms that apply to an ongoing and organized pattern of concerted activity among individuals (for instance, signals such as "As the captain of this team, I . . ." will frame the situation with respect to team rules and procedures). A third kind of sociocultural frame is the use of signals to structure an interaction in terms of accepted, expected, and normal forms of interpersonal conduct in a situation (for example, "Come on, don't be so stand-offish," "Pay attention to what I'm saying," "Are you here today?" and the like all represent verbal sanctions that seek to reframe an interaction into a normal mode for interpersonal behavior in a particular context).

Personal frames concern the use of gestures to create varying types and degrees of intersubjective contact with others. One class of gestures concerns those that mark friendship (smiles, informal demeanor, etc.) and thereby delimit the range of behavioral options of participants. Another type of personal frame is the use of gestures to communicate biographical information about either personal life history and/or prior activities leading up to a particular interaction (for example, telling stories of one's past, recounting previous events, and recalling similar circumstances all frame an interaction in a biographic mode). And a final type of personal frame occurs when gestures allow actors to penetrate the emotional layers of a person (crying, holding hands, and certain kinds of facial gesturing signal a framing of a situation in a more intimate mode).

This rough classification of frames does not, of course, correspond to Goffman's but seems consistent with his general idea and with Mead's concept of the generalized other(s). Goffman's analysis, I think, is much too concerned with how framing is used as a manipulative tool among people presumably rather like himself—clever and sophisticated actors (who apparently have no core self). As a result, he misses the far more fundamental (and perhaps less clever) insight that interaction cannot proceed easily without some degree of physical, demographic, and sociocultural, and, under certain conditions, personal framing. The crucial point is not so much that people shift and manipulate frames, although they do indeed do this, but that they signal and interpret to achieve a relatively stable "framework" for emitting other gestures during the course of the interaction—a view that is closer to Mead's generalized other. Thus, it is this view of Goffman's idea of framing that I will use as I approach a synthetic model of interactional processes.

Much of Goffman's analysis of frames represented a frontal attack on the hyperrelativism and solipsism of phenomenology and ethnomethodology, on the one side, and the excessive sociocultural determinism of conventional sociology, on the other.[7] For Goffman actors are not constructing, *de novo*, indexical and reflexive accounts in each and every situation, nor are they mechanical dupes who conform to the dictates of cultural norms and social structure in making their "definitions of situations." Goffman's analysis tries to fall somewhere between these extremes and is useful for this reason. Yet I do not see great incompatibility, as Goffman did, between frame analysis and Garfinkel's ethnomethodology.

Indeed, frames only establish definitional parameters and, by themselves, are insufficient to assure the smooth flow of interaction. Garfinkel's great contribution is the recognition that actors implicitly construct an account of "what's real" within the framing of a situation. As I emphasized in Chapters 4 and 5, humans need to feel that an external and factual world exists "out there." Framing only takes interactants so far; they also need to use their stocks of ethnomethods to create the presumption that they share the same universe. Frames reduce the complexity of this task and give it focus, but they are not a substitute for what I term "account-making" and "account-taking."

My adaptation of ethnomethodological ideas will, however, be selective and involve some reformulation. An account, as defined in Chapter 7, is an implicit and typically unacknowledged sense, feeling, and presumption among actors that they share, for the purposes at hand, common external and internal worlds. Accounts are created through signaling and interpreting ethnomethods, which are buried in other signals—pauses, assertions, pointed questions, patterns of conversational turn-taking, inflections, verbal fillers, and the like—but they send a subtle message—let pass, don't question, leave alone, accept at face value, etc. And, as others implicitly interpret this message, they tacitly agree (or disagree) to follow its instructions. Out of this process, as it continually undergirds interaction, especially conversations, actors avoid questioning discordant information and so bypass points of ambiguity and other problematic features in interpersonal activities. In this way, they save themselves a great deal of interpersonal labor and, equally important, create a de facto presumption of

[7] Both of these criticisms are, I think, reasonable, although Goffman produces his own extreme conceptualization of the cynical, clever, and manipulative actor who apparently uses morality for his or her amoral (and I guess immoral) purposes.

reality that plugs any gaps of uncertainty. This sense of reality constitutes an implicit account of what's real and gives actors the tacit feeling and presumption that they share a common backdrop for their other interactional activities.

In addition to developing an "account of what's real," actors also seek to assert implicitly that their actions are sincere, normatively correct, and efficient in a given context. Conversely, they tacitly interpret each other's actions in terms of their seeming authenticity, conformity to relevant norms, and efficiency with respect to means-ends schemata. These ideas come to us, of course, from Jürgen Habermas (1970a, 1970b) and are labeled "claim-making" and "claim-taking." Unlike Habermas, however, I see these processes as typically being unconscious and tacit. For much like ethnomethods, claims are signaled "between-the-lines" and rarely are stated boldly "out front." Indeed, to make them conscious, deliberate, and explicit (for instance, "I know that I'm right on this"; "How can you pretend to be . . ."; "How can you be so out of it!"; etc.) will set off a cycle of claiming, counterclaiming, and discourse—a situation that, I contend, most interactants wish to avoid. For as people quietly signal that their actions are sincere, normatively correct, and efficient in a given context, they implicitly ask each other to accept what is occurring without further questioning. Conversely, by accepting these claims during the process of interpretation and by not making challenges, they avoid the need for a considerable amount of interpersonal negotiation.

Thus, contrary to Habermas's emphasis on the process of "discourse," individuals are usually disposed to accept each other's claims, unless they are openly contradictory or in violation of contextual interpretations of what is factual and what is appropriate in the situation, or as is sometimes the case, unless someone is spoiling for a fight or operating with a chip on their shoulder—thereby assuring "discourse." And even then, actors tend to avoid challenges and counterclaims, if they can. Thus, in actual interaction, people seek to bypass the "discourse" considered by Habermas to be so desirable in his "ideal speech act."

In my view, validity claims are much like ethnomethods in that they tacitly mark the flow of interaction with just enough information about sincerity, normative appropriateness, and efficiency to stave off requests for more fine-tuned and in-depth role-taking and negotiation. But, much like breaching experiments with ethnomethods, an interaction will stall and cycle around questions of sincerity, norms, and means-ends if actors challenge each other's implicit claims. And once this process of claiming is no longer implicit, then actors will need to spend a considerable amount of energy renegotiating their respective claims. Moreover, like breaching and subsequent interpersonal efforts at reconstructing a sense of facticity with ethnomethods, discourse over validity claims will disrupt other interactional processes, holding them in suspension and eventually forcing a reframing, reaccounting, reritualizing, and restaging of the situation.

This completes my review of the key concepts in the theories examined in previous chapters. I have tried to conform to the way the concepts are used by various theorists, but obviously I have altered and extended the definition of some of them. We are now in a position to examine a composite model that attempts to pull these concepts together into a dynamic set of processes.

A Dynamic Model of Interactional Processes

In Fig. 8.1, the key concepts on interactional processes are arranged into an analytical model.[8] Juxtaposing the concepts in this manner and delineating their causal connections highlights the dynamic interrelations among what are often considered contradictory theories. As with the composite model in Chapter 5, the closer the variables in the model *and* the more direct the causal path connecting them, the greater is their causal influence on each other. Moreover, Fig. 8.1 is designed to complement Fig. 5.1 on motivation. In essence, Fig. 8.1 elaborates upon the very last variable in Fig. 5.1—that is, signaling and interpreting. As actors mobilize energy, they signal and interpret in terms of the dynamics outlined here.

As is emphasized with the three variables on the left of the model, actors use their deliberative capacities to project self-references in a situation (as denoted by arrow *a*). Drawing from both core and peripheral self, individuals create self-references in the situation that, as we see shortly, guide the processes of role-making, stage-making, ritual-making, and to a lesser degree, frame-making, account-making, and claim-making. In using their deliberative capacities to project self-references, actors draw from their stocks of knowledge at hand (causal path *b-a*); and as they do so, they use their stocks to impose a frame on a situation (path *b-d*), which, in turn, helps them select relevant role conceptions (*d-i*) and staging procedures, ethnomethods, and claims (via the causal paths denoted by arrows *m*, *n*, *o*, and *p*).

As is indicated by the causal paths at the top of the model, I see role-making as circumscribing the staging and ritual activities of actors (arrows *m* and *n*) and frame-making as guiding their accounting and claiming signals (arrows *o* and *p*). Of course, as arrows *i* and *j* emphasize, role-making

[8] This model is a significantly revised version of the one in J. Turner, 1986a, 1986c.

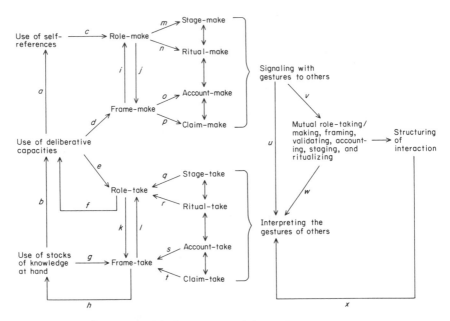

Fig. 8.1. A composite model of interactional dynamics.

and frame-making exert mutual effects on one another: as actors seek to use stocks of behavioral sequences and syndromes to make a role consistent with self-references, these stocks help them impose a frame, while conversely, as actors use stocks of knowledge about physical, demographic, sociocultural, and personal frames, these stocks impose limits on the kinds of roles that they can make for themselves. In turn, individuals use staging and ritual as major, though not exclusive, vehicles for signaling their role, while employing ethnomethods and validity claims as partial means for communicating how they have framed the situation. The end result is a collage of gestures, operating at many different verbal and nonverbal levels, that signals information that is interpreted by others.

As arrow *u* underscores, such interpretation is reflexive. Individuals interpret their own gestures and, to varying degrees, filter and interpret the signals of others through the prism of their own framing, role-making, ritual, accounting, and claiming activities, especially as these are circumscribed by self-references. Yet interpretation is not wholly, or even principally, reflexive; the gestures of others are interpreted by using deliberative capacities and stocks of knowledge to role-take, frame-take, stage-take, ritual-take, account-take, and claim-take. As causal path *b-e* indicates, I see role-taking as a more conscious and deliberative process in which in dividuals use stocks of knowledge to assess the roles that others are attempting to make for themselves, especially with respect to their staging and ritual activities (arrows *q* and *r*). Role-taking is not always conscious, but it is rarely far below people's capacity to think about and articulate the "meaning" of others' gestures. In contrast, as causal arrow *g* suggests, frame-taking is more implicit, especially when the accounting and claiming activities (arrows *s* and *t*) are the basis for interpreting the framework being imposed by others on a situation. However, if actors rely primarily upon role-taking (causal arrow *k*) to understand another's gestures, then this process of frame-taking is more explicit and amenable to conscious reflection (as is indicated by causal path *e-k*).

Just as role-making and frame-making circumscribe other signaling processes, role-taking and frame-taking initially guide the process of interpretation. Actors will attempt, at least initially, to determine the role(s) and frame(s) of other(s). To do so, they will rely heavily upon the staging, ritual performances, accounting, and claiming of others, but I would argue that unless these can suggest role and frame as well, the process of interpretation will be disrupted, and actors will become more conscious and reflective about "what is wrong" (as is denoted by feedback paths *f* and *h-b*). When role-taking proves ineffective, then, actors will more consciously scrutinize the gestures of others for their role-making content; and in particular, they will be attuned to what the staging and ritual activities of others tell them about the underlying role(s) being asserted by others. Similarly, when frame-taking is ambiguous, actors will delve further into their stocks of knowledge to figure out what the accounting and claiming activities of others tell them about the frame being imposed by others.

Whether interpreting is problematic or not, it influences the process of signaling (via such paths as *h-b-a*, *h-b-d*, *h-b-d-i*, *f-a-c*, *f-d*, and *f-d-i*). If framing is problematic, actors will signal this through their own gestures, particularly with ethnomethods and validity claims. And, if role-taking is ambiguous, individuals will signal this to others, especially through staging and ritual. Of course, when interpretations have created clear roles and frames as well as understandable accounts, claims, stages, and rituals, then signaling will reflect this fact and will, in all probability, proceed without great effort or conscious deliberation.

The end result of these signaling and interpreting processes is mutual role-taking/making, framing, validating, accounting, staging, and ritualizing (arrows *v* and *w*). It is from such mutual agreements over roles, frames, accounts, stages, claims, and rituals that an interaction becomes structured. Such structuring, or ordering of interaction in time and space, can feed back (via loop *x* as it connects to other causal paths) and circumscribe interpreting and signaling processes. Indeed, as I will argue in later chapters, most interactions occur within a structured context where the relevant and appropriate roles, frames, claims, accounts, stages, and rituals are known and understood, thereby greatly facilitating both interpreting and signaling.

Conclusion

Such are some of the general implications of the causal paths delineated in Fig. 8.1. The model pulls together diverse lines of thinking on interaction; and even if the specific causal connections are viewed as incorrect or in need of revision, the general thrust of the model reconciles very different theories under the conceptual canopy provided by Mead and Schutz. The important thing about such a model as that in Fig. 8.1 is that it states arguments in explicit terms, thereby encouraging corrective criticism and revision. Equally important, it suggests some interesting propositions about interactional processes. Let me now turn to these in my concluding remarks.

As I noted in Chapter 5, it is not possible, nor desirable, at this point to develop an extensive list of propositions, since all of the necessary models have not been developed. But, as I did for the process of motivation, it is useful to present a series of preliminary generalizations that emphasize certain causal paths in the model. Later, we will want to reformulate these in light of the variables introduced from the analysis of motivational dynamics in Chapters 3–5 and from the discussion of structuring processes to come in Chapters 9–11. And so, as a way of summarizing the essential elements in the model presented here, I offer the following list of generalizations:

1. The degree of interaction between two or more actors is an additive function of their level of signaling and interpreting.
   a. The level of signaling is an additive function of the degree of role-making, frame-making, stage-making, ritual-making, account-making, and claim-making.
   b. The level of interpreting is an additive function of the degree of role-taking, frame-taking, stage-taking, ritual-taking, account-taking, and claim-taking.
2. The level of role-making in an interaction is a primary function of the degree of effort to affirm self-references and a secondary function of the degree of effort to impose frames.
3. The level of role-taking in an interaction is a primary function of the

degree of visibility in the ritual-making and stage-making gestures of others and a secondary function of the level of ability in using stocks of knowledge to understand the frame-making gestures of others.

4. The level of frame-making in an interaction is a primary function of the level of ability in using appropriate stocks of knowledge to make claims and construct accounts and a secondary function of the degree of intensity in role-making.

5. The level of frame-taking in an interaction is a primary function of the degree of visibility in the claim-making and claim-taking gestures of others, and a secondary function of the degree of intensity in role-taking with others.

6. The level of stage-making/taking in an interaction is an additive function of the level of role-making/taking and ritual-making/taking.

7. The level of ritual-making/taking in an interaction is an additive function of the level of role-making/taking and stage-making/taking.

8. The level of account-making/taking in an interaction is an additive function of the level of claim-making/taking and frame-making/taking.

9. The level of claim-making/taking in an interaction is an additive function of the level of account-making/taking and frame-making/taking.

IV

Structuring Processes

9

Early Models of Interpersonal Structure

As MOTIVATED ACTORS signal and interpret, they sustain social interaction across time. Although the persistence of interaction at a single point in time is the most basic unit of sociological analysis, it is the linking together of interactions at different points in time that is more sociologically interesting. Such sustained structuring is accomplished through "chains of interaction" where, in a literal sense, individuals "pick up where they left off" from past encounters. These chains involve remobilization of past motives, remaking of roles, reframing, restaging, reaccounting, revalidating, and retaking of roles in a manner that repeats the basic form of the previous interaction.

This repetition of the basic form of an interaction is facilitated by the processes that were termed "structuring" dynamics in Chapter 2 (see Fig. 2.1). That is, structuring processes guide and circumscribe the remobilization of motives, remaking and retaking of roles, and so on, so that individuals do not have to work so hard at reconstituting and reconstructing an interaction. If structuring processes are well established, the motivational energies and interactional activities of actors can be channeled in relatively clear and unambiguous ways. Structuring thus reduces the intensity of negotiations over motives, stages, roles, frames, and other motivational and interactional processes. Without structuring, every reencounter of individuals would involve so much interpersonal work that they would exhaust themselves. The social order depends, in fact, on some degree of structuring of those interactions that must be repeated.

Avoiding the Micro-Macro Debate

At this point, it is tempting to offer an explanation of how to fill the micro-macro "gap" by an analysis of structuring that reconciles the motives and gestures of individuals with the organizational properties of populations of actors. I will, however, resist being a "Br'er Rabbit" who is trapped by this conceptual tar baby. Instead, I will address a more limited and decidedly micro question: What interpersonal processes order the form and pattern of interactions among individuals across time and in space?[1] Perhaps my analysis will suggest lines of inquiry that might reconcile micro and macro sociology, but such issues lie beyond the scope of the present project.

When one looks at the works of the early theoretical masters for insights into the micro processes of structuring, however, the micro-macro question immediately resurfaces, for most early work on "structure" is decidedly macro or else seeks to bridge the micro-macro gap. In examining early conceptual work to see what leads it offers a micro analysis of structuring, I will translate selectively in order to highlight various theorists' insights into micro dynamics. In a very real sense, I embark on an odyssey reminiscent of Talcott Parsons's work, but there are several major differences in our respective approaches. First, my analysis of structuring dynamics is built upon the detailed analysis of both motivation and the interactional processes of signaling/interpreting. Second, my effort is not designed to leap, like Superman or Max Weber, "in a single bound" from unit acts to macrostructures. Third, I approach those writers on whom Parsons commented—particularly Spencer, Durkheim, and Weber—with entirely different conceptual eyeglasses, bringing into focus only the aspects of their work that deal with micro processes. And fourth, I include the important figures whom Parsons ignored—Georg Simmel, George Herbert Mead, and Alfred Schutz. Thus, my general strategy is the same as Parsons's, but the results of our analyses are very different.

Weber's Action Theory

At the risk of belaboring the critique presented in Chapter 1, I begin my review of early models of microstructuring with a reexamination of Max Weber's "action" approach (Weber, 1978: 3–62). To perform this examination, the model presented in Fig. 1.1 is redrawn in Fig. 9.1 in order to

[1] I stress "interpersonal processes" because macrostructural conditions—population size, density, and differentiation; distributional inequalities; networks, etc.—set the parameters within which individuals interact. To some extent, these macrostructural conditions determine the values and weights of the variables discussed in the models for micro dynamics that I have been developing. But, as I have emphasized, it is important to isolate the variables for either micro or macro analysis separately, *before* we begin deciding the degree to which their values and weights influence each other. Otherwise, the fundamental properties of micro dynamics get conceptually mixed up with those macro processes that determine their values and vice versa. Thus, I am not arguing that macrostructure is irrelevant, only that such concerns are premature. Moreover, I am *not* asserting that the model of structuring toward which I am moving explains macrostructures; it does not, although I suspect that the microstructuring processes to be outlined in Chapter 11 influence some of the values for macrostructural models in the same way that macrostructural conditions influence micro dynamics.

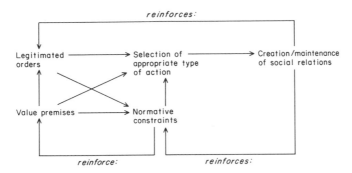

Fig. 9.1. Weber's model of structuring processes.

place Weber's analysis of structuring processes in its best possible light. In this revised model, Weber's approach emphasizes the importance of values and norms, and the selection of a type of action, whether instrumental-rational, value-rational, affectual, or traditional. For Weber, then, social action becomes structured when actors adjust their responses to each other by selecting courses of action in terms of reference to values and norms. In turn, such structuring reinforces norms and values, while at the same time legitimating the more macro "order" within which interaction occurs.[2]

Though there is an implicit model of motivation in Weber's analysis—that is, value orientations become internalized as needs and thereby circumscribe actors' selection of means—there is relatively little emphasis on the process of interaction. Indeed, interaction becomes structured *because* actors are able to invoke similar value premises and to develop normative frameworks for ordering their actions across encounters.

Thus, much like Parsons's (1937) early review of Weber, we are left with the conclusion that interaction becomes structured in terms of norms. This is not exactly a conceptual breakthrough (though in this age of hyper-micro analysis and overreaction against functionalism, theory has tended to underemphasize the importance of norms). The major problem with Weber's model is not the emphasis on norms per se, but the failure to provide details on the interpersonal processes by which the norms are created, sustained, or changed. Instead, norms are simply a "given" and operate as a macrostructural parameter on the choice of action.

Weber's approach is thus macrostructural, despite definitional assertions that sociology is the study of meaningful action (Weber, 1978: 23). Weberian sociology is concerned, not with interaction processes, but with

[2]I am perhaps "Parsonizing" Weber here and in Fig. 9.1. Or, perhaps even worse, I am "Turnerizing" Weber, but if Fig. 9.1 does not seem a reasonable representation of Weber on microstructuring, then he probably does not have a theory of micro dynamics.

the macrostructural dynamics of legitimated orders, although it occasionally posits a motivational dynamic in actors' perceptions and choice of means.[3] Even so, there is little emphasis on the *process* of motivation; it just appears as a kind of intervening cognitive variable inserted between macrostructure, on the one side, and action choices, on the other. Moreover, Weber does not really examine the interpersonal processes that link motivated actors to each other.

Yet Weber's approach does leave us with an important variable—norms. Interaction is indeed structured by norms; and however conceptually chic it is these days to ignore or criticize "normative theorists," the structuring of interaction in time and space *always* reveals a heavy normative element. Our goal is to understand in more detail the processes by which norms operate to structure interaction among motivated actors.

Spencer and Durkheim's Converging Models of Interpersonal Structuring

In *The Structure of Social Action* (1937), Parsons rejects Herbert Spencer and embraces Emile Durkheim. Like most sociologists in his time and today, Parsons assumed that there are fundamental differences between Durkheim and Spencer. Such conclusions are based upon a rather superficial analysis of their respective works and on the presumption that Spencer was an individualistically oriented "utilitarian" and Durkheim a more collectively oriented "normative" theorist. In their personal and social philosophies, this is indeed the case, but examination of their actual works on sociology shows clearly that their sociologies are virtually the same (J. Turner, 1984b). Indeed, I have argued elsewhere that Durkheim "borrowed"—to put it politely—the core ideas of his sociology from Spencer, whose key insights appeared twenty years before Durkheim's work came into prominence (J. Turner, 1985b; Turner and Beeghley, 1974). I do not wish to dwell on this theme, except to indicate that it has guided my decision to examine their converging schemes together.

As many commentators have noted, Durkheim's work underwent considerable transformation from the early macro analysis of the division of labor and the rules of sociological method (Durkheim, 1893, 1895) to the later micro emphasis on cognition and ritual (Durkheim and Mauss, 1903; Durkheim, 1912). This movement between macro and micro levels of analysis should, therefore, provide a useful model of how interaction be-

---

[3] The best illustration of this is, of course, Weber's analysis of the "Protestant ethic" and the emergence of capitalism.

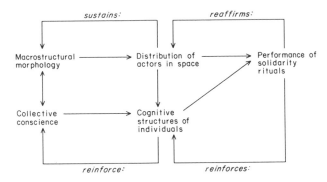

Fig. 9.2. Durkheim's model of interpersonal structuring.

comes structured. That is, in looking at Durkheim's work as a whole, there should be a heavy emphasis on how interpersonal activity sustains—or creates and changes—patterns of structural differentiation and integration among individuals. In Fig. 9.2 I have redrawn the model in Fig. 3.6, where my concern was with motivational processes, to reflect the present topic— the structuring of interaction.

For Durkheim, there is always a macrostructural background to inter- personal behavior, which consists of the morphological features of a situ- ation (Durkheim, 1893)—the number of people co-present, their organi- zation into types of structures (kin, community, etc.), their pattern of arrangement (differentiated, autonomous, interrelated, dependent, etc.), and the nature of their interconnections (loyalty to common ideas, con- tract, exchange, obedience to law, etc.). Durkheim's concept of the "col- lective conscience" has always proved difficult to interpret—even by Dur- kheim himself as he delved further into social psychology. At the more structural level, the "collective conscience" denotes the "volume," "den- sity," "determinateness," and "content" of those ideas that actors share, whereas at the more micro level, it concerns the cognitive structures of in- dividuals who are seen by Durkheim as mapping their perceptions and dis- positions in a manner that reflects the macrostructural or morphological features of their environment (Durkheim and Mauss, 1903; Durkheim, 1912).

As the model in Fig. 9.2 emphasizes, macrostructural morphology de- termines the distribution of actors in space. Also it is reciprocally related to the collective conscience; that is, macrostructural morphology deter- mines the form and content of the collective conscience and is, in turn, rein- forced by the collective conscience. As is also evident in Fig. 9.2, both the collective conscience and the distribution of actors circumscribe an individual's cognitive structures. Together, the distribution of actors and their respective cognitions determine the nature of the rituals performed to reinforce social solidarity. When actors are co-present, when they reveal similar cognitions about their situations, when they share common values, beliefs and norms, and when they are connected to a larger macrostructural reality, they are likely to emit rituals in their interpersonal relations. Such rituals derive from a fundamental need to affirm their common "group inclusion," as the model on motivational dynamics in Fig. 5.1 emphasized. Such ritual performances also structure interaction across time by reinforcing actors' patterns of co-presence, their cognitions, and their commitments to common ideas (note feedback arrows in Fig. 9.2).

If we extend and extrapolate Durkheim's analysis somewhat, the structuring processes implied by this model can be made more explicit. First, there is a "normative element" in Durkheim's approach. Actors share commitments to common ideas about rights and duties and use these as a basis for structuring interaction across time and in space. This normative portion of Durkheim's work is, of course, what Parsons (1937) stressed. Second, there is an ecological/demographic element. The number of individuals and their distribution in space influences the nature of interpersonal rituals. Structuring thus involves the ordering—and the maintenance of this ordering through ritual—of spatial relations. As Goffman (1959) was later to stress, such "staging" is an important aspect of interpersonal structuring. Third, there is a cognitive element. Although this is easily the most poorly conceptualized element of Durkheim's work, it nonetheless alerts us to the processes by which actors "categorize" each other and situations in a manner that influences their interpersonal relations. And fourth, there is an interpersonal element, emphasizing the significance of rituals. Such rituals are the vehicle for realizing deep-seated motives for group-inclusion and for structuring interpersonal relations that can meet these needs over time. For Durkheim, then, ritual is the major structuring force in interaction because it meets needs for group inclusion (solidarity), while at the same time it is the interpersonal mechanism by which the norms, cognitive categories, and ecological/demographic patterns are reinforced and maintained.

In sum, with this simple extension of Durkheim's ideas, several critical structuring processes are exposed: using norms, ordering space, categorizing others and situations, and performing rituals. Durkheim's movement into micro sociology never exhausted the explanatory power of these variables, nor did his treatment allow him to bridge the gap between his early macrostructural work on system size, differentiation, and integration (Durkheim, 1893) and his more micro analysis of cognitive structures and ritual (Durkheim, 1912; Durkheim and Mauss, 1903). Yet there are several

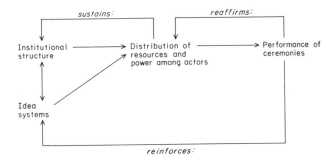

Fig. 9.3. Spencer's model of interpersonal structuring.

important conceptual leads in Durkheim's work, and, as will become evident, they will all be incorporated into a more general modeling of structuring.

Without denying the power of Durkheim's thought, I must stress that Spencer's *Principles of Sociology* (1874–96) anticipated many of Durkheim's ideas. In Fig. 9.3 I have outlined Spencer's concepts in a manner that emphasizes their convergence with Durkheim's.

Indeed Durkheim and Spencer's theories of macrostructural dynamics are virtually identical, with the important exception that Durkheim stressed the normative element more than Spencer. Both presented models of macrostructure that emphasized population growth, ecological concentration, competition, functional differentiation, and integration. And much like Durkheim's search for the interpersonal and cognitive dynamics underlying these macro processes, Spencer argued that institutional structures, especially as these determine the distribution of resources and power among actors, are always the product of "subinstitutional" processes revolving around "ceremony" (Spencer, 1874–96, 2: 3–36).

For Spencer, "ceremony" denotes ritual activities and other signs that mark the course of an interaction (see J. Turner, 1985b: 116). In particular, ceremony can include stereotyped performances (ritual) and/or symbols (badges, fashion, trophies, etc.) to signify the level of inequality between actors. The greater the inequalities produced by the macro institutional structure, the more clearly differences in the resources among actors are marked by distinctive symbols and the more ritualized interactions become (see J. Turner, 1985b: 116–22). Such rituals and signifying objects reinforce patterns of inequality and the larger macrostructure that generates these patterns of inequality.

As is evident in Fig. 9.3, Spencer also viewed "idea systems"—that is, law, values, standards of aesthetics, beliefs, religious dogmas, and language—as exerting considerable influence on the performance of those rituals feeding back and legitimating the broader macrostructure. Spencer's analysis of idea systems is not as detailed as Durkheim's, but, despite what many critics claim, he does recognize that ideas are an important mechanism of social control and that they are crucial for sustaining inequalities.

Spencer's model is not as robust as Durkheim's, but it too stresses the importance of ritual in structuring interaction. Moreover, in a somewhat different fashion than Durkheim's more phenomenological approach, Spencer argued that actors are categorized not only in terms of rituals but also in terms of signifying signs such as badges, fashion, and other objects. And finally, contrary to Durkheim's and most contemporary sociologists' assessment of Spencer's work, he does recognize the normative element as an important structuring force.

In sum, from Durkheim's and Spencer's analyses of subinstitutional processes, the significance of norms, ritual, and mutual categorization, and the ordering of space emerge as important structuring dynamics. While neither developed a clear conceptualization of how interaction is organized in terms of these processes, they both recognized that macrostructural properties of society depend upon the operation of these micro dynamics.

Simmel's Resource Transfer Model of Structuring Processes

More than Spencer, who is incorrectly considered the dominant utilitarian of this early period in sociology, it is Georg Simmel (1907) who employed utilitarian ideas in a sophisticated exchange model of structuring processes. This model was intended as a critique of Marx's labor theory of value, but my concern is not so much with the attack on Marx as with the conceptual leads provided by Simmel for understanding how chains of interaction are sustained across time. In Fig. 9.4, I have redrawn the model in Fig. 3.3, where my concern was with motivational processes. Here, I emphasize how Simmel's analysis can provide insight into the structuring of interpersonal activity.

Simmel viewed interaction as an exchange of valued resources, with actors being differentiated in terms of the respective value of the resources they hold. Actors who possess valued and desired resources will be in a position to extract valued resources from others, particularly when they can use "generalized" objects of value, such as money, in exchange relations with others. As I indicated in Chapter 3, these ideas anticipated most of modern exchange theory. They also provided insight into a key structuring process: stabilization in the transfer of resources (Freese, 1986). For interaction to be structured, Simmel implicitly argued, the exchange of re-

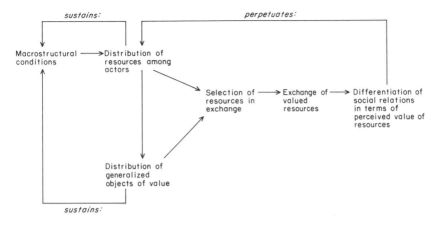

Fig. 9.4. Simmel's model of exchange structures.

sources among actors must be stabilized over time. The structuring of interaction thus depends upon agreements among individuals over the ratios of various resources that are to be exchanged at each encounter.

As Fig. 5.1, the composite model of motivation indicates, the exchange of material and symbolic resources is a part of any interaction, with actors being motivated to realize a profit in each situation. What Simmel clearly recognized is that these motivational forces influence the degree to which interaction becomes structured over time, for if the transfer of resources among actors creates an acceptable level of profit for each, then this ratio of payoffs becomes a tacit expectation for the exchange payoffs at their next encounter. And, if this expectation is repeatedly realized, it becomes even more salient as the yardstick for measuring what will occur in subsequent encounters.

This stabilization of resource transfers becomes a powerful structuring force because it is tied to those motivational energies that mobilize actors during interaction. Thus, to the extent that the transfer of resources among actors can be stabilized over time, interaction will reveal a structure—each actor will emit those behaviors that in the past brought the expected gratifications. Conversely, an interaction will be very quickly "unstructured" when expected resources are not received.

While I have extended Simmel's (1907) argument slightly, this is his basic position. For Simmel, inequalities in resources do not necessarily lead to conflict (as Marx argued), especially if actors find that resource transfers yield some level of profit. Indeed, when each actor finds the resources of another valuable, even if the ratio of exchange is unequal, then resource transfers will represent a stabilizing (as opposed to conflict-producing) force in human interaction.[4] Only when expectations are not met, either through a failure of others to provide resources at the customary rate or through an escalation of the expectations themselves, do resource transfers become a source of the tension and/or conflict that can restructure social relations. Marx's great failing, I think, was his inability to recognize what Simmel saw; at the micro interpersonal level of interaction, resource transfers, even among unequals, tend to stabilize around an acceptable ratio of payoffs for each actor; and as a result, these stabilized transfers give interaction a form or pattern across time. In contrast, Marx took a more macro view, emphasizing the inequality in the societal-level distribution of resources.

Mead and Schutz on Structuring

The respective schemes of George Herbert Mead and Alfred Schutz both sought to link the more micro processes of signaling and interpreting to the macrostructural dimensions of the social universe. Their efforts were limited, however, by a conceptual inventory more suitable to a micro approach. Thus, Mead's (1934) lectures are more an analysis of "mind, self, and interaction" than a conceptualization of "society," and Schutz (1932) is more concerned with the mental "orientations" of actors than with the properties of social structure. Yet, because their schemes are tied to sophisticated models of interactional processes, they are particularly useful for my purposes—the analysis of structuring in face-to-face interaction. For contrary to the arguments of some contemporary theorists (e.g., Blumer, 1969; Garfinkel, 1967), I do not think their models are of great use in understanding macrostructural properties per se, but as long as we confine analysis to the micro level, we can find a number of conceptual leads in their work.

In Fig. 9.5, I have modeled those concepts used by Mead to analyze "society." For Mead, "society," or "institutional patterns," is sustained by "concerted" and "coordinated" interaction among individuals, while interaction is circumscribed by existing institutional structures. Structure and interaction are thus opposite sides of the same coin, but more interesting than this kind of metaphorical assertion are the conceptual details of how this mutual feedback occurs.

[4] Though Simmel did not explore the issue in these terms, the legitimacy of an unequal exchange depends upon whether or not actors' general sense of "justice" is being violated. If either party sees an exchange as "unjust," then it will be difficult to legitimate and stabilize. This issue was, of course, Marx's point: the labor theory of value explains why actors should feel injustice. But Simmel's counterpoint was that perhaps subordinates do not always see unequal exchange relations as unjust or worthy of incurring the high costs of trying to change them.

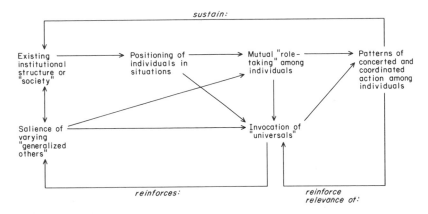

Fig. 9.5. Mead's model of interaction and society.

As Baldwin (1986) has noted, there is an ecological dimension to Mead's work; my reading of the scattered references to this dimension is that institutional structures—that is, established and stable patterns of organization—determine the spatial distribution of interactants and physical objects in a situation. Such ecological processes circumscribe the kind of mutual role-taking that can occur, but role-taking is influenced even more by those generalized other(s) that are viewed as salient by interactants. For individuals to be linked together across time, then, they must create or invoke a "community of attitudes" or a generalized perspective for organizing their conduct. Such a perspective involves more than developing normative expectations about appropriate sequences of behavior; it also requires utilizing common orientations, dispositions, and meanings to frame a situation.

In addition to the constraints of the generalized other(s) and of a situation's ecology, Mead (1934: 82–89, 125, 269) appears to have seen the invocation of "universals" as facilitating the structuring of an interaction. By "universals," Mead meant several things; in the context of structuring, they are standardized markers—e.g., words, gestures, and objects—that stimulate similar perspectives, orientations, dispositions, and meanings among actors. Universals are, in a sense, categories, because they allow actors to ignore the idiosyncratic and unique aspects of objects and gestures in order to place them in some more general class of objects and symbols requiring certain types of responses. To the extent universals can be invoked, interaction is facilitated. For interaction to become structured, Mead seems to imply, the physical props, the gestures of others, and the others themselves need to be classified or categorized as instances of a more general or "universal" type. When this is done, it is easier to resume an old interaction or enter an ongoing one.

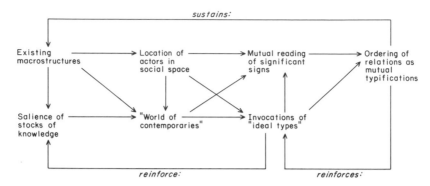

Fig. 9.6. Schutz's model of interaction and social structures.

Alfred Schutz (1932: 176-202) was much more explicit and detailed about the importance of what he called "typifications" in interaction situations. In Fig. 9.6, I have modeled Schutz's early line of argument in a manner that highlights its convergence with Mead's model. For Schutz, actors possess in their "stocks of knowledge at hand" a "world of contemporaries" who are the relevant types of actors who can potentially be implicated in a situation. These are "ideal types" of persons toward whom an individual is prepared to respond in certain predictable ways. People impute to such categorized individuals "because-of" and "in-order-to" motives (see pp. 81–83 in Chapter 6), thereby facilitating the process ordering social relations. Such typifications can, of course, be readjusted and revised as circumstances warrant, but they are useful in reducing the need for fine-tuned reading of gestures. Moreover, they enable actors to structure interactions, since past encounters have established the relevant typifications of others as belonging to general classes or categories; as the interaction is renewed, these categories can serve as a basis for reestablishing social relations. Additionally, situations can be typified with respect to the physical props that are present, as well as by types of people. Actors can then move into and out of social relations with ease, because all elements of a situation can be seen as instances of an ideal type. Under these conditions individuals can proceed to interact with a certain level of confidence about the likely responses of others, while at the same time being sure of how to organize and orchestrate their own responses.

In the model presented in Fig. 9.6, then, existing macrostructural parameters dictate the relevant stocks of knowledge, the location of actors in space, and the cast of potential others ("world of contemporaries"). In turn, these variables determine the ideal types that are invoked as a basis for interpreting gestures. Thus, in Schutz's view, the more a situation can involve mutual typifications of actors as representatives of categories, the more likely will these social relations be ordered in a way that reproduces existing institutional structures.

Admittedly, I have stretched Mead's and Schutz's arguments with some interpretive license. Yet the models presented in Figs. 9.5 and 9.6 are what emerged as I pondered the question of what concepts Mead and Schutz use to explain the structuring of interaction. Somewhat to my surprise, an emphasis on categorizing the elements of a situation becomes the most visible line of argument: drawing on stocks of knowledge and generalized others, actors construct categorical typifications of people and of other features of the setting—physical props, spacing of others, and the like. Thus, they do not need to engage in fine-tuned role-taking during each and every interaction in a chain nor to treat each new situation as novel.

I should also mention two other conceptual leads in Mead's and Schutz's respective approaches. First, the concepts of the "generalized other" and, to a lesser extent, "stocks of knowledge" suggest a normative element in the structuring of interaction. However, the complex set of cognitive variables denoted by these terms is never adequately sorted out in either Mead's or Schutz's scheme. Hence, in their present conceptual clothing, I am not sure that these concepts increase our understanding of how interaction is structured. Second, the notion of ecological space and distribution of actors is mentioned by both Schutz and Mead, but they do not elaborate upon these ideas. We are left, then, with a hint about an important structuring dynamic—regionalization of actors in space—but we will have to turn to more contemporary theories to appreciate the significance of this variable.

Conclusion

Though these early theories about structuring are rather imprecise, they isolate five important dynamics: the creation and use of norms; the ordering of space; the emission of rituals; the categorization of situations and others; and the stabilization of resource transfers. I have, of course, selectively pulled concepts from these early theorists' larger projects and given disproportionate weight to those variables that I sense are important. My review may not be entirely true to each theorist's actual intent, but as I indicated in Chapter 2, my goal is to use theorists' ideas in new ways, not to provide yet one more summary and commentary on the early masters. With these five dynamics as clues to how interaction becomes structured, our task is now to examine more contemporary theories to see how early conceptual leads have been extended and supplemented.

10

Contemporary Models of Interpersonal Structure

MOST CONTEMPORARY ANALYSES of structure in interpersonal relations are intended to bridge the micro-macro gap. Typically, a particular set of interpersonal practices is seen as *the* dynamic by which social structure is created and sustained. Moreover, macrostructures are often viewed as understandable only with reference to these interpersonal practices, although there is almost always a conceptual caveat noting how macrostructures feed back and constrain the very micro processes that produce and reproduce them. My sense is that all of these bridges between micro and macro are rather flimsy, consisting of provocative metaphors like "society is symbolic interaction" (Blumer, 1969); "structure is produced and reproduced by human agency" (Giddens, 1984); "society is ultimately composed of behaviors among men as men" (Homans, 1974); "social structures are chains of interaction rituals" (Collins, 1981); and so on.

Though these metaphors do not detail how the macro is constructed from the micro, they nonetheless provide important insights into the processes by which interaction is structured over time and space. Whether the concepts denoting this structuring of interaction are in fact adequate for understanding long-term and large-scale organization among populations of individuals is debatable—and in my view doubtful. But the insights into the microstructuring of interaction remain, and in this chapter, I review representative models of interpersonal structuring.

The Hidden Legacy in Parsonian Action Theory

Apparently, Talcott Parsons considered incorporating the ideas of Georg Simmel into *The Structure of Social Action* but decided against doing so, presumably because Simmel's work did not "fit" into the scheme that he was proposing. If this historical note is accurate, I find Parsons's conclusion rather surprising, since Simmel's (1907) *The Philosophy of Money* could have provided Parsons with the critique of Marx that he seemed to want and the sophisticated revision of utilitarianism that he clearly needed.[1] Moreover, Simmel could have provided the early Parsons with a concept that he was to rediscover 40 years later in his action theory—the notion of "generalized symbolic media of exchange" (Parsons, 1963a, 1963b, 1970; Parsons and Platt, 1975). Unfortunately, by the time Parsons had recognized the significance of symbolic media in exchange transactions, he had moved to a macro functionalism, leaving individuals in interaction far behind. Yet, even in Parsons's use of the concept of generalized symbolic media of exchange, there is an implicit model of structure. If we take this tacit model and blend it with the functional ideas for which Parsons is both famous and infamous, then an interesting theoretical lead on structuring processes emerges. Parsons did not develop this model as explicitly as I have outlined it in Fig. 10.1, but its dynamics capture the essence of what a latter-day Parsonian analysis of structuring might have revealed.

The early functional model in Parsons's (Parsons, 1951; Parsons, Bales, and Shils, 1953) ever-evolving scheme is delineated in part of the middle and all of the bottom portions of Fig. 10.1, whereas the later model, more reminiscent of Simmel, is found in some of the middle and all of the top portions of the figure. Social systems reveal four functional needs, or "imperatives," of adaptation, goal attainment, integration, and latency (Parsons, Bales, and Shils, 1953), and individuals can be viewed as located in subsystems having primary relevance for meeting these functional needs. This location in a "functional sector" determines the means (and, the "media" as well) that actors use in their interpersonal dealings with each other. Such interpersonal relations involve exchanges of resources that are constrained by values and norms, while being conducted in terms of the "symbolic media" appropriate to a functional sector (that is, "power" for goal attainment, "money" for adaptation, "influence" for integration, and "commitments" for latency). When these exchanges of resources in terms of generalized media are sustained across time, the structure of the resulting "social system" reinforces the relevance of values/norms and the use of generalized media, while at the same time meeting functional needs for adaptation, goal attainment, integration, and latency.

Obviously, Parsons never presented his argument in this way, but if he had seen more clearly the leads provided by Simmel, he might well have paused much earlier in his career to consider the significance of resource transfers in interpersonal relations. And perhaps he would have delayed his conceptual rush from "unit acts" (Parsons, 1937) to a universe of action systems incorporating the entire "human condition" (Parsons, 1978).

[1] Indeed, I think that Parsons's "unit act" involves a very utilitarian actor, albeit one with morals and a sensitivity to social conditions.

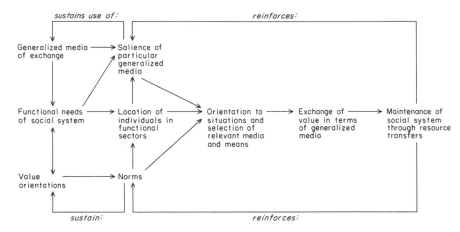

Fig. 10.1. Parsons's implicit exchange theory of structuring.

Thus, the model in Fig. 10.1 is, at best, implicit in Parsons's work, representing what a more detailed analysis of interaction might have looked like if he had been pushed to provide one. What, then, are the conceptual leads in this model for a composite model of interpersonal structuring?

First, Parsonian theory stresses the normative element. Exchange relations and transfers of resources are guided by norms; and if these transfers prove sufficiently profitable over time and/or meet system needs, they reinforce norms and the more general value orientations that help structure interaction. Second, Parsons's implicit model adds the notion that interactions that become structured involve the stabilization of resource transfers through the use of generalized symbolic media. Thus, when individuals select a course of action, they do so in terms of generalized media that will facilitate the exchange of values. Just what exchange media are relevant is jointly determined by norms, the functional location of actors, and, of course, the resources possessed by others. To appreciate this second conceptual lead, we do not have to accept Parsons's typology of "generalized symbolic media" or his presumption that their use is tied to the four functional imperatives of all action systems. Rather, the important point is that interaction is more easily structured when actors "know" the relevant media for an exchange of resources and when they agree upon what generalized media are to be used across exchange transactions. Such knowledgeability about media presupposes that individuals categorize situations in terms of the kind of media —power, influence, approval, honor, money, etc.—that are relevant.

This brings us to a third conceptual lead in Parsons's model: the categorization of situations and the use of this categorization to select means and media in interaction. Again, in order to appreciate Parsons's insight, we do not have to accept his typologies on how actors classify and orient themselves to situations—say, in terms of the "pattern variables" (Parsons, 1951). Rather, we need only recognize that the structuring of interaction depends upon mutual categorization that is then used to select the appropriate means and media for completing the transfer of resources and for giving predictability to subsequent transfers.

I should not extend Parsons's ideas further, because it would be all too easy to impose my biases on his scheme,[2] thereby making it unrecognizable as Parsonian. The important point in this exercise is that there are interesting ideas in Parsonian theory for a model of structuring. Even though his approach emphasized "structure" over the interpersonal processes implicated in structure, it does contain several implicit concepts about interpersonal processes, and Fig. 10.1 makes the best case for their importance to a theory of structuring.

The Exchange-Theoretic Model

Contemporary exchange theory has been consistently concerned with the question of how interpersonal processes are implicated in the emergence, maintenance, and transformation of social structures (e.g., Homans, 1961, 1974; Blau, 1964; Emerson, 1986, 1972a, 1972b, 1962; Willer, 1981). While the terminology among exchange theorists varies somewhat, the main questions have been how exchanges of valued resources create patterns of differentiation, especially with respect to power and prestige, and how such differentiation becomes "integrated" or "balanced" into a structural pattern. These concerns, along with the central concepts of virtually all exchange theories, are outlined in Fig. 10.2.

Exchange theories see the existence of macrostructures—that is, relatively stable networks and patterns of differentiation among actors in a population—as determining the distribution of valued resources among actors. Such macrostructures are presumed to be the result of past micro exchanges, as is emphasized by the feedback arrow across the top of Fig. 10.2. In terms of their respective resources, actors in micro encounters find each other "attractive"; that is, they perceive others' resources as valuable, and they are therefore willing to give up some of their own resources to secure them. In order to strike the best deal possible, individuals often engage in mutual impression-management to hide their desire for the resources of another and to indicate the desirability of their own resources.

[2] One reviewer remarked at this point: "I think you already have!"

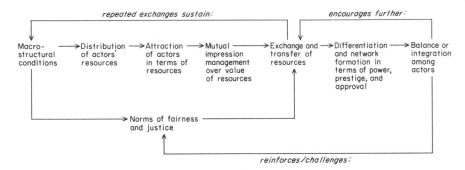

Fig. 10.2. Contemporary exchange theory on structuring.

Out of these efforts come actual exchanges, but these are guided by norms of "justice" and "fair exchange" as they have evolved from past exchanges and been institutionalized in macrostructures.[3] In turn, patterns of differentiation and network formation among actors emerge from these exchanges, as circumscribed by considerations of justice and fairness.

The degree of differentiation among actors in terms of power and prestige is shaped by the respective values of their resources and the number of actors from whom they can secure these resources. Power differences are most likely when the respective resources of actors are of very different value and when those who find the resources of another particularly valuable cannot secure them elsewhere. Prestige differences also follow from these same general conditions, but in a more mitigated form. Peer relations are most likely when these two conditions—inequality and scarcity of alternatives—do not exist, with the result that actors merely exchange approval for approval. In the short run, exchanges tend to become "integrated" (Blau, 1964) or "balanced" (Emerson, 1972b), since actors come to accept their respective payoffs as judged by the "market value" of their resources and by norms of fairness and justice. Such integration and balancing stabilize the rate of exchange, thereby sustaining macrostructures and norms of fairness/justice.

From an exchange perspective, then, stabilization of resource transfers through balancing and integration (that is, acceptance of payoffs) is what structures an interaction. Such stabilization is facilitated by norms that specify what rates of exchange are fair and just. Thus, as long as interactions involve profitable exchanges of resources that are defined as fair, they will be repeated. And as they are repeated, structuring occurs, in two sen-

---

[3] Another reviewer asked of exchange theorists: "Why do macrostructural conditions lead to norms of fairness and justice? I think that exchange theories arbitrarily throw this in, as a vague recognition of 'cultural' factors which are not explained by their theory."

ses. First, repetition of exchanges sustains existing macrostructural conditions that in turn influence the distribution of resources and actors, while reinforcing those norms that define what is fair in a situation. Such maintenance of macrostructures circumscribes what is possible in subsequent exchanges by "loading the dice" in terms of the distribution of resources among actors and the relevance of particular justice norms. Second, repetition of exchanges, per se, will produce structure without reference to its consequences for macrostructural processes. If actors receive rewards at one point in time, then they will be likely to anticipate and accept their respective payoffs at their next encounter, as long as established ratios of resource payoffs and norms of fairness are not violated.

As is evident, these conceptual leads are similar to those provided by Parsons's implicit model, without all of the functional trappings of Parsonian action theory. In fact, when one takes the functional imperatives out of Parsons, it looks very much like what he rejected in 1937, a modern-day version of utilitarianism. Nonetheless, the critical point is that the structuring of interaction depends upon the stabilization of resource transfers in terms of the ratios of resources exchanged,[4] the ability of each actor to realize some profit, and the assessment by each actor that the exchange is fair and just with regard to relevant norms.

Collins's Exchange-Ritual Model

In Chapter 4, I summarized Randall Collins's (1986, 1981, 1975) model of motivational processes. In this model the "need for group membership" was seen to be the guiding force behind people's conversational exchanges. That is, conversations are typically about group inclusion/exclusion issues, with individuals "spending" their "emotional energy" and "cultural capital" in order to sustain and perhaps enhance their position in an ongoing group context. In Fig. 10.3, I have redrawn the model presented in Fig. 4.5 to emphasize its implications for structuring processes.

For Collins, macrostructural conditions constrain what can occur in micro situations. Such conditions typically determine the number of people co-present in an interaction situation, the distribution of people in space, the distribution of relevant resources among actors, especially their level of emotional energy and cultural capital, and the length of time that actors will be co-present. Such macrostructural conditions are built up from past interactions that, as they are strung out across time in chains of interaction,

---

[4] Of course, some exchange theories also present theories of conflict (e.g., Blau, 1964); and in fact, I would argue that most conflict theories are a subtheory of exchange (see J. Turner, 1986b: 230).

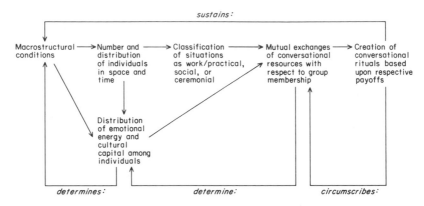

Fig. 10.3. Collins's interaction ritual model of structuring.

create those macrostructures that circumscribe each subsequent interaction among individuals. Such interactions are conceptualized as "interaction ritual chains" in which individuals classify situations as work/practical, social, or ceremonial; mobilize the appropriate emotional energy (e.g., sentiments, feelings, dispositions) and cultural capital (e.g., memories of past conversations, control of physical props, vocal styles, knowledge, authority); spend this energy and capital in conversational exchanges with others; and realize some level of profit (e.g., positive emotions and/or enhanced capital) with respect to their place or position in an ongoing group context.

Collins sees this process as a "ritual," but in a rather idiosyncratic way. Because the conversational exchanges among individuals revolve around a clear focal point—group membership—they represent a "ritual performance" toward a sociological "totem," the group. Conversations thus address a common focus (group membership) and arouse people's emotions with respect to their sense of involvement in groups. In other words, the basic motivational force in human interaction—need for group membership—is linked to how people interact—ritualized conversational exchanges using emotional energy and cultural capital to sustain/enhance their sense of group membership.

Interactions become linked together over time as actors' respective profits from one conversational encounter become stored as a memory and are subsequently used to classify situations and mobilize a given level of energy/capital in the next encounter. Over time, as encounters are linked together in a "chain," the exchange of conversational resources becomes somewhat stabilized as actors accept their place in the ongoing organization of an interaction context. If there is a great inequality in the organization of this context—that is, some control much more cultural capital and can mobilize more emotional energy than others—then conversations become highly "ritualized" in another sense of this term: stereotyped sequences of behaviors that allow subordinates to invest as little capital and energy in the situation as possible, while freeing superordinates from the responsibilities of constantly monitoring the action of subordinates. Such stabilization of resource transfers and ritualization help sustain the distribution of energy and capital among actors and, hence, the larger macrostructure.

Despite several points of ambiguity in this portrayal of structuring, it does offer a number of important conceptual leads. First, structuring revolves around resource transfers, especially with respect to issues of group membership. Second, when such transfers are stabilized through established ratios of payoffs and rituals, they become even more structured, making it easier to link encounters together in chains of interaction. Third, categorization or classification of situations facilitates structuring by indicating what emotional and cultural resources are relevant to a conversational exchange and what rituals are most appropriate for such exchanges. And fourth, just what categories and resources are employed in an encounter is circumscribed by demographic/ecological conditions, especially the number and distribution of actors in space and time. These represent, as I will emphasize in the next chapter, critical processes in the structuring of interaction.

The Interactionist Model

With a few notable exceptions (e.g., Shibutani, 1986), interactionist theorizing has tended to assert the explanatory primacy of interpersonal processes, without actually demonstrating how structure is created and sustained. At best, Mead's model of motivation and signaling/interpreting (see Figs. 6.1 and 9.5) is recast somewhat, as it has been extended by contemporary theorists. Even then, some of the more promising concepts in Mead's approach—such as "universals"—become recessive in contemporary interactionists' portrayal of structuring processes. Nonetheless, my representation of the interactionist model indicates that here too we can find some interesting conceptual leads for a more general model of structuring.

Fig. 10.4 outlines what I see as the critical elements in interactionists' conceptualizations of structuring. Social structures are sustained through a series of reinforcement processes arising out of people's efforts to construct patterns of "joint action" (Blumer, 1969). These reinforcement pro-

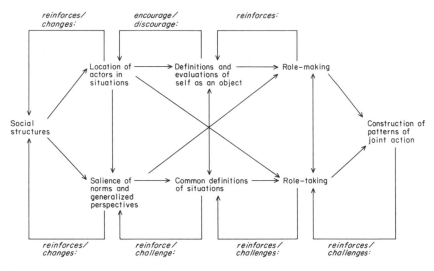

Fig. 10.4. Interactionist models of structuring.

cesses, as denoted by the many feedback loops in the model, indicate the implicit behaviorism in all interactionist theorizing. That is, individuals find rewarding those behaviors that increase the accuracy of role-taking and role-making, that confirm self as an object, that sustain definitions of situations, that affirm the salience of norms and generalized perspectives guiding conduct, and that place actors in positions and roles. Conversely, if efforts at joint action do not provide this reinforcement, they will produce pressures for changes in social structure.

Thus, for interactionists, social structure is a process revolving around key reinforcement patterns. Once created, however, social structure dictates the relative locations (positions) of actors in situations as well as the relevant norms and perspectives. In turn, the position of actors determines which aspects of self will be seen as relevant in an interaction, whereas the increased salience of norms and generalized perspectives (meanings, attitudes, orientations, feelings, and dispositions) influences the "definitions" of situations (Thomas and Zaniecki, 1927) that individuals can develop. Such definitions are reciprocally related to self in that one's self-conception circumscribes what one sees as important in a situation, while being influenced by these very perceptions. Role-making is primarily influenced by self, as qualified by norms, generalized perspectives, common definitions, and role taking, whereas role-taking is principally influenced by common definitions of situations, as circumscribed by actors' relative positions, and by their efforts to make a role for themselves.

As the extreme left and right portions of the model in Fig. 10.4 stress, interactionist theorizing sees social structure as a process of active construction of joint acts across time; past joint actions result in relative positioning of individuals in status-roles and make certain norms and perspectives more salient than others. There is, then, a heavy normative element in interactionist theorizing, although most interactionists remain suspicious of this concept.[5] Moreover, there is a pronounced emphasis on position in a larger network of positions, although once again interactionists would not use these terms. Social structures are also created and held together by people's ability to construct common definitions about the elements of a situation. That is, through mutual role-taking, they can agree upon the categories of others and objects that exist in a context and that, as a consequence, dictate the range of appropriate responses, norms, and perspectives to be invoked in a situation.

What makes interactionism unique is the emphasis on self and its effects on needs to make a role and to define a situation so as to reinforce those dimensions of self that individuals see as particularly relevant. In other words, a social structure will be sustained to the extent that it enables people to maintain positive self evaluations about those dimensions of their core and peripheral self that they see as important.

There are, I think, some useful conceptual leads here, although they will need to be blended with concepts from other perspectives to develop a more general theory of structuring. The behaviorism in interactionist theory requires, I believe, incorporation into a more comprehensive exchange-theoretic framework, where actors are seen as negotiating not only over positions in groups as well as norms and definitions, but also over confirmations of self. Moreover, while interactionist concepts of role-making and role-taking tell us much about what people do when they interact (see Chapter 8), they do not provide an explicit structuring dynamic. Concepts like norms, definitions of situations, and generalized perspectives do not add much conceptual enlightenment beyond functional analyses of structure, and, in fact, tend to be used by interactionists in rather vague and metaphorical ways. At best, these concepts argue that actors orient themselves to situations in terms of common cognitions. Before refining further the concepts of interactionist theory, however, let us examine some additional approaches that, along with those discussed thus far, may provide the conceptual tools for developing a more refined model of structuring.

---

[5] The prominence of "norms" varies with the interactionist in question. At one extreme is Blumer (1969) who would see norms as one of many "objects" of reflection in an individual's deliberations over a course of action, whereas at the other extreme would be Stryker (1980) who would at least acknowledge that there are norms regulating (to varying degrees) people's behavior.

Goffman's Model

As I outlined in Fig. 7.2, Erving Goffman (1959, 1967, 1974) provided many of the key concepts for the model of interpersonal signaling and interpreting presented in Fig. 8.1. Goffman also provides critical insights into the processes that structure interaction across time and space. In Fig. 10.5, I have recast the ideas in Fig. 7.2 to emphasize the process of structuring.

Unlike many micro theorists, particularly in some versions of symbolic interactionism, Goffman always recognized that interaction occurs within a macrostructural context that, as indicated in Fig. 10.5, determines not only the distribution of actors in space and time, but also the salience of shared cultural orientations, though, as with interactionist theory, the properties of these cultural orientations are left rather vague. Under the spatial, temporal, and cultural constraints determined by the macrostructure, individuals seek to frame situations and present themselves in a favorable light; frames further circumscribe the range of potential responses in a situation, and self-presentations provide the motivational energy for the interaction to proceed. All these factors together allow individuals to ritualize and regionalize their interaction. Ritualization involves the emission of stereotyped sequences of gestures. By the use of space and physical props regionalization circumscribes the emission of these rituals providing the physical cues for different types of gesturing sequences (for example, a backstage region will require different opening, closing, and sequencing rituals than a frontstage region).

Thus, if people can create agreements over the spacing and juxtapositioning, their use of physical props, and their timing of the interaction in space, then their next interaction can proceed smoothly, since they "understand" what the physical and temporal parameters of their interaction "mean." Similarly, if they can agree to use common sequences of gestures for opening, ordering, and closing their interaction, then their subsequent interaction will involve considerably less interpersonal work, because they now "know" how to proceed. In turn, these processes of regionalizing and ritualizing feed back and sustain the macrostructure by ordering people in space and time, while reaffirming shared cultural orientations. Thus, ritualized and regionalized interactions reinforce the very macrostructure that initially encouraged the use of certain rituals as well as the ordering of space and time. As interactions in more and more contexts are regionalized and ritualized, structure is built up.

Despite Goffman's rather imprecise portrayal of macrostructure and cul-

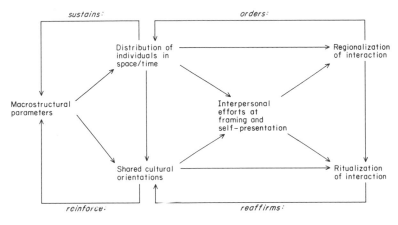

Fig. 10.5. Goffman's model of interpersonal structuring.

tural orientations, his analysis provides two conceptual leads for understanding structuring processes. Those interactions that can be ordered in space/time and that can be sequenced in a predictable (ritual) form will be more readily repeated and linked together in chains of interaction. And, as individuals in a society acquire knowledge of what juxtaposition, physical props, spacing, staging, and behavioral sequences "mean" in varying contexts, they can organize their responses without great interpersonal effort. Indeed, a complex society that requires considerable movement of individuals into and out of many different kinds of situations depends upon a high level of knowledgeability about the meaning of diverse rituals and regions.

Giddens's Structuration Model

Though as I summarized in Chapter 4 (see Fig. 4.3), Anthony Giddens has developed a useful theory of motivational processes, he has, curiously, had comparatively little to say about interactional processes revolving around signaling and interpreting. Part of the reason for this conceptual gap resides in Giddens's critical assessment of interactionist theory, which, in his view, has focused on face-to-face interaction to the exclusion of structural and motivational issues. He attempts to correct for these deficiencies by blending concepts from psychoanalytic theory, interactionism, and phenomenology/ethnomethodology into a theory of motivation. Unlike so much of motivational theory, he conceptually integrates the forces that mobilize human agents with those that structure their interaction in time and space. It should not be surprising, therefore, that his model of

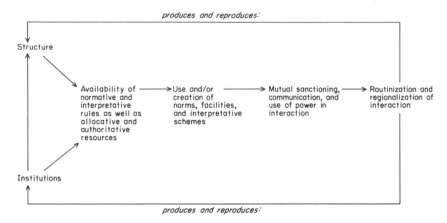

Fig. 10.6. Giddens's structuration theory.

"structuration" will prove useful in developing a composite model of structuring.

In Fig. 10.6, I have outlined in skeletal form his model of structuring, at least as I see it. I have removed much of Giddens's (1984, 1979) vocabulary, which often becomes obtuse, but Fig. 10.6 is true to his essential line of argument (for my more detailed review of his approach, see J. Turner, 1986b: 546–78). For Giddens, "structure" denotes the "rules" and "resources" that individuals use to extend their interaction across space and time. Rules are "generalizable procedures" that people employ as a methodology or formula for organizing their responses, whereas resources are "facilities" that actors can draw upon to get things done during an interaction. There are two basic kinds of rules: normative rules are used to create rights and obligations in an interaction; interpretative rules are employed to generate "stocks of taken-for-granted knowledge" in a context. Similarly, there are two types of resources: authoritative resources are those organizational capacities that actors possess and draw upon in a situation to control and direct the pattern of interaction; allocative resources are those material features of situations—props, artifacts, goods, etc.— that actors use to coordinate their responses and accomplish tasks.

As indicated in Fig. 10.6, the "structure" of a situation consists of various rules and resources that individuals can employ to organize their interactions. In this process, actors create norms, facilities, and interpretative schemes. While rules and resources are "transformational"—that is, they are capable of being combined and recombined to create varying norms, facilities, and interpretative schemes—there is often an institutional constraint on what rules and resources are available to actors and on how they can be transformed. Giddens (1984: 31, 1979: 107) offers a typology of institutions in terms of various configurations of rules and resources, but for my purposes here I need only stress that he sees many interaction contexts as lodged in institutionalized patterns that have been built up from past interactions and that now circumscribe the rules and resources available to individuals.

The norms, facilities, and interpretative schemes thus created are, in turn, used for mutual sanctioning, communication, and use of power. Emerging from these interpersonal activities is an ordering of interaction in terms of routines and regions. This ordering is made possible by available rules and resources and is motivated by deep-seated needs for ontological security and a sense of trust (see Fig. 4.3 for the details). Routinization organizes an interaction across time; regionalization orders an interaction in space. And, as situations become routinized and regionalized, actors reproduce the very structures and institutions that determine the resources and rules available to them. Giddens's discussion of routines and regions is detailed and worth further examination, since I believe these two concepts denote important structuring dynamics. Let me begin with routinization.

For Giddens (1984: 72), "the routinization of encounters is of major significance in bending the fleeting encounter to social reproduction and thus to the seeming 'fixity' of institutions." Routines thus stretch interaction across time by enabling actors to interact in predictable ways during a single encounter or in successive ones. Giddens emphasizes five interpersonal mechanisms by which actors sustain routines: (1) the use of rituals that mark the opening, sequencing, and closing of a particular pattern of interaction; (2) the use of "turn-taking" methods to assure that conversations proceed in a predictable form maintaining the routine; (3) the use of "tact" to create the appropriate sense of decorum necessary for sustaining routines; (4) the use of signals to mark individuals' respective (status) positions in a situation, thereby allowing them to preserve their sense of identity and the routine; and (5) the use of frames as markers for indicating what range of behaviors and demeanors is appropriate for maintaining a routine.

Regionalization derives from Giddens's view that interaction reveals a geographical element as well as a serial ordering of responses across time. Giddens (1984: 110–44) introduces the concept of "locale" to highlight certain dimensions of spatial structuring. Locales vary in terms of their physical and symbolic boundaries, their degree of connectedness to broader institutional patterns, their span and extension of physical space, and their duration across time. And so, as individuals interact, they use rules and resources to mark the geographical boundaries of their interaction, to connect their use of space to broader institutional patterns, to partition the space in which the interaction occurs, and to decide upon the time period during which space will be used. Such "staging" practices enable actors to increase the predictability of their responses, thereby meeting basic motivational needs for security and trust, while reproducing structure and institutions.

In sum, then, Giddens (1984) provides three important conceptual leads for developing a more comprehensive model of structuring processes. First, there is a normative element, recast here into a provocative view of norms as transformable tools for ordering interaction. Second, there is the concept of routines or routinization, which emphasizes that the structuring of interaction will be difficult unless the responses of individuals become highly predictable and habitual. And third, there is the notion of regionalization, which stresses the significance of ordering actors in space for the maintenance of interaction across time.

Conclusion

The theoretical approaches summarized in this chapter supplement and advance the insights of those early theoretical masters examined in the previous chapter. I have stressed what I see as key insights; and we are now ready to pull them together into a composite model of structuring and to use this model to generate some tentative "laws" or principles of structuring dynamics. In doing so, it will be necessary to detach these structuring dynamics analytically from motivational and interactional processes. That is, quite apart from what motivates interaction or what actors do when they signal and interpret, how is interaction ordered across time and space? Naturally, structuring is embedded in motivational and interactional processes, and I will mention this along the way. For the present, however, I will give structuring dynamics the same treatment I have used in previous chapters for motivational and interactional dynamics, continuing to explore each of these processes as if they could be separated into discrete conceptual entities. I will save for Chapters 12 and 13 a more explicit examination of the causal connections among motivational, interactional, and structuring dynamics. Then we will be ready to put the conceptual pieces back together again, and in the process, move toward a theory of social interaction.

11

Toward a Synthetic
Model of Structuring

AS PEOPLE MOBILIZE their motivational energies and engage in mutual role-taking and making, staging, validating, ritualizing, and framing, they often create an emergent property: structure. Such structure is not a "thing," however, but a process in which individuals produce and reproduce patterned sequences of interactive responses. And once created, these established sequences become, in a sense, a "mental template" or "schema" for how those individuals will interact when they resume contact. When such cognitive schemes can be learned by others, then successive sets of actors can enter situations and repeat the lines of behavior created by others, often in the distant past. Thus, the process of structuring is, on the one hand, an overt patterning of behaviors in time and space and, on the other hand, a mental modeling of information about what interactive sequences apply to varying types of situations.

Structuring as a Distinctive Property of Interaction

This dual quality of structuring presented Durkheim with a conceptual dilemma, since he could not satisfactorily reconcile his earlier pronouncements that a "social fact" is an "external and constraining thing" (Durkheim, 1895) with his later recognition that "the collective force is not entirely outside of us; . . . but rather, since society cannot exist except in and through individual consciousness, this force must penetrate and organize itself within us" (Durkheim, 1912: 209). Just how to reconcile the conclusions that society or structure exists both as an external and visible reality and as a mental construction has often confounded analyses of "social structure." Part of the reason for this confusion, I think, is that when addressing the topic of structure, theorists become too macro and emphasize large-scale and long-term interactive patterns; yet, curiously, when they try to connect these macro dimensions of structure to individuals, they typically become too micro and delve into the properties of human consciousness and cognition. The result is conceptual flip-flopping between the majesty of the macro structural order and the inner workings of individual mental constructions.

This in turn creates the gap between micro and macro sociology; and although there may be both an ontological and a metaphysical basis for this gap, it is probably wider than necessary. In recent years, efforts have been made to examine the micro foundations of the macro order, but these have tended toward a micro extremism that emphasizes talk and conversation, while defining away most alternative conceptions of structure as reifications and hypostatizations. Or, as the models presented in the last chapters have revealed, macrostructural processes are conceptualized in rather imprecise terms—structural parameters, cultural orientations, norms, generalized perspectives, functional needs, and the like. The result is for macrostructure, as well as "structural" considerations in general, to exist as vague pronouncements alongside more precisely conceptualized micro processes—thereby creating another kind of conceptual gap.

None of this is necessary. For the time being, let us accept the existence of a discontinuity in our conceptualizations of face-to-face interaction and the organization of populations. Then let us recognize that to address the topic of structure we must choose either a micro or a macro perspective and that those alternatives will yield diverging conceptualizations and different kinds of insight into the operative dynamics of the social universe. With these simple guidelines in mind, my micro analysis of structuring addresses a very modest question: how is it that individuals are able to pattern and sequence their interactions across time and space?

Part of the answer to this question is contained in the previous chapters on motivational and interactional dynamics. But, as this chapter will emphasize, we cannot explain patterns of interaction solely in terms of either those forces motivating individuals or those processes enabling individuals to signal and interpret. Additional concepts are required and can be found, as I have indicated, in the works of the theorists discussed in Chapters 9 and 10. All that remains, then, is a synthesis of these works into a composite model of structuring that suspends consideration of how to bridge the micro-macro gap.

The Dynamic Properties of Structuring

My examination of the early masters and representative contemporary theorists yields six general conceptual rubrics for understanding how structuring operates. I will label these (1) categorization, (2) regionalization, (3) normatization, (4) ritualization, (5) routinization, and (6) stabilization of resource transfers. These processes are "energized" by motivational dynamics, and they are conducted by virtue of the interactional processes of staging, validating, accounting, role-taking and making, ritual-taking and making, and framing. As I emphasized above, however, structuring is an emergent property that requires some new concepts or, at the very least, a number of extensions of those concepts used to understand motivation and signaling/interpreting. These six concepts represent my best guess as to basic interpersonal processes that create, sustain, and perhaps change patterns of interaction.[1] Several are elaborations of concepts in earlier models of motivation and signaling/interpreting, which is not surprising, since structuring is implicated and embedded in motivational and interactional dynamics (see Fig. 2.1). For the moment, however, let us view motivational, interactional, and structuring processes as discrete dynamics, saving for the next chapter a review of their mutual embeddedness.

Categorization

As many theorists have emphasized and as I have noted in several places, individuals often seek to view situations and each other in terms of consensually agreed upon categories. By visualizing situations and individuals as examples or instances of a category, the need for fine-tuned signaling and interpreting is greatly reduced. For once persons and contextual elements are categorized, the appropriate responses are, in a very literal sense, preprogramed and can be emitted without great deliberative effort. Individuals carry in their stocks of knowledge information about how they are supposed to orient themselves and behave, in general terms, in given types of situations. Without this information, structuring of interaction would be difficult; each situation and individual would be unique, requiring new responses at different points in one encounter and at each new encounter. But by invoking relevant categories, individuals can enter new situations and emit appropriate responses to strangers, thereby reproducing those structures through which different actors pass.

This structuring dynamic is implicit in Weber's (1978) and Parsons's (1951) view that actors engage in "types of action"—instrumental-rational, value-rational, affectual, appreciative, etc. It is, of course, made explicit in Parsons's conceptualization of the pattern variables as mechanisms for typifying social systems and in his later view of functional imperatives/requisites and generalized media as a means for initially classifying situations in terms of their functions and media. Schutz's (1932) critique of Weber (and by extension, of Parsons also) explicitly recognizes that interaction is greatly facilitated when others can be typified as representatives of an ideal type, but unlike Weber and Parsons, who emphasized just a few categories, Schutz maintained that the categories are more subtle and complex. Similarly, interactionist notions about "definitions of situa-

---

[1] I emphasize "interpersonal" since macrostructures clearly constrain what can occur during social interaction. But, if we are focusing only on the micro dynamics of structuring, then these six concepts denote what I see as the critical processes involved.

tions" argue that actors categorize, but here, too, there is no presumption of a limited number of categories.

There is, then, clear consensus that actors simplify situations by categorizing them, but the question of how they do so remains problematic. Do they create new categories for each situation? Do they carry in their stocks of knowledge a few provisional categories? Or do they carry complex sets of categorical elements that are combined and recombined in each situation? I suspect that the answer to all these questions is affirmative. Yet my sense is that, although actors do indeed construct highly fine-tuned and situationally specific schemes of classification, the production and reproduction of structure depend more on the use of a few general categories. For if there are too many categories, their very purpose—that is, to simplify—is obviated.

Despite Parsons's and Weber's provocative formulations on the categorization of social situations, I think that Collins (1975) has been the most theoretically insightful. For Collins, individuals initially assess situations as being one of three types: work/practical, ceremonial, or social. This simplifies the organization of responses, since individuals now "know" the range of behaviors most relevant to the situation. Of course, they may also carry in their cognitive structure, or develop during the course of interaction, more fine-tuned and contextual conceptions for each of these three general types of situations, thereby facilitating further the organization of behaviors during prolonged interactions. But initially—which is the critical moment for the reproduction of an interaction—individuals rely upon a few general categories.

Though Collins does not explore the issue in any detail, these three categories, and various refinements and subtypes that may subsequently be invoked by actors, are a critical force behind the structuring of an interaction. For if actors are to order their responses during one interaction sequence and at subsequent encounters, they need to classify the situation as involving work/practical, ceremonial, or social demeanors. Moreover, if actors are to enter new situations, there must be markers (words, nonverbal gestures, physical props, etc.) informing them of the relevant category.

Not only do people classify situations, but they also classify or typify each other. While the typification of others is implied by the categorization of the situation, Schutz's (1932) argument should alert us to another dimension of categorization: the classification of individuals as representatives of categories. My sense is that such classification varies according to the degree of intimacy with which people view each other. At one extreme, they can see each other as intimates with whom they feel in true intersubjective contact, while at the other, they can view each other as categories whose subjective states they presume by virtue of their being instances of respective types of individuals. And perhaps there is some middle category where people see each other as types, and yet at the same time, as persons about whom they should know some personal specifics. I hypothesize, therefore, that individuals simultaneously classify situations as work/practical, ceremonial, or social and others as intimates, persons, or categories. Table 11.1 summarizes what is involved in the nine possible categories that result.

The critical point is that the structuring of interaction is dramatically facilitated when one of these nine types can be used by individuals to organize their responses. Once again, such categorization makes responses predictable, enables people to enter new situations and understand what is expected, and allows them to pick up old interactions where they left off. Of course, I am not precluding the possibility (indeed, the likelihood) that situations change, that they shift from one type to the other, or that they involve categorical elaboration and fine-tuning. Indeed, the course of interaction often changes the structure of situations, but even such transformations are structured, in at least two senses: actors use markers (words, nonverbal cues, physical props, spacing, etc.) to signal movement to a new category; and new categories provide their own guidelines for the reordering of responses. Thus, to a great extent, micro interactions are structured by individuals' capacity to categorize them into relatively few types (as illustrated in Table 11.1) and at the same time to mark movements to new sets of categories or refinements of existing ones. Of course, as we will see later, these capacities to categorize are influenced by the other structuring processes.

Regionalization

As Goffman (1959) was the first to emphasize, the ecology and demography of an interaction are critical variables. The structuring of an interaction is, therefore, particularly likely to be influenced by such considerations as the span of space in which the interaction occurs, the physical props that exist, the objects dividing space into "regions," the number and distribution of individuals in regions, and the movement of people into and out of the overall space and its various subregions.

These ecological and demographic variables will, to some extent, determine the flow of interaction: a large space will have different interaction patterns than a small one; a space divided into many regions (offices, corridors, elevators, desks, etc.) will produce very different interactions than an open space; a crowded space with many people will generate different interactions than a sparsely populated one; a region allowing constant movement and turnover of participants will reveal dramatically different interactions than a place where movements are more restricted. Thus, as

TABLE 11.1

A Provisional Typology of How Humans Categorize

	TYPES OF SITUATIONS		
	Work/practical	Ceremonial	Social
Categories	Others as functionaries whose behaviors are relevant to achieving a specific task or goal and who, for the purposes at hand, can be treated as strangers	Others as representatives of a larger collective enterprise toward whom highly stylized responses owed as a means of expressing their joint activity	Others as strangers toward whom superficially informal, polite, and responsive gestures are owed
Persons	Others as functionaries whose behaviors are relevant to achieving a specific task or goal but who, at the same time, must be treated as unique individuals in their own right	Others as fellow participants of a larger collective enterprise toward whom stylized responses are owed as a means of expressing their joint activity and recognition of each other as individuals in their own right	Others as familiar individuals toward whom informal, polite, and responsive gestures are owed
Intimates	Others as close friends whose behaviors are relevant to achieving a specific task or goal and toward whom emotional responsiveness is owed	Others as close friends who are fellow participants in a collective enterprise and toward whom a combination of stylized and personalized responses are owed as a means of expressing their joint activity and sense of mutual understanding	Others as close friends toward whom informal and emotionally responsive gestures are owed

LEVELS OF INTIMACY IN DEALING WITH OTHERS

independent forces in their own right, demography and ecology circumscribe the potential range of interaction structures that can emerge in a situation. I will refer to these demographic and ecological forces as "regionalization."

Although demographic and ecological variables circumscribe the range of what is possible, the actual structuring of the interaction sequence across time is the result of shared conceptions of what space, regions, numbers, movements, and objects actually "mean." The structuring of an interaction, therefore, requires relatively stable ecological and demographic conditions *and* general consensus over what these conditions indicate as the appropriate lines of conduct.

My argument is that, through socialization and interactive experience, competent actors develop stocks of knowledge about interactive ecology. They then use this knowledge to regionalize interaction in time, thereby contributing to its structuring. In Fig. 11.1, I have constructed a rough schematic view of the cognitive structure that generates these meanings. I visualize individuals as carrying in their more general stocks of knowledge a subset of information about the meanings of varying ecological and demographic conditions. This information is cognitively organized along four dimensions: the meaning of space in varying contexts; the meaning of objects in different spatial settings; the meaning of the division or organization of space in different contexts; and the meaning of interpersonal demography—varying numbers, distributions, and movements of people in different settings. For an interaction to become structured, actors must agree what the space in which they are located signifies (a floor of offices, classroom, football stadium, etc.); they must accept the significations of objects in this space (desks, doors, carpets, chairs, nameplates, turnstiles, etc.); they must understand what the division of space into regions means (offices, corridors, conference rooms, sections, rows of chairs, etc.); and they must know what the number, distribution, and movement of people in the situation indicates (e.g., crowds at a stadium, receptionist in an office, students in a classroom, etc.).

Though this may all seem obvious, regionalizing is a complex and subtle process. For example, in order for a classroom to structure interaction, students and professors must "know" what the room signifies, what chairs and other props are to be used for, what the ordering of space into student and teacher sections signifies, and what the number and movement of people signify for classroom activity. Moreover, students and professors understand the significance of such variables as a large or small class, a seminar or lecture arrangement of props, a podium or non-podium lecture style, formal or casual dress and demeanor of a teacher, and so on. This juxtaposition of objects and people in space thus stimulates a particular

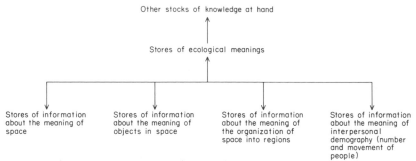

Fig. 11.1. The cognitive structure of regionalizing dynamics.

kind of interaction that reproduces varying types of "classroom structure." Similarly, the constellations of objects and people in office space, bars, stadiums, street corners, workplaces, department stores, grocery stores, and the likes all signal that certain kinds of interaction are to ensue. The fact that people "know" the meaning of these constellations enables the interaction to proceed smoothly and to be repeated at subsequent points in time.

Without regionalization, actors would need to work very hard to figure out what they are supposed to do. For regionalization offers a host of cues that tell people how to orient themselves and that indicate which range of norms, rituals, categories, and resources are most relevant. Without understanding of interactive ecology and demography, a much greater burden falls upon interpersonal signaling and interpreting, forcing actors to "work at" and "work out" their respective sequences of responses. But when they can use standardized ecological and demographic cues, the interaction can flow more readily and can be more easily resumed at a future time.

Normatization

As is evident in reading Table 11.1, categorization implies that certain kinds of responses are "owed" to others. Thus, categorization helps specify what obligations are relevant and salient in an interaction, whereas the invocation of normative obligations facilitates the organization of responses in terms of categories. However, because the concept of "norms" is so problematic in contemporary theorizing, I should pause and provide a more detailed appraisal and conceptualization.

In recent decades, the concept of "norms" has been identified with the imputed deficiencies of functional theorizing (Turner and Maryanski, 1978), and as a consequence, theorists are reluctant to develop "normative" theories. Such fears of being labeled "functionalist," "consensus theorist," or some similar epithet are misguided, because we can hardly deny that people do indeed develop and use normative agreements about what should occur in situations. To ignore this obvious fact is, to me at least, rather absurd. The real question is not whether individuals organize their conduct in terms of norms—they do—but rather, what the nature of norms is and how they are employed by individuals to structure interactions.

The major problem with most "normative" theories is that norms are viewed as *the* primary force holding structure together. In order to carry this excessive explanatory burden, norms have tended to be conceptualized as consensually accepted expectations that are unambiguously tied to positions in a network of positions. As such, norms guide the conduct, or "role behavior," of each individual occupying a status position in a social system (Linton, 1936; Parsons, 1951). The criticisms of this line of argument are well known and need not be repeated, but I do wish to emphasize one simple point: the critics have often "thrown the baby out with the bathwater." It is one thing to recognize that norms are not so clear, consensually agreed upon, and neatly tied to status positions, but it is quite another to assert that norms do not exist or that they are insignificant in creating and sustaining structure. How, then, can we resurrect the concept of norms in a manner that helps explain structuring processes?

Anthony Giddens's (1984, 1979) view of structure as rules and resources that actors draw upon to produce and reproduce patterns of interaction is, I think, a good place to begin reconceptualizing normative dynamics. His recognition that norms provide not only information about rights and obligations, but also more generalized "interpretative schemes," is a useful conceptual lead. Thus, as I begin to discuss the normative element, I will borrow three points of emphasis in Giddens's (1984) structuration theory. First, norms are not so much prepackaged sets of expectations tied to specific positions (although this does occur as a limiting case) as they are cataloged stores of information about obligations, rights, duties, and interpretative perspectives. Second, norms are "generative" in the sense that actors carry in their stocks of knowledge understandings about the procedures by which normative information is categorized, stored, retrieved, assembled, and reassembled for use in situations. And third, norms are "facilitative" in that actors construct normative agreements by drawing upon their stores of information about rights, duties, obligations, and interpretations and by using these agreements to order their current and subsequent responses in situations.

This shift in emphasis stresses the generative and transformable nature of normative behavior, as actors actively negotiate or, as is often the case, renegotiate their general interpretations of, and respective obligations in, specific contexts. Sometimes, of course, individuals confront situations where generative and transformable options are very limited, since past interactions have created relatively clear and consensual "rules" and "ex-

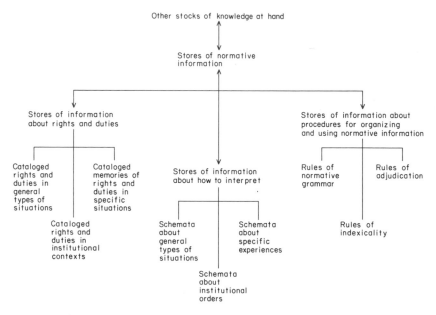

Fig. 11.2. The cognitive structure of normative dynamics.

pectations" about what should occur. But even here, these established normative expectations constitute only a general framework within which actors can create more fine-tuned agreements about how they should interpret and act in a situation.

This concern with the process of constructing and reconstructing normative agreements, even within contexts heavily imbued with normative content, is why I am using the term "normatize." I want to represent the concept of norms as a verb—that is, as an active, dynamic process—rather than as a noun. Yet the fact that I convert the term "normatize" into the noun "normatization" forces the recognition that people do indeed create norms that appear to be, in Durkheim's words, "a thing" limiting options and circumscribing conduct. This "thing" is transformable, but often at costs far exceeding what people are willing to pay. Hence, as part of their stocks of knowledge, people carry around in their heads prepackaged normative orientations that they draw upon in predictable ways and use to guide their conduct.

In light of these considerations, how are we to conceptualize less metaphorically "normatizing" and "normatization"? Fig. 11.2 outlines my sense for the cognitive elements involved.[2] I visualize "normative infor-

[2] Once again, I invite "structuralists," who are supposed to know about these things, to join me in trying to explain more adequately the generative processes involved in creating expectations that guide behavior (that is, norms).

mation" as a subset of more general stocks of knowledge, which, like all such stocks, are acquired through past interactions and experiences. In turn, this subset of general stocks of knowledge consists of three interrelated stores of information: (1) knowledge about rights and duties, (2) knowledge about how to interpret, and (3) knowledge of the procedures for using (1) and (2).

Stores of information about rights and duties comprise individuals' cataloged information about what to expect in situations. By cataloged, I mean that the information is stored in a somewhat systematic way (perhaps as ordered gestalts) and that it can be retrieved (remembered) and made available for use in a situation. My guess is that individuals catalog information along three lines: stores of rights and duties that apply to general types of situations and to all individuals within a given culture and society (norms of politeness, address, demeanor, decorum, conversational turn-taking, spacing, etc.); norms of rights and duties in those highly ordered institutional contexts evident in all societies (economy, kinship, religion, politics); and norms of the rights and duties negotiated and selectively remembered in specific situations over the course of a lifetime. As individuals interact, then, they invoke normative information about expectations of people in general, modify this information in terms of any institutional context that may (and may not) be relevant, and then qualify this information even further in terms of actual experiences in the same or in similar situations.

This process of filtering and focusing information about rights and duties is both facilitated and circumscribed by the other two subsets of normative information. Taking information about interpretation first, I view actors as ordering their knowledge about how to interpret situations and others into schemata, or somewhat loosely organized gestalts of interpretative elements revolving around the relevant attitudes, meanings, feelings, dispositions, and other orienting cognitions in a situation. These interpretative gestalts both filter each actor's perceptions of a situation and order the retrieval of information about rights and duties. There are, I think, three basic kinds of interpretative schemata, similar to the catalogs of information about rights and duties: those about situations in general, those concerning institutional contexts (family, economy, religion, etc.), and those ordering specific past experiences in actual interactive contexts. Actors use these three schemata simultaneously to denote a situation as an instance of a past experience, as an element of an institutional order, and as a general type or category of interaction (such as work/practical, ceremonial, social); and on the basis of this denotation, they select information about the rights and duties that are relevant and that are to be used in interactive negotiations with others.

This selection of rights and duties as well as their use in interaction also occurs in terms of procedures for organizing cognitive elements in general and normative elements in particular. My belief is that there are three general types of such cognitive rules or procedures for cataloging, ordering, combining and recombining, retrieving, and using information: grammatical rules specifying how interpretative gestalts and pieces of information about rights and duties are to be strung together to create a set of expectations; rules of indexicality or context indicating the kinds of rights, duties, and schemata appropriate to varying types of situations; and rules concerning adjudication of potentially discordant information about rights and duties, interpretative schemata, normative grammar, and contextual inferences.

In sum, then, there is a complex set of cognitive dynamics revolving around the process of normatizing situations. Perhaps I have delved too far (or perhaps not far enough) into what these cognitive dynamics might be, but the critical point is that norms do not just exist; rather, they are produced and reproduced by virtue of the cognitive capacities of active agents. The major criticism of normative theories is that it is hard to determine where the norms structuring interaction come from. In my view, norms are the joint outcome of the motivational and interactional processes discussed in the previous chapter, the cognitive processes schematically represented in Fig. 11.2, and the other structuring dynamics discussed in this chapter. This argument will become more evident in later chapters, but lest I be accused of being a traditional normative theorist, it is important here to stress the generative nature of normatizing.

Thus, in terms of the processes denoted in Fig. 11.2, the normatization of a situation revolves around the capacity of actors to invoke a similar interpretative schema for organizing their perceptions, to agree upon their respective selection of rights and duties, and to employ similar procedures for creating, contextualizing, and adjudicating normative elements. Obviously, this process has to be incredibly complex and subtle; and yet individuals pursue it without great interpersonal difficulty. Part of the reason for this apparent ease is that competent actors have cognitively cataloged their past experiences about rights and duties and interpretative schemata and, in the process, acquired knowledge about the procedures for organizing normative elements. As a result, they can invoke without undue stress the relevant schemata and the appropriate rights and duties, while attending to any problems of normative organization. Only when actors cannot agree on rights and duties, schemata, and organizing procedures does interaction become stressful and difficult to structure. In general, actors are highly motivated to normatize situations because it enables them to structure their interaction in ways that meet the basic motivating needs (such as ontological security and trust) outlined in Fig. 5.1 and to avoid consuming more energy than necessary to signal and interpret with respect to all of the interactional processes delineated in Fig. 8.1. Moreover, as we will see later in this chapter, normatizing also facilitates the operation of other structuring processes.

Ritualization

Rituals are stereotyped sequences of behavior that symbolically denote and emotionally infuse the ongoing flow of interaction. With the concept of "stereotyped," I wish to emphasize that the meaning of the behavioral sequence is "understood" (often only implicitly) by others and that the general direction of the behavior is thereby highly predictable. With the concept of "symbolically denote," my intent is to stress that these stereotyped sequences of behavior mark some aspect of group involvement. That is, rituals are about group inclusion, and they operate as a mechanism for denoting some dimension of a collective context. Finally, with the concept of "emotionally infuse," I argue that rituals mobilize feelings and motivational energy. As is suggested by Fig. 5.1, where motivational dynamics are outlined, anxiety is reduced to the extent that interaction succeeds in producing a sense of inclusion, trust, and security. All of these deep-seated needs are, I think, met by ritual activity; thus it should not be surprising that they are "emotionally charged" behaviors.

To ritualize an interaction is thus to create stereotyped sequences of gestures among individuals that symbolically mark the implicit solidarity of ongoing interaction and that meet each individual's basic needs for group inclusion and, to a lesser extent, trust and security (as well as needs for gratification, self-confirmation, and facticity—as we will see in the next chapter). Moreover, in creating stereotyped sequences, each individual's gestures become more predictable, thereby reducing the interpersonal work involved in signaling/interpreting, while at the same time holding at bay the emotional energy associated with anxiety and a failure to meet basic needs.

During interaction, four types of rituals are most critical for structuring the flow of mutual gesturing: opening and closing rituals, forming rituals, totemizing rituals, and repair rituals. Opening and closing rituals are sequences of behavior that mark the initiation and termination of an interaction. The structuring of any one interaction, or its resumption later, is greatly facilitated by the ability of actors to understand when an interaction is being initiated and terminated. Moreover, there are usually ritualized ways of "telling" others as part of the opening ritual how long the interaction will last, whereas the closing "tells" actors how easy it will be to pick up the interaction again at a subsequent time. Structuring interaction thus involves not only opening-closing behavioral sequences, but also implicit subrituals that inform actors as to the nature, duration, and resumption of the interaction.

A forming ritual involves the use of stereotyped behavioral sequences to order the interaction between its opening and closing. Such rituals indicate the form that the interaction should take, supplementing clues already given in opening gestures and previous closing gestures. Forming rituals give individuals a sense of "where an interaction is going" and "what's likely to happen." Moreover, they can be used to mark shifts in the form—for example, from a formal to a more personal mode.

A totemizing ritual is a reaffirmation of group involvement and involves behavioral sequences that make the interaction, and potentially the group, the focus of attention. Such rituals typically revolve around "totems" in the sense that individuals will use symbols—objects, words, nonverbal gestures—as representations of *the* relationship and/or *the* group. I thus see totems as more than reverent responses toward physical objects; certain kinds of responses make totems of other people (for example, a warm embrace or a verbal sequence affirming friendship). In these cases, the other person is a totem toward whom rituals are addressed, but the rituals are not so much a "worship" of the person as of the relationship or group in which both actors are implicated. When, for example, someone says "I love you," he or she is affirming the relationship (as one involving intimacy) as much as the person. Indeed, the recipient of these vows of "love" is serving as a totem. Such totemic rituals usually require reciprocity if they are to be effective in structuring interaction. That is, actors need to serve as totems for each other; and so, when someone says "I love you," there is an implied reciprocal ritual, such as "I love you, too," in which the roles of worshiper and totem are reversed. But again, what is being "worshiped" here is the relationship as much as either individual.

These totemic rituals tend to be the most emotionally infused of all rituals because they make the referent of the situation explicit—that is, the relationship and structure of the ongoing enterprise. As a result, when totemizing rituals are not performed, or go unreciprocated, the sense of common attachment to the group is undermined and anxiety increases, thereby fueling additional emotions such as anger, frustration, and hurt.

Other rituals are also totemizing, but less explicitly so. Indeed, a failure to use a conventional ritual can often be a "slap in the face" not so much for an individual as for the relationship among individuals. For example, when someone ignores a closing ritual, the next encounter between these individuals cannot proceed without a sense that the relationship has been disrupted and must now be reconstructed. Or, if someone violates a forming ritual, this "attacks" the structure of the relationship, and so invites disproportionate emotional reactions from others. Thus, as becomes clearly evident when opening-closing and forming rituals are not performed, they too evidence totemizing elements.

Since disruption of interaction is inevitable in human affairs, repair rituals are an essential part of structuring. Structuring cannot endure without a set of behavioral sequences to signal efforts at restoring a breached interaction. In each actor's stocks of knowledge are inventories of repair rituals that they can use to "smooth over" a disrupted interaction. Some of these are generic and apply to most contexts ("Excuse me," "I'm so sorry," "Please forgive me," "Sorry, I didn't know," etc.), whereas others are specific to a particular type of situation (work/practical, ceremonial, social) or level of intimacy.

Structuring thus depends upon agreement and understanding among actors as to what opening and closing behavioral sequences are acceptable, what forms of interactive dialogue are appropriate, what gestures affirm their relationship, and what kinds of gestural sequences will repair a disrupted situation. The more actors share knowledge of rituals and the more readily they can emit them, the more likely an interaction is to reveal continuity and the more likely is it to be resumed with ease at subsequent points in time. Moreover, as individuals acquire knowledge about classes of situations and the ritual repertoires appropriate to those situations, they can more readily move in and out of interactions with persons whom they have not met before. For if structure is to be elaborated beyond chains of repeated interaction among the same people, individuals must have generalized and appropriate rituals for how to open, proceed, close, and repair their interactions, thereby enabling them to reduce the level of interpersonal work needed to keep an interaction going while at the same time allowing them to meet basic needs for group inclusion, trust, and security.

Routinization

Social structure depends upon "habits," or routinized behavioral sequences where, without great mental and interpersonal effort, actors do pretty much the same thing in time and space. In the context of interaction, routines involve repetitive sequences of mutual signaling and interpreting that are customary and habitual for the parties involved. Such repetitive sequences are typically punctuated with rituals that if emitted sufficiently often, become highly routinized. But the structuring of interaction depends upon more than such perfunctory rituals; it also requires less emotionally infused behavioral sequences that "fill in" time and give predictability to movement in space. Anthony Giddens (1984) has been the most perceptive of contemporary theorists in recognizing that routines are important for the reproduction of structure as well as for meeting people's deep-seated needs for ontological security and trust (that things are as they appear and that they are predictable). For as individuals "do the same thing in the same place," their responses reveal continuity and predictability, thereby enabling others to react in an equally predictable fashion.

Routines typically emerge as a natural part of interactions that must be sustained. Thus, as people work, live family life, attend school, and interact in other institutional contexts, they tend to routinize a great proportion of their interactions in these contexts. For example, students tend to sit in the same spot in a college classroom, take notes in similar ways, and interact in a routinized manner with those around whom they habitually sit. Such routinizing helps reproduce "classroom structure," but it also provides students (and teachers) with a kind of "ontological security blanket," thereby reducing the potential anxiety associated with those situations where one must be alert and attuned to the gestures of others.

As people create routines in most of their daily contexts—working, playing, eating, sleeping, etc.—they order their lives; and as these behavioral routines bring people together at predictable times and places, they similarly order their interactions. The result is that they can "go on automatic pilot" as they interact, without great deliberation about gesturing and interpreting. Each person simply behaves "as they always do," thereby easing the interpersonal strain on each other and making it easy to resume the interaction later. In a sense, routines are a sort of interpersonal "dead time" that "fills in" structured interactions between those episodes where individuals must be interpersonally alert, awake, alive, and attuned. Without routines, interaction would be exhausting; and thus interactive structures, especially longer term ones, depend upon each party routinizing their responses in order to conserve energy.

But routines are, at least latently, a potential source of emotional arousal, which suggests that they are tied to deep motivational needs. For if people's interactive routines are disrupted, they are often "upset" and "frustrated" to a degree far beyond what might be expected if routines were simply a way to save interpersonal energy. This seemingly disproportionate reaction signals that routines are important to meeting basic needs for security and trust as well as other needs, such as the "profits" in exchanges associated with a given routine. Recognition of this dynamic indicates that people are actually highly motivated to create those "dull routines" that they often complain about but rarely seek to change.

Thus, routines are not just the by-product of other behavioral activities. Actors are motivated to create routines; and they can do so because they carry in their stocks of knowledge information about the kinds of routines appropriate for various types of situations and about the ways of implementing these routines. This knowledge is, of course, built up from past experiences, but it is supplemented indirectly through observation of others, media, and additional sources of information. And so, for those major contexts of activity in human affairs—work, family, and school, for example—competent actors develop a sense for the relevant ways to go about establishing routines. This knowledgeability, and the motivation behind its implementation, is thus an important dynamic of structuring. Routines make responses predictable and in so doing meet fundamental needs for trust and security (see Giddens's model in Fig. 4.3).

Stabilization of Resource Transfers

Actors are motivated to realize a profit in those material and symbolic resources implicated in an interaction (see Fig. 5.1); and as they come to accept a given type and ratio of resource transfer in a particular interaction setting, structuring is facilitated. For if a setting yields an acceptable rate of profit for the individuals involved, they are motivated to stay in this setting and emit those interactive sequences that have been profitable. Moreover, if the types and ratios of resources transferred are accepted by individuals, these become normative expectations that are used to order subsequent interactions. Knowing what types of resources are to be exchanged and what the rate of exchange will be reduces considerably the uncertainty of a situation (and hence, the potential anxiety associated with a failure to meet needs for security, trust, and self-affirmation) and the amount of interpersonal negotiation that will be required for actors to feel comfortable. However, when exchange ratios are in doubt, considered "unfair," damaging to self, or constantly subject to renegotiation, it will be difficult to structure an interaction over time. For under these conditions actors will be motivationally mobilized to change the situation and unwilling to accept as appropriate existing interactive sequences.

As denoted in the model of motivational dynamics in Fig. 5.1, exchanges will revolve around securing those material and symbolic resources that maintain a sense of group inclusion, confirm and affirm self-conceptions, promote a sense of facticity, provide for a sense of ontological security, and create a sense of trust. Thus, to the degree that resource transfers can stabilize around acceptable ratios of those valuable resources, an interaction will be more readily structured.

Just what resources are defined as relevant and salient for meeting these needs is related to people's personal biographies and, more importantly, to the context of an interaction. My view is that individuals carry in their stocks of knowledge understandings about the "generalized" material and symbolic resources most relevant to a context and that they seek to negotiate a level of these resources that will provide them with a sense that they are a part of ongoing group activity, that the responses of others are predictable and trustworthy, that things are as they appear, that self has been affirmed, and that a factual world exists "out there."

Many interaction contexts do not require great negotiation, since they are mediated by generalized reinforcers, such as money. But even in these situations (e.g., the purchase of a product), other resources are being exchanged. For example, if one observes the conversation surrounding a simple purchase ("Hello," "How are you?," "What can I do for you?," "A good choice," "Come back again"), money is not the only medium of resource transfer. In fact, conversational exchanges are probably more visible than the actual transfer of money. Hence, "friendliness" and "courtesy" are more than interpersonal tactics to smooth the transaction; they are part of the resource transfer itself, and they facilitate its stabilization. This becomes particularly evident when one party in a financial transaction is viewed as being "rude" or "cold"; under these conditions the offended party will be upset and less likely to pursue or renew the interaction, thereby lessening the possibility that the interaction will become structured.

Other structuring processes help to define what resources are relevant for a context and just how they are to be exchanged. I see rituals as particularly important in this respect, because they open and close a transfer in a manner that makes it predictable, mutually including, self-sustaining, and factual, while at the same time confirming that "things are as they appear." Particularly when the exchange is unequal (say, conformity is exchanged for help), ritual orders the resource transfer in a way that simultaneously makes responses predictable, saves people's dignity, acknowledges their mutual inclusion, sustains appearances, and creates a sense of facticity. Conversely, stabilization of resource transfers reinforces those rituals (as well as other structuring dynamics) that enable actors to determine the relevance of resources and acceptable rates of exchange.

In sum, then, the structuring of interaction depends upon actors' mutual capacity to categorize, regionalize, normatize, ritualize, routinize, and stabilize their responses toward each other. As I have argued, this capacity presupposes that individuals have stores of information about these dynamics and that they can use them appropriately in their signaling and interpreting activities. If such is the case, then basic motivational needs can be met, and the processes of signalling and interpreting are simplified. In light of these considerations, we are now in a position to construct a com-

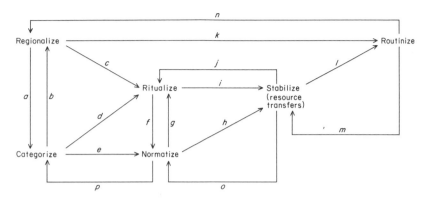

Fig. 11.3. A composite model of structuring dynamics.

posite model of these dynamic elements in the process of structuring interaction.

A Dynamic Model of Structuring Processes

All of the structuring dynamics discussed thus far are interrelated. As the values for one of these variables increase or decrease, the values for the others will change in the same way. The purpose of an analytical model, however, is to delineate the causal paths through which these mutual effects operate and to suggest hypotheses about the most crucial interrelations among these structuring dynamics. Of course, as I have indicated throughout this chapter and as I will begin to explore in more detail in the next chapter, many of these interrelations are with other interaction processes—motivation, signaling, and interpreting. For the present, I offer the composite model in Fig. 11.3 as my best estimate of the dynamic causal relations among just the six structuring variables.

In juxtaposing the variables in Fig. 11.3, I am arguing that proximate variables *and* those connected by a causal path exert the most influence on each other; and the closer the variables and the shorter the causal paths connecting them, the greater the causal effects. Moreover, since the structuring process flows from left to right, the initial structuring of an interaction successively involves regionalizing and categorizing, then ritualizing and normatizing, and then stabilizing resource transfers and routinizing responses. This implies the hypothesis that structuring will be particularly difficult to initiate without categorization and regionalization.

The feedback paths delineated in the model complicate the analysis of structuring dynamics, however. For once an interaction is structured through the processes flowing from left to right in the model, the feedback effects of variables on each other become critical to the reproduction and maintenance of structure. As is evident, these feedback effects create a number of cycles (e.g., paths like *p-e* and *p-e-h-o*) that become nodes around which a pattern of interaction is created and sustained. In fact, the nature of a structured interaction will vary in terms of which configuration of cycles is most evident in a particular situation. Indeed, if one was so disposed (and I am not, for the present), it might be possible to develop a typology of structured interactions in terms of varying configurations of cycles.

With these general features of the model as a backdrop, let me now examine in more detail some of its key causal paths. When individuals first initiate an interaction, or renew an old one, the issues of regionalizing and categorizing become immediately salient. At this initial point in an interaction, people use situational ecology and demography as cues to establish the appropriate categories of response (see Table 11.1). That is, by noting the span of space, the division of this space into regions, the existence of significant physical props, as well as the number, distribution, and movement of people, actors categorize a situation in terms of ceremony, work, or socializing and the degree of intimacy that is appropriate (as is denoted by causal arrow *a*); and conversely, as actors categorize, the "meaning" of a situation's demography and ecology becomes more clearly defined and brought into sharper focus (causal arrow *b*).

Several feedback processes reinforce (or potentially disrupt) the mutual effects of regionalization and categorization. As feedback loop *n* underscores, routines help to sustain regionalization; as individuals develop habitual ways of positioning and moving in space, they reproduce the organization of an interaction, and in so doing, they reinforce the appropriateness of those categories used to orient actors (via causal path *n-a*). While regionalization helps create and sustain those very routines that reproduce routinization (causal arrow *k*), other processes are also involved in creating routines (note the processes being funneled through *l*, all of which will be examined shortly). Just as regionalization is influenced by feedback from routinization, categorization is connected to normatization: as actors categorize, they invoke a relevant range of normative elements (as denoted by causal arrow *e*), and, as they normatize a situation, they reinforce (or perhaps, challenge) the relevance and salience of categories (feedback loop *p*). Of course, there are more protracted feedback causal cycles in which the process of categorization is implicated (for example, path *d-i-o-p*), but these tend to influence categorization through their feedback effects on normatization.

Thus, to the extent that actors can regionalize and categorize an interaction, and subsequently reinforce these through the processes channeled through feedback loops n and p, the structuring of an interaction is greatly facilitated. Conversely, if regionalization and categorization are not mutually reinforcing, or are not reinforced through feedback loops n and p, then structuring will prove difficult. For without regionalization actors cannot easily order their activities in space; without successful categorization they will have difficulty stretching the interaction across time. The rationale behind these conclusions will become more evident as we move further into the dynamics of the model.

Regionalization and categorization both have a direct effect on the degree of ritualization (causal arrows d and c); and categorization has an indirect effect on ritualizing through the process of normatizing (causal path e-g). Once actors have regionalized and categorized an interaction, they are more likely to "know" the appropriate opening, forming, closing, totemizing, and, if necessary, repairing rituals. The knowledge and use of these rituals enable individuals to sequence responses in a predictable way, while providing them with the necessary behavioral repertoires to repair a breached interaction. Knowledge of such rituals not only facilitates the ordering of responses at one point in time; it also allows individuals to pick up an interaction at subsequent points in time. Moreover, knowledge of those rituals appropriate to generic classes of situations (as indicated by regionalization and categorization) gives actors the capacity to enter new situations with strangers. By enabling sets of actors to enter and exit basic types of interaction settings with relative ease, rituals expand the potential scope of structuring.

Ritualizing an interaction has direct reciprocal causal effects with normatizing (as indicated by causal arrows f and g) and indirect effects with categorization (path e-g-f-p). As actors categorize, they are better able to invoke those stores of information about rights and duties, interpretative schemata, and procedures for ordering normative elements that are most relevant for a particular context (see Fig. 11.2). In so normatizing a situation, individuals can better select (via arrow g) the germane opening, closing, forming, totemizing, and repairing rituals. Conversely, as is indicated by causal arrow f, the emission of rituals reinforces normatizing efforts by infusing them with the emotional content that springs from the way rituals are implicated in motives for group inclusion, trust, and security. This line of argument will be discussed more extensively below and so, at this point, I simply want to emphasize that rituals operate to emotionally infuse interaction by serving as a vehicle for attaching basic motive states to those norms circumscribing the flow of an interaction (Durkheim, 1912).

This consequence of rituals for structuring is, as I noted earlier, also evident in stabilizing resource transfers (as is signaled by causal arrow i). By creating stereotyped sequences of gesturing, rituals order negotiations over, and exchanges of, material and symbolic resources; and in so doing, they help individuals secure a sense of trust, group inclusion, self-affirmation/confirmation, security, and facticity. Moreover, rituals reduce the costs, especially to self-esteem, of exchanges among unequals by regularizing their respective interpersonal demeanors, although at times "ruthless" resource holders force their inferiors to engage in elaborate and demeaning rituals. (In the short run such degrading rituals may stabilize the resource transfer as dramatically unequal, but in the long run this inequality will be likely to motivate efforts to restructure the exchange.)

Once resource transfers are stabilized through ritual—and other structuring processes, especially normatizing and routinizing (to be discussed shortly)—they feed back and circumscribe the range of potential rituals that can be emitted in a situation (as indicated by feedback loop *j*). Because resource transfers revolve around meeting some of humans' most basic motivational needs, their stabilization exerts a very powerful force on the emission of rituals that reinforce the existing nature and rate of exchange.

Stabilization of resource transfers also bears this kind of direct reciprocal relationship to normatizing processes (via cycle *h-o*), while at the same time, revealing a more inclusive cycle incorporating the effects of norms on rituals (cycle *o-g-i*). My comments above have already incorporated the dynamic of the latter cycle, so let me concentrate for the moment on the *h-o* cycle. A great deal of the literature on exchange processes has emphasized the importance of such issues as "justice," "equity," "equality," and "nonrationality" in exchange transactions (e.g., Cook and Emerson, 1978; Cook and Hegtvedt, 1983). This emphasis underscores the fact that for different contexts actors invoke implicit rules about the "appropriate," "fair," "equitable," and "just" transfer of resources, especially under conditions of inequality. These "norms of fair exchange," as Blau (1964) termed them, mitigate against the potential tensions associated with the advantages that some actors typically enjoy in exchange relations. For if actors could push their advantage to the extreme, it would be difficult to stabilize a pattern of resource transfer over extended transactions. Those at a disadvantage would eventually seek to leave the relation or engage in retaliatory action. Of course, these events often do occur in actual exchanges, but they do not facilitate structuring; on the contrary, they destructure interaction until norms of fairness are adhered to by the advantaged parties.

Thus, in order for social relations to stabilize, actors must accept as fair and reasonable the ratios of resources exchanged. My reading of the rather large literature on this topic reveals that actors possess in their stocks of normative knowledge rather complex and contextually based norms about what would constitute fairness in different types of situations and that these are employed as a yardstick for evaluating the transfers of resources. If an exchange falls within the guidelines of these norms, then an interaction is more easily stabilized, as is emphasized by causal arrow *h*. As resource transfers are stabilized in terms of these justice considerations, norms of fairness are reinforced (as indicated by feedback loop *o*), thereby giving them greater salience at subsequent exchanges or in new exchanges with different actors under similar conditions. The cycle denoted by causal path *h-o* becomes, I hypothesize, self-sustaining for those situations in which individuals regularly must participate, and, as norms of fairness are reinforced, they become part of the repertoire of categories that individuals use to typify situations (as is emphasized by feedback arrow *p*). As a result, when actors categorize situations, the relevant norms of fairness are invoked without great deliberation; only when they are violated (as is often the case in actual situations) do individuals become cognizant of them (and use them to destabilize and destructure the interaction).

The stabilization of resource transfers with rituals and norms encourages routinization of an interaction, as is stressed by causal arrow *l*. For when actors accept the ratios of resource exchanges and consider them fair, while ordering and punctuating the interaction with rituals, it becomes much easier to do the same thing at each subsequent encounter. Habit is thus not mere inertia; rather, it is also an implicit acceptance of a ratio of payoffs that are normatively regulated and ritualized. Such routinization feeds back, as denoted by loop *m*, to stabilize further the exchange of resources. Of course, if routines are disrupted by a dramatic change in the ratio of exchange payoffs, they become a source of destruction to the exchange relation itself (loop *m*) and perhaps to the norms (feedback path *m-o-h*), the rituals (path *m-o-g-i*), the categories (paths *m-o-p-d-i* and *m-o-p-e-h*), and the regionalizing (path *n-c-i*) that ultimately regulate resource transfers.

Conclusion

Such is a preliminary review of the causal dynamics among these structuring processes. Obviously, the composite model presented in Fig. 11.3 presents only the broad contours of these dynamics, but it does represent a reasonable synthesis of the models presented in Chapters 9 and 10. And, as I have done for the models of motivation and interaction, it is useful to conclude by presenting a list of the abstract principles suggested by this composite scheme.

In general, the degree to which an interaction among individuals is ordered in space and across time is a positive and additive function of the extent to which these individuals categorize, regionalize, normatize, ritualize, routinize, and stabilize resource transfers. From this come the following, more specific corollaries.

1. The degree to which individuals reveal consensual agreements about the level of intimacy, ceremony, and socializing required in a situation (*categorize*) is a positive and additive function of the extent to which they regionalize and normatize.

2. The degree to which individuals share knowledge about the meaning of the objects, physical divisions, and distributions of people in space (*regionalize*) is a positive and additive function of the extent to which they routinize and categorize.

3. The degree to which individuals construct agreements about the rights, duties, and interpersonal schemata appropriate to a situation (*normatize*) is a positive and additive function of the extent to which they categorize, ritualize, and stabilize resource transfers.

4. The degree to which individuals agree upon the opening, closing, forming, totemizing, and repairing behavioral sequences relevant to a situation (*ritualize*) is a positive and additive function of the degree to which they regionalize, categorize, normatize, and stabilize resource transfers.

5. The degree to which individuals develop compatible as well as habitual behavioral and interpersonal responses to a situation (*routinize*) is a positive and additive function of the extent to which they regionalize and stabilize resource transfers.

6. The degree to which individuals accept as appropriate a given ratio of resource transfers in a situation (*stabilize*) is a positive and additive function of the extent to which they normatize, ritualize, and routinize.

V

Theoretical Synthesis

12

The Intersection of Micro Dynamics

AT THIS POINT, it might seem useful to construct a grand model, splicing together the three composite models developed in Chapters 5, 8, and 11. In this way, I could address the causal paths connecting the three models in an explicit manner and thereby realize the conceptual promise implied by the sensitizing model in Fig. 2.1. In fact, such an exercise was my original intent for this chapter, but when I actually pieced the models together and added additional causal paths, this "composite of the composites" became unwieldy. An analytical model allows for increased complexity, but it must never abandon parsimony; and as I immediately recognized, parsimony was lost with a "grand synthesis." And yet, as I have argued throughout, it is necessary to explore the causal relations outlined in Fig. 2.1. How, then, is this to be done?

The Limits and Uses of Analytical Models

The best strategy, I think, is to pursue the problem more discursively by developing propositions to describe the crucial causal connections among motivational, interactional, and structuring processes. These propositions are "suggested" by the models already summarized, and so I will be consistent with the strategy advocated in Chapter 2. But there is a lesson in all of this: analytical models have limitations in that as ever more reality is subsumed, the models become too complex and convoluted, and therefore less useful.

However, I do think that it has been useful to break micro dynamics down into its constituent processes and then to examine these separately. For, as I have indicated in earlier chapters, much micro theorizing collapses these three processes together and, as a result, does not do full conceptual justice to the complexity of any of them. With these discrete models, I have been able to develop more detailed and robust conceptualizations; as a result, the ideas in the models can be more precisely and explicitly reconnected than in previous conceptualizations. Analytical models are, therefore, useful in extracting the key elements of phenomena that are mutually embedded in the empirical world and in suggesting propositions that can explicitly denote the crucial causal forces behind this embeddedness. The previous chapters have sought to realize the former. Now, let me turn to the latter and develop some tentative propositions on the relations among motivational, interactional, and structuring processes. In this discussion, I will make repeated reference to the causal paths denoted in the models of Figs. 5.1, 8.1, and 11.3, above.

The Motivational Basis of Interactional and Structuring Dynamics

Some General Considerations

Before launching into a more detailed review of the causal paths suggested by Fig. 2.1, I should offer several general hypotheses on the nature of the effects among motivational, interactional, and structuring processes. As Parsons's action theory recognized, especially the formulation of the cybernetic hierarchy (Parsons, 1958, 1961), interaction and its structuring into social systems require the mobilization of energy by individuals. Rather than Parsons's psychoanalytic view of this process, however, I rely more upon Mead's (1934) behaviorist position. That is, those processes of signaling, interpreting, and structuring that (1) promote a sense of group inclusion, trust, and security, (2) mitigate against anxiety, (3) provide material and symbolic gratification, (4) create a sense of facticity, and (5) affirm self-conceptions will be retained in the behavioral repertoire of individuals and will be repeated at subsequent points in time, thereby enabling actors to structure their interaction across time and space. Conversely, those interactions and structures that do not meet these needs will be less likely to be retained in the repertoire of individuals, and structuring of the interaction will be less likely to occur. It is, of course, a rare interaction or structure that can meet all these motivating needs fully and simultaneously; hence, we need to qualify this line of argument in several respects.

First, the fewer *the number* of fundamental needs realized in an interaction, the less likely will it be repeated at subsequent points in time. Moreover, the fewer the number of needs being met in an interaction, the greater will be the desire of individuals to leave the interaction. If they cannot leave (because of either micro or macrostructural forces), the greater will be their desire to change the nature of the interaction or structure, at least up to the point of futility where withdrawal, apathy, and other defense mechanisms set in. The viability of an interaction situation and its repetition at subsequent points in time is thus connected to its capacity for reinforcement—that is, for meeting the fundamental needs denoted in Fig. 5.1.

Second, when an ungratifying interaction cannot be avoided, individuals will be more likely to keep their signaling/interpreting brief and perfunctory, while trying to exit the situation as soon as possible. If these interpersonal strategies are not allowed (as is the case with coercive total institutions), then severe behavioral pathologies will emerge among individuals and the interaction and/or structure will be sustained largely through coercion rather than positive reinforcement. Of course, such situations or structures are rare; in fact, individuals typically find ways under even the most adverse circumstances to create interactions and informal structures that meet fundamental needs (e.g., the "informal system" in bureaucracies or the "inmate subculture" in prisons).

Third, the *configuration* of needs being fulfilled is also a crucial factor. An interaction or structure infrequently realizes all fundamental needs simultaneously and to the same degree; so, depending on the configuration of needs being met, the profile of an interaction and its subsequent repetition will vary. The model in Fig. 5.1 provides some clues as to the most relevant configurations and their effects on interactional processes and their subsequent structuring. One crucial configuration is exposed if we split the model vertically at anxiety, which is a mediator between more unconscious needs for a sense of group inclusion, trust, and security, on the one hand, and more conscious needs for material/symbolic gratification, self-confirmation, and sense of facticity, on the other. Another crucial configuration can be seen in the three rows across the top, middle, and bottom portions of the model. This split highlights the connections among needs for (1) gratification and group inclusion, (2) self-confirmation, anxiety, and trust, and (3) ontological security and facticity. Depending upon which of these vertical or horizontal configurations is most salient, the nature of interaction and structuring will vary. At this point, I am not prepared to offer a detailed and systematic review of the effects of varying configurations; rather, I only want to indicate that the pattern of needs being met, or not met, is an important variable. This conclusion will become more evident shortly, when I do explore the effects of at least some of these configurations.

The ease of signaling and gesturing in a situation, as well as the likelihood of the repetition of such interactions at subsequent times and places, is thus a positive and additive function of the number of motivational needs fulfilled, while the general nature of interaction and structuring is related to both the number and the configuration of needs being accommodated. There is, then, a behaviorist basis for the maintenance of an interaction and structure as well as for its change and alteration. George Homans (1961) made this point long ago, and Mead (1934) argued the same position even earlier (see J. Turner, 1982; Baldwin, 1986), but the general point is not useful unless the domains of value—that is, types of needs or realms of gratification—are specified (Emerson, 1986; J. Turner, 1986d). The model in Fig. 5.1 does this; and when viewed in the context of interactional and structuring processes, it provides us with some general clues about the motivational basis of interaction and structuring. Let me now turn to a review of the more specific paths connecting motivational to interactional and structuring dynamics.

Some Specific Causal Paths

If one places Fig. 5.1 on motivational processes with Fig. 8.1 on interactional processes side by side, several interesting causal paths emerge; the most interesting, I think, are those moving horizontally from left to right across the models. Since motivational forces influence structuring dynamics through their effects on signaling and interpreting, it is also possible to provide insight into the motivational basis of structuring (see Fig. 11.3). The three rows of variables—top, middle, and bottom—of Fig. 5.1 represent the major lines of causal influence of motivational processes on signaling/interpreting and indirectly on the structuring processes outlined in Fig. 11.3. Each of these three causal paths is examined below.

The effects of needs for trust, anxiety reduction, and self-confirmation. As is denoted by the middle portions of Fig. 5.1, people need to avoid the sense of anxiety that comes with a failure to confirm self and to realize a sense of trust or predictability in the responses of others. As these needs mobilize energy, individuals use their deliberative capacities to make self-references in an interaction situation. In turn, these self-references about those aspects of self that must be confirmed and affirmed, especially as further fueled by anxiety and a lack of predictability, motivate individuals to role-make. As Fig. 8.1 argues, they often do so through ritual and staging. That is, they not only employ opening, forming, totemizing, closing, and repairing rituals, but they also manipulate spacing, props, and movement to assert the role that will best confirm/affirm salient aspects of self. Thus, the greater the needs for achieving a sense of trust, for reducing anxiety, and for confirming self, the more likely will rituals and staging be used to make a role for oneself.[1] Conversely, if needs for self-confirmation, anxiety reduction, and trust are low, then the use of ritual and staging to make roles for oneself will be correspondingly less evident.

By virtue of their effects on role-making, needs for trust, anxiety reduction, and self-confirmation will influence structuring processes, particularly regionalizing, ritualizing, and routinizing. Specifically, the greater are

[1] Perhaps more than other processes, staging is circumscribed by the macrostructure, which orders space and determines the distribution of people in most micro settings.

efforts at role-making among individuals, the more likely is a situation to become structured in terms of those props, spacing arrangements, movements, and rituals that regionalize and ritualize the interaction in a manner that confirms self. As a result, the situation is more likely to be routinized in ways that provide predictable responses from others with respect to their sense of self. It is for this reason that physical props, relative positioning, patterns of movement, rituals, and routines take on emotional significance for individuals when lost or disrupted. For, as emotional outbursts often emphasize, these staging, ritual, and routinizing procedures represent signals marking an individual's ability to make roles that sustain salient dimensions of their self-conception.

As the bottom half of Fig. 8.1 indicates, actors use each other's efforts at ritual and staging as one vehicle for role-taking, or seeing the situation from another's perspective. Such role-taking will, in turn, influence one's own self-references as these determine role-making efforts. And if the interaction can be routinized, then it becomes even easier to role-take, since the responses of others are habitual and hence easier to understand. Thus, to the extent that a situation can result in mutual role-making and role-taking that confirm each actor's self, it will be repeated; and as a result, it will be more likely to become structured in terms of patterns of regionalizing, ritualizing, and routinizing that will be difficult to alter because of their embeddedness in motivational needs.

The effects of needs for group inclusion and symbolic/material gratification. The top of Fig. 5.1 denotes needs for group inclusion and symbolic/material gratification. Needs for group inclusion influence those for gratification through their effects on anxiety and more indirectly through their effects on trust and self-confirmation. Conversely, the sense of group inclusion is influenced by the capacity of individuals to receive those material and symbolic rewards indicating that they are part of the ongoing flow of an interaction.

As actors mobilize energy to realize needs for gratification and group inclusion, especially as these are influenced by trust, anxiety, and self, they use their deliberative capacities to role-make in ways that sustain self-references and, to a lesser extent, to frame-make. Thus, I would hypothesize that actors' efforts to realize a material and symbolic profit in an interaction stem from a combination of needs for group inclusion, self-confirmation, and anxiety reduction and that the primary vehicle for realizing this profit is found in stage-making and ritual-making activities. Thus, as needs for group inclusion increase, anxiety will escalate. In turn, this increase in anxiety will lead to efforts at manipulating spacing, movement, and physical props to assert one's place in the group and using rituals in a manner that symbolically signals one's involvement in the group. These tendencies are escalated even further to the extent that needs for self-confirmation become implicated.

To a lesser degree, needs for group inclusion can influence frame-making as individuals try to order cognitively a situation so that a sense of group involvement is implied by their accounts and claims. Thus, as individuals use ethnomethods to create a sense of reality or facticity, they construct accounts in a way that implicates them in this reality; and as they make claims about sincerity, means-ends, and normative appropriateness, they assert their sincere involvement in the group and their willingness to use normatively appropriate means to various ends.

Both the primary causal path through role-making and this secondary one through frame-making have effects on the process of structuring. If needs for group inclusion drive role-making, then regionalizing, ritualizing, and routinizing will enable individuals to stabilize resource transfers that mark materially and symbolically their inclusion in the structure. In particular, exchanges will revolve around the acquisition of physical props and positions that enhance one's sense of group involvement and the use of totemizing rituals that reaffirm one's solidarity with others in the group. In turn, such stabilization of resources, when coupled with successful re-gionalization and ritualization, will facilitate routinizing a situation. As indicated in Fig. 11.3, such routinization feeds back to stabilize resource exchanges and regionalization, thereby giving individuals an increased sense that they are habituated in an ongoing group context. The less crucial causal path through frame-making influences structuring by allowing actors to create an account that facilitates categorizing a situation as one in-volving their participation and by enabling actors to make claims that nor-matize the situation in a manner that defines their activities as appropriate to the ongoing context. Such categorizing and normatizing embed actors in a situation, while creating structuring conditions that will encourage further ritualizing, stabilizing of resource transfers, and routinizing in ways that allow individuals to see themselves as part of the existing structure of an interaction.

Role-taking and, to a lesser extent, frame-taking are influenced by these structuring processes as they unfold to meet needs for material/symbolic gratifications that signal group inclusion. As actors read each other's ef-forts at staging and ritual-making, they take on each other's sense for how they want to be involved in the group. As a result, they can better orches-trate their own role-making activities to fit into the group vis-à-vis others' needs to do the same thing. To a lesser degree, frame-taking through the interpretation of the accounts and claims signaled by others invokes those relevant stocks of knowledge that can be used to make complementary roles and to impose compatible frames on a situation. Moreover, if both role-taking and frame-taking are circumscribed by routines, then it is even easier to understand and predict the responses of others. As a result of these processes, actors are more likely to feel a sense of compatibility and common involvement in the group, while at the same time they can better understand what material and symbolic resources will mark their respective positions in the ongoing interaction.

The effects of needs for ontological security and facticity. The bottom portions of Fig. 5.1 indicate that needs for a sense of ontological security are connected to needs for a sense of facticity through needs for anxiety reduction and self-confirmation and affirmation. That is, with an escalating need to feel that "things are as they appear," anxiety levels increase. In turn, this increased anxiety has a primary influence on needs to create a sense that there is a fixed world "out there" and exerts a secondary influence on needs to perceive that salient elements of self-conceptions are indeed appropriate to the structure of the situation. Equally important are the two feedback loops at the bottom of Fig. 5.1, because they emphasize that as people interact with others, their ability to create a sense of common external and intersubjective worlds is the primary vehicle by which needs for a sense of ontological security are realized. Thus, even if salient needs to confirm self are implicated in these causal processes, the critical feedback process is the extent to which actors' signaling and interpreting can create a perception of facticity and, in turn, a feeling of ontological security. My hypothesis is that as needs for ontological security increase, so do needs for facticity; and as needs for facticity escalate, actors will mobilize energy and use both their deliberative capacities and stocks of knowledge in redoubled frame-making/taking and role-making/taking. If needs for facticity predominate over needs to confirm self, then the emphasis will be on patterns of frame-making that revolve primarily around the use of ethnomethods to construct an account of "what's real" and secondarily around the use of claims to assert sincerity, normative appropriateness, and means-ends rationality. To the extent that needs for self-confirmation are escalated by needs for ontological security, however, claim-making will become an increasingly visible part of efforts to frame a situation. Moreover, role-making will increase as actors try to create a sense of facticity and security through the use of rituals and staging activities.

I am arguing, then, that the use of ethnomethods to construct a frame for an interaction stems principally from needs for ontological security and facticity, whereas needs for self-confirmation, as these are aroused by the anxiety associated with increased ontological insecurity, are the major force behind the use of validity claims to impose a frame on a situation and, to a lesser extent, the use of rituals and staging techniques to make a role that preserves the appearance of matters being what they seem to be. In sum, then, signaling will revolve primarily around ethnomethods when needs for security and facticity are high and around assertions of validity claims as well as ritual and staging when needs for self-confirmation increase as a consequence of deep-seated ontological insecurity.

These motivated efforts to use ethnomethods and validity claims to construct frames have a significant impact on structuring processes. My hypothesis is that account-making and claim-making are the most significant interactional forces behind categorizing and normatizing. More specifically, I propose that as needs for security and facticity escalate signaling to construct accounts, actors will seek to typify each other and the situation as an instance of a category. I also hypothesize that as ontological insecurity fuels needs for self-confirmation, actors will use validating techniques to normatize a situation in terms of standards of appropriateness, means-ends rationality, and sincerity. In other words, needs for facticity and security, as these influence account-making, are the primary motivational force behind categorization, while needs for self-confirmation, as stimulated by the anxiety associated with ontological insecurity and as manifested in animated claim-making, are the principal motivational forces behind normatizing. As actors frame-make, then, they categorize and normatize in ways that will allow them to feel that things are as they appear, that there is a common external and internal universe, and that there is reason to believe the appropriateness of self-definitions in this universe.

Needs for ontological security and, to a lesser extent, facticity also structure a situation through their effects on anxiety, self-confirmation, and role-making. As ontological insecurity escalates, actors' sense of self "does not seem as it should" in a situation; as a result, they will redouble their efforts to make a role for themselves through staging and ritual-making, which, in turn, increases the likelihood that they will ritualize and regionalize their interaction. As they regionalize the interaction, they also encourage routinization. All of these structuring processes create the perception and feeling that things are as they appear: routinization provides a sense of habit and predictability; ritualization orders the sequence and flow of an interaction; and regionalization structures the juxtaposition of individuals in space.

Categorizing and normatizing a situation facilitate frame-taking since, as actors can invoke similar categories and norms, they can more readily impose a framework on the situation. Without an existing structure to a situation, however, needs for facticity and security will escalate efforts to use stocks of knowledge to frame-take by reading the gestures of others with respect to the accounts and claims that they signal (see bottom of Fig.

8.1). More specifically, needs for security and facticity will increase the use of stocks of knowledge to account-take, whereas needs for self-confirmation, when influenced by needs for ontological security, will increase efforts at claim-taking. These activities are, in turn, used to determine how best to construct frames. Similarly, ritualizing, routinizing, and regionalizing a situation allow actors to more readily role-take, especially with respect to their place vis-à-vis others. As a consequence, they can better know which frames and roles would be most appropriate in a situation.

The Interactional Basis of Structuring and Motivational Dynamics

Some General Considerations

The processes of signaling and interpreting are not just neutral vehicles through which motivational forces operate to structure interaction. They constitute an emergent reality and reveal their own dynamics, somewhat independently of motivational and structuring processes. One of the most obvious, but nonetheless important, properties of signaling and interpreting is that these processes consume time and energy. Just how much one can signal and interpret is constrained by the time available to actors and by the amount of physical energy that they can mobilize. While motivational processes influence these constraints, there is an upper limit on the amount of time and energy that actors are able or willing to spend, no matter how motivated they are.

My sense is that people wish to conserve energy in most situations. Except for highly salient encounters, people generally do not desire to work very hard at signaling and interpreting; as a result, they use gestures in a manner that preserves their time and energy. Thus, one of the basic reasons that individuals role-make/take, frame-make/take, stage-make/take, ritual-make/take, account-make/take, and claim-make/take is to save themselves a lot of interpersonal work. I would hypothesize, then, that the more actors can mutually agree upon roles, frames, stages, rituals, accounts, and claims, the less the interpersonal energy and time required in the interaction. Moreover, the more these interpersonal practices can lead to regionalized, categorized, normatized, ritualized, stabilized, and routinized structural patterns, the less the interpersonal energy and time expended in the interaction.

Of course, the desire to save time and energy can be obviated by powerful motive states or by external demands of the situation. But in general individuals seek to reduce the anxiety associated with unfulfilled need-states (see Fig. 5.1); and so, as they use role-making/taking, framing, accounting, validating, and ritualizing practices to structure their interaction, they lower anxiety and minimally fulfill other basic needs. For to be highly mobilized is tiring and time-consuming; and hence, interactional and structuring processes operate to stave off physical and emotional exhaustion. This may appear to be an obvious point, but it is one of the most powerful forces of social order. Let me now turn to more specific causal paths in Fig. 8.1 on interactional processes and see their effects on structuring and motivation.

Some Specific Causal Paths

As a general rule, the above considerations lead to the following principle: the more that actors can mutually frame, role-make/take, validate, account, stage, and perform rituals, the greater the likelihood that they will be able to categorize, regionalize, ritualize, normatize, stabilize (resource transfers), and routinize their interaction over time. And the more they can realize these latter states, the less time and energy are necessary to sustain an interaction and the less likely are fundamental needs to be activated during the course of the interaction at any point in time.

What, then, are the specific causal paths through which these events transpire? One way to answer this question is to examine each structuring process in terms of the specific signaling and interpreting processes that create and sustain it. In so doing, we can also suggest the consequences of these interactional processes, not only on structuring, but, indirectly, on motivational dynamics as well.

The interpersonal basis of regionalizing. The most obvious signaling and interpreting bases of regionalizing are the processes of stage-making and stage-taking. As Figs. 8.1 and 11.1 show, actors carry in their stocks of knowledge stores of information about the meaning of objects, people, divisions, and movements evident in space. They use this knowledge, especially about role-conceptions that actors share, in order to stage a situation as part of the process of role-making. Staging, then, is part of a more inclusive process of signaling what role an individual is seeking to play; and without such role-making, the contextual meaning of spacing, positioning, movements, use of props, and other staging signals would be difficult to determine. These considerations lead to the hypothesis that the more individuals seek to role-make in a situation, the greater is their ability to determine the meaning of each other's staging efforts (through role-taking); and as a result, the more likely they are to regionalize a situation and thereby to structure their interaction across time.

Such role-making is, as is outlined in Fig. 8.1, connected to individuals' capacity to develop situational self-references and to impose frames. That is, role-making is facilitated if actors can use their self-conception to provide situational self-references and if they can impose frames, especially physical and demographic ones (see Table 8.1). Regionalization is thus secondarily related to the ability of individuals to generate situational self-definitions and frames that can, in turn, be used to focus their role-making/taking and stage-making/taking activities.

In using self-definitions and frames to organize their role-making/taking and stage-making/taking activities, individuals can also meet motivational needs for confirmation of self and a sense of group inclusion. For knowing and understanding one's place in space makes it easier to develop self-definitions and a sense of group membership. Of course, if role-making/taking and stage-making/taking are unsuccessful, then these needs for self-confirmation and group inclusion escalate (at least to the point of futility where apathy and withdrawal set in) and encourage further efforts at role-making and frame-making in an attempt to determine, literally, "where one stands" in a situation.

The interpersonal basis of categorizing. As is delineated in Table 11.1, actors will tend to categorize, at least initially, a situation in terms of its level of intimacy and its context. This occurs primarily as a result of people's frame-making and frame-taking activities, although role-making and role-taking are also involved. As actors invoke physical, demographic, socio-cultural, and personal frames (see Table 8.1), they typify others as categories, persons, or intimates and define the context as work/practical, ceremonial, or social (see Table 11.1). While framing involves the use and interpretation of many kinds of gestures, it is particularly facilitated by people's efforts to construct an account through ethnomethods and to create consensus over validity claims about norms, means-ends, and sincerity. The accounting activities of actors create a diffuse background sense of who exists, what is known, and what is possible in a situation, whereas the validating efforts of participants structure the situation in terms of the kinds and levels of sincerity, the relevant normative elements, and the appropriate means to various ends (whether social, work/practical, or ceremonial). These considerations suggest the following hypothesis: the more signaling and interpreting revolve around framing, especially accounting and validating, the greater is the likelihood that actors will categorize an interaction and use these categories to order their responses in the present and at future encounters.

Thus, by framing and thereby categorizing situations, actors reduce the necessary level of interpersonal work at any given point in time; and in so doing, they create expectations about what should and will occur at subsequent points in time. These effects of framing activities are often supplemented by role-making, especially the use and interpretation of staging maneuvers and rituals. For as I emphasized in Chapter 11 and as the causal arrows *a* and *b* between "Regionalize" and "Categorize" in Fig. 11.3 underscore, the physical props, the number and distribution of people, and the spacing arrangements are, by themselves, sufficient to categorize a situation. In a sense, highly ordered spatial situations reveal preprogramed rituals, frames, accounts, and claims that individuals simply reproduce without great deliberation or expenditure of energy. Yet, even in such highly circumscribed situations, more fine-tuned categorizing occurs as a result of mutual accounting and validating as these enable actors to initially frame and reframe a situation. I would hypothesize, then, that the more visible a situation's ecological, physical, and demographic dimensions and the greater the level of consensus over the meaning of these staging dimensions, the more readily will actors be able to frame and categorize an interaction; and if the interaction persists, the more rapidly and easily will they be able to reframe and fine-tune the situation in terms of accounting and validating efforts.

Not only does framing (and, on some occasions, staging) a situation create categories that ease the process of interaction, these interpersonal procedures feed back and meet several fundamental motive-states of individuals. Framing creates a sense of facticity, especially when account-making and taking have been extensively used to construct and fine-tune the categories. By knowing the appropriate levels of intimacy with respect to others, individuals can more readily achieve a sense of intersubjective facticity; and by understanding the social, ceremonial, or work/practical nature of the situation, they can more easily achieve a sense of an external and factual world "out there." In turn, achieving a sense of facticity meets more deeply-seated needs for ontological security.

The interpersonal basis of normatizing. As individuals frame situations, particularly with respect to claim-making and taking, they perform much of the interpersonal work for normatizing their present and future interactions. By mutually asserting and interpreting the appropriateness of their conduct in terms of rights/duties and the "rationality" of their means as these are related to ends, individuals draw upon stocks of knowledge and use these to negotiate over the expectations and interpretative schemata that will guide their conduct (see Fig. 11.2). Moreover, as they mutually make and take accounts, they resolve (or think they do) potentially discordant elements in their respective interpretations; as a consequence, they make even more explicit the operative rights and duties as well as the rules for organizing the elements of an interpretative schema. Hence, it can be hypothesized that the more actors can successfully validate each other's claims over appropriateness and sincerity, while at the same time using ethnomethods to construct an account, the greater is the likelihood that they will reach agreement over the operative rights and duties, the interpretative schemata, and the organizing rules; and as a consequence of this signaling and interpreting activity, the greater is their capacity to normatize the situation.

Role-making and taking also contribute to normatizing in several respects. First, as individuals try to make a role for themselves, they communicate to each other how they expect to be treated, thereby encouraging mutual agreement over rights and duties. Second, during role-taking, actors achieve understanding of the perspective behind each other's efforts to role-make, thus increasing their capacity to employ similar interpretative schemata and corresponding rights and duties. Third, in using rituals strategically during the process of role-making, they negotiate over the duration, form, and referent of their interaction, thereby providing additional information about the rights and duties as well as the interpretative schemata that are most salient in a situation. These considerations would suggest the hypothesis that the more actors can successfully role-make and accurately role-take, the greater is their ability to understand the expected behaviors and perspective associated with their respective roles, and thus, the greater is their capacity to normatize a situation.

These interpersonal dynamics also influence motivational processes. In particular, the use of stocks of knowledge to understand the claims and accounts of others enables individuals to achieve a greater feeling of facticity and, indirectly, ontological security. For as individuals use validating and accounting procedures to develop a common interpretative schema and agree on the procedures for organizing this schema (see middle and right of Fig. 11.2), they increase their sense of intersubjectivity and their perception that there is a factual and orderly world "out there." To some extent, role-taking creates the same feeling, since as people interpret each other's roles and the perspective associated with these roles, they reinforce their sense of intersubjectivity as well as their perception of an orderly world composed of compatible roles. Role-making does more, however. It also enables people to meet needs for self-confirmation by establishing a role that reinforces their conception of themselves as a certain kind of person who has a particular set of rights and duties.

The interpersonal basis of ritualizing. There is, of course, an obvious relationship between ritual-making and ritual-taking, on the one hand, and the ritualizing of an interaction, on the other. As people use and interpret rituals, they develop standardized opening, closing, forming, totemizing, and repairing sequences for that situation. Such standardized sequences give a predictability to each actor's responses, but by themselves these do not mean very much. Rituals only "make sense" when they occur in a meaningful context and when they have clear referents in this context. As Fig. 8.1 indicates, rituals have reciprocal causal relations with staging and accounting activities; and it is in this association with accounting and staging that they "make sense" for individuals. An account creates a sense of "what's real" and the rituals used (and interpreted) by actors are geared toward sustaining this account. In particular, rituals will be used to gloss over presently unclear details, repair breached interpersonal sequences, and assert a given account. And, out of this use of rituals, both the account and the rituals take on greater clarity. That is, the ritual strings together, and if necessary repairs, the elements of the account, whereas the emerging account becomes one of the primary contextual referents of the rituals.

Similarly, stage-making and stage-taking are causally implicated in rituals. The numbers, movements, and juxtapositioning of people, as well as the presence of physical props, all provide contextual cues that dictate what rituals are to be employed. Conversely, the use of rituals is one of the principal vehicles by which staging activities occur. Movement into, or out of, a setting will be marked by rituals; varying patterns of juxtapositioning among actors in space will be managed by rituals; and physical objects and props take on their meaning through the kinds of rituals used to mark their significance.

Rituals are thus connected to accounting and staging dynamics. Additionally, because rituals connect processes involved in both framing and role-making/taking processes (see causal arrows in Fig. 8.1), they have enormous significance for making and taking roles as well as for imposing frames in an interaction. For role-making/taking (to a considerable extent) and framing (to a lesser degree) occur through ritual-making and ritual-taking. Thus, as rituals are emitted, they help actors order those other structuring processes—categorizing, regionalizing, and normatizing—that reveal direct causal effects on ritualizing (see Fig. 11.3).

These causal dynamics indicate that the ritualizing of an interaction is connected to the ability of actors to use staging and accounting techniques in conjunction with rituals. More formally, I would suggest the following hypothesis: the more actors can use rituals to construct accounts and to stage a situation and, by implication, to frame as well as role-make/take, the more these rituals will reveal contextual meanings and referents; and as a consequence of the latter, the more likely they will become a basis for ritualizing an interaction in the present and at future points in time.

Ritualizing an interaction through the use of ritual, staging, and accounting techniques also has a number of consequences for motivational processes. In fact, I would argue that ritual-making and ritual-taking have more comprehensive consequences for motivational processes than all other interpersonal and structuring processes. For, as I suggested in Chapter 11, rituals and ritualizing not only reduce the amount of interpersonal energy and anxiety produced in a situation; they also meet needs for facticity, ontological security, symbolic/material gratification, group inclusion, self-confirmation, and trust. Let me elaborate.

As rituals are used to construct accounts, they help create a sense of facticity by highlighting elements of what's real; in so doing, they also emphasize that "things are as they appear" and contribute to a sense of ontological security. Moreover, by ordering the sequences of responses, especially as this ordering meets needs for facticity and ontological security, rituals promote a sense of trust and predictability. Additionally, since rituals are part of the role-making process (see Fig. 8.1), they also enable actors to confirm and affirm self; perhaps more importantly, they allow individuals in situations of inequality to reduce the costs to their dignity of subordination by virtue of confining the emission of gestures to a necessary few. Rituals are also important in providing individuals with a sense of symbolic gratification, since the solidarity-producing consequence of ritual itself is a symbolic reward. Such is particularly likely to be the case with respect to group inclusion as well as self-confirmation and affirmation. For example, even a simple and perfunctory ritual greeting (such as "How are you?") can subtly sustain both one's self as an object of worth and one's sense of being included in the ongoing flow of the context. Rituals also mark the exchange of more material rewards, since interpersonal negotiation and bargaining are almost always conducted in highly ritualized terms. For instance, most exchanges, especially those over material rewards, reveal clear opening/closing procedures. And, because symbolic and material gratifications so often revolve around issues of people's membership and place in a group, rituals and ritualizing are therefore the principal mechanism for promoting a sense of inclusion and solidarity with others in an ongoing context. For these reasons, then, ritual-making and taking, as they influence the ritualization of a situation, are crucial for meeting the full range of fundamental human needs outlined in Fig. 5.1.

The interpersonal basis of stabilizing resource transfers. As noted above, ritual-making and taking are at the center of resource exchanges, although, as I noted in Chapter 11, other interpersonal and structuring processes are also important (see causal arrows *h* and *m* in Fig. 11.3). During signaling and interpreting, rituals, as circumscribed by staging and accounting activities, are the key dynamics. Rituals sequence the exchange (particularly as they contribute to the ritualization of a situation); stage props and positioning are frequently the objects of exchange, but even if such is not the case, staging orders the juxtaposition and props of each actor in the exchange (especially as these influence regionalizing); and accounting enables individuals to create a sense of an external and intersubjective order, while providing the procedures for repairing the sense of order within which the actual exchange can occur (particularly as accounting enables actors to categorize and normatize a situation). Thus, it is reasonable to hypothesize that the more actors can use rituals and, at the same time, construct accounts and stages, the greater is their ability to stabilize the transfer of resources over time.

Resource stabilization through rituals, accounts, and staging has important effects on motivational processes by helping individuals meet needs for symbolic and material gratification. If the resources exchanged revolve around group membership, they can allow individuals to meet needs for group inclusion and, indirectly, trust and predictability. Furthermore, the use of rituals and accounts to stabilize resources can help actors realize needs for facticity by providing them with a feeling that there is a regular ratio of payoffs and a sense that there is an orderly flow of resources in a fixed world. Finally, because ritual and staging techniques are part of the more inclusive role-making process, they will inevitably have consequences for self-confirmation and affirmation. For as individuals seek to use staging and rituals to stabilize resource transfers, they attempt to sustain a conception of themselves as a certain kind of person who is, in the particular situation, deserving of a given resource payoff. To the extent that ritual and staging stabilize the transfer of resources, then, much of the ambiguity and anxiety over "putting oneself on the line" in each and every encounter is eliminated, allowing actors to confirm self without undue effort and without arousing great anxiety.

The interactional basis of routinizing. If individuals are to behave and interact in much the same way during each encounter, it is necessary for them to role-make/take and frame-make/take in the same manner. Indeed, it is crucial to the smooth flow of the interaction that they not "think about" their framing and role-making/taking activities. Habitual staging and ritual help keep role-making and taking implicit, whereas unbreached accounting and unchallenged claiming practices sustain tacit frames. Let me examine these points in more detail below.

Routinization requires that actors do "the same thing in the same place." This kind of habitual conduct is possible when staging and rituals are unambiguous. That is, for routinization to occur, the ecology, demography, and physical structure of space must be much the same over time; and equally important, such habituated staging must invoke the same opening, closing, and forming rituals. Thus, as actors move through their mutual staging of the situation, past experiences (as accumulated in their stocks of knowledge) lead them to emit and interpret the same rituals, which reciprocally reinforce the salience of their staging practices. Similarly, routinizing depends upon a reciprocal and reinforcing relationship between accounts and claims. The validity claims of each actor must be accepted and unchallenged, while the accounts of "what's real" by each actor must be uncontested; even if they are not, there must be clear repair rituals for patching any breaches in the account back together. Thus, it is reasonable to propose the generalization that the more actors' staging and ritual activities, on the one hand, and their accounting and validating practices, on the other, can become mutually reinforcing, uncontested, and unreflective, the greater is the likelihood that their interaction will be routinized in space and across time.

As with those other interpersonal processes structuring an interaction, these dynamics have implications for meeting basic motivational needs. The unconscious and habitual use of staging, ritual, accounting, and claiming procedures has, I think, the greatest impact on needs for a sense of ontological security and, indirectly, on needs for a feeling of trust. As actors, without great deliberation, order their responses into habitual sequences in space and time, they create an implicit sense that their relations "are as they appear" and that their responses to each other are predictable. To a lesser extent, the habituation of interpersonal procedures creates a sense of facticity, especially when accounts are accepted and when the repair rituals for breached accounts are unambiguous and easily implemented without undue anxiety or thought. To an even lesser degree, the habituation of interaction helps meet needs for symbolic/material gratification by assuring actors that exchange payoffs will be as they always have been.

The Structuring Basis of Motivational and Interactional Dynamics

Some General Considerations

In the above analysis, I have already touched upon the many ways that structuring of an interaction feeds back and influences the mobilization of motivational energies as well as the flow of signaling and interpreting. Here, I will mention some of the general implications of these feedback processes; in the next section, I will elaborate upon some of the more specific processes discussed earlier.

It is a rare interaction that occurs outside of an existing structure. Past interactions typically regionalize, categorize, normatize, ritualize, stabilize, and perhaps even routinize the interpersonal options of individuals. Through socialization, modeling, memory, and other dynamics that organize human cognitions, these structuring processes have become part of actors' stocks of knowledge. Indeed, at the cognitive level, they represent some of the more organized gestalts that actors employ as they mobilize energy, signal, and interpret. And, as actors use this knowledgeability, they reproduce both cognitively and behaviorally the structure of an interaction. Thus, as I noted at the beginning of Chapter 11, structure is both an overt interpersonal process of mobilizing energy to signal and interpret in ways that reproduce this structure and a "mental template" about how best to organize responses. It is this latter, more cognitive dimension of structure that enables individuals to reproduce even those structures that others have created in the distant past and that they now enter for the first time. For as micro-chauvinists are prone to emphasize, society ultimately rests on—and perhaps is nothing more than—signaling and interpreting by motivated and cognitively competent actors in concrete settings.

In my view, this conclusion is too extreme. We will never, I suspect, understand macrostructures in the terms that I have outlined in these pages. There are dimensions to the aggregations of populations of actors and to their combined interactions in micro settings that require an entirely new level of analysis—macrosociology. In fact, these macrostructural dynamics operate as parameters on structuring processes at the micro level; and I would argue that understanding these macrostructural constraints is theoretically more important in reducing the micro-macro gap than are further pronouncements by micro-chauvinists that society is nothing more than "symbolic interaction," "interaction ritual chains," "behavior of men as men," "communicative action," "ethnomethods," and similar hyper-micro positions. For me, then, it is important to recognize that macro patterns of population aggregation, differentiation, and integration circumscribe the use of structuring dynamics (see J. Turner, 1987, N.d.*b*). At present, I am not prepared (although I am preparing)[2] to offer an answer to the question of how macrostructural dynamics constrain interpersonal structuring processes. For the time being, I simply wish to emphasize that structuring is a product of both interactional and macrostructural dynamics, but once a situation is structured by these dynamics, it constrains the mobilization of energy as well as signaling and interpreting activities. More formally, it can be hypothesized that the more that macrostructural conditions and past interactions have increased the degree of regionalization, categorization, normatization, ritualization, resource stabilization, and routinization in a situation, the less is the amount of motivational energy expended in signaling/interpreting.

Some Specific Causal Paths

The effects of regionalizing. As a situation is regionalized, the number, spacing, and movement of individuals are given meaning, as are the divisions of space into regions and the distributions of physical objects and props. In turn, role-making/taking is facilitated, because the range of stag-

---

[2] For my more preliminary statements on macro dynamics, see J. Turner, 1986a, N.d.*b*. My planned "sequel" to this book (J. Turner, N.d.*a*.) will be on these macro processes.

ing and ritual procedures that can be used is circumscribed. Moreover, since regionalization orders people in space, it creates physical and demographic frames (see Table 8.1), thereby facilitating the process of framing. Thus, the more a situation is regionalized, the more it constrains the processes of role-making through restrictions on ritual and staging options and of framing through the imposition of physical and demographic frames—thereby decreasing the level of interpersonal energy that actors must mobilize in the situation.

Regionalization also influences motivational processes directly. By constraining role-making/taking and framing, regionalization determines how all motivational needs are met, particularly self-confirmation/affirmation and group inclusion. By organizing space, the location of self in the structure of a situation is established; as a result, the role-making options of individuals are made less ambiguous, thereby reducing the level of anxiety. And, by ordering space and dictating the range of rituals that can be used in a situation, the relative positioning and procedures for reaffirming one's place in the flow of interaction are determined, thus facilitating one's sense of group inclusion.

In addition to meeting needs for self-confirmation/affirmation and group inclusion, the organization of space has secondary effects on other motive forces. Facticity is encouraged when the meanings of spatial organization are unambiguous; and in turn, this helps create a sense that the world is as it appears, especially in its physical, ecological, and demographic dimensions. Moreover, as behavioral options are circumscribed by regionalization, trust is more readily achieved, because people's responses become more predictable. And finally, as regionalization determines the meanings of physical objects, it helps to define what is materially valuable and gratifying in the situation. Thus, to the degree that a situation is regionalized, it meets basic motivational needs by (1) defining the staging procedures necessary for self-confirmation, (2) ordering the spatial dimensions of group inclusion, (3) providing meanings about space necessary for creating a perception of facticity, (4) creating a set of physical parameters for realizing ontological security, (5) increasing the level of predictability so necessary for trust, (6) defining the range of material rewards necessary for gratification—and, in doing all of the above, reducing the level of diffuse anxiety.

The effects of categorizing. As actors typify situations in terms of the appropriate degree of intimacy with others and the requirements for work/practical, ceremonial, or social demeanor, the processes of role-making/taking and framing are made considerably easier. If actors understand demeanor requirements and intimacy levels (see Table 11.1), then the kinds of roles that they can make through staging and ritual are delimited and focused. Similarly, the nature of claims and accounts used to frame a situation is also circumscribed. The result is that signaling and interpreting are facilitated, because individuals negotiate over roles and frames within a much narrower range of options.

As categorization facilitates role-making/taking and framing, it also meets basic motivational needs directly, and indirectly through its effects on interactional processes. Let me first examine the indirect effects. Since all needs are realized through either role-making/taking or framing (see causal paths in Fig. 8.1), categorizing a situation will have indirect consequences for meeting all motive states in individuals. More formally, if role-taking/making and framing are circumscribed by categorizing, then: (1) self-confirmation will be facilitated as categories determine the range of roles to be asserted; (2) material/symbolic gratification will be encouraged as categories circumscribe the staging and ritual practices used to focus actors' attention on those materials and symbols that can bestow gratification; (3) facticity will be encouraged as categories dictate the kinds of accounts that can be used to frame the encounter; (4) ontological security will be realized as categories constrain the imposition of frames necessary for sustaining the appearance that "things are as they seem"; (5) trust will be sustained as categories make role-making/taking and framing of responses more predictable; (6) group inclusion will be achieved as categories define the use of ritual and stages that locate actors in a situation; and (7) anxiety will be reduced as categories facilitate the realization of all the preceding.

Turning to more direct effects on motivation, without regard for the processes of signaling and interpreting, categorizing a situation reduces anxiety by lowering the uncertainty about how to orient one's demeanor in relation to others. In so doing, categorizing helps define how basic needs are to be met. Thus, to the extent that actors can use common categories in a situation, categories are more likely to define those types of symbols and materials that can yield rewards, those behavioral options that can produce self-confirmation, those types of relations that can generate a sense of group inclusion, those types of procedures that are relevant in constructing a sense of facticity and ontological security, and those typical responses that increase predictability and, hence, trust.

The effects of normatizing. If individuals normatize a situation, then the relevant rights and duties, interpretative schemata, and organizing procedures are clarified, with the result that role-making/taking and framing are constrained and simplified. And the more that normative constraints delimit framing and role-making/taking, the more explicit are the interpretations of staging procedures, the nature of appropriate rituals, the procedures for creating accounts, and the communicative discourse necessary for validating claims.

In circumscribing signaling and interpreting in this way, normatizing also works to meet basic motivational needs directly, as well as indirectly through its effects on signaling and interpreting. It does so by specifying how people are supposed to act, interpret, and reconcile potentially discordant expectations with respect to (1) the appropriate procedures for confirming self, (2) the relevant interpretative schemata and procedures for constructing a sense of facticity, (3) the expectations critical for achieving a sense of predictability and trust, (4) the duties and prerogatives required to fit in the group and feel included, (5) the procedures for going about achieving symbolic and material gratification, and (6) the interpretative schemata and expectations so necessary to feeling ontological security.

The effects of ritualizing. Appropriate rituals become more explicit as situations become structured by virtue of either macrostructural constraints or past interactions. Each basic type of ritual has varying effects on interactional processes, as can be summarized by the following set of hypotheses. The more opening, closing, and forming rituals are specified in a situation, the more clearly defined are the meanings of, and behavioral options in, a stage setting. The more forming and repairing rituals are specified, the more explicit are the procedures for repairing and constructing accounts and reconciling validity claims. The more clearly specified are opening, closing, and forming rituals, the more explicitly defined are the boundaries of relevant frames and reciprocal roles.

Both directly, and indirectly through the processes delineated by the above hypotheses, ritualizing has a number of important effects on basic motivational processes, which I present here as propositions. First, the more clearly specified are totemizing rituals and, to a lesser extent, opening, forming, and closing rituals, the more readily can individuals achieve a sense of group inclusion. Second, the more that forming and repairing rituals are specified, the easier it is for actors to construct and sustain a sense of facticity and, in the process, to meet needs for ontological security. Third, the more opening, closing, and forming rituals are specified, the more predictable the responses of each actor are, and as a result, the more likely actors are to achieve a sense of trust. Fourth, the more totemizing rituals are specified, the more clearly denoted are the objects and symbols necessary for achieving a sense of gratification. Fifth, the more clearly specified are opening, closing, forming, and repairing rituals, the more explicitly marked are the sequential procedures for realizing a sense of self-confirmation. And finally, the more all rituals are specified and meet other motivational needs, then the more those conditions for reducing diffuse anxiety are likely to be realized.

The effects of stabilizing resource transfers. The principal direct effect of resource stabilization on signaling and interpreting is to circumscribe interpersonal rituals, staging, and claims; indirectly, through its effects on these processes, it also influences framing and role-making/taking. For, as individuals establish, or have established for them by macrostructural forces, a ratio of payoffs over particular symbols and material objects, their interpersonal options are constrained.

With respect to rituals, enduring exchange relations are always ritualized, with clear opening, closing, forming, repairing. And if the exchange is highly valued by at least one party, totemizing rituals will also be evident. Such rituals are influenced by the value to each party of the resources exchanged and the degree of inequality in each party's payoffs, leading to the following hypothesis: the greater the value of the resources and the more unequal the payoffs in a stabilized transfer of resources, the more explicit and delimited is the use of rituals during the course of interpreting and signaling, and as a consequence, the more limited are the role-making options of actors and the more focused are the frames imposed by actors.

With respect to claim-making and claim-taking, stabilized transfers of resources restrict the claims that individuals can make in a situation, *unless* they wish to change the nature of resources exchanged and the ratio of payoffs (an occurrence that happens frequently, but usually at high cost). An existing ratio of payoffs for clearly defined resources constrains the range of means-ends rationales, modes of sincerity, and assertions of normative appropriateness that actors can make. Such is the case because the symbols and objects being exchanged in a particular ratio all dictate the relevant ends that means can meet, the subjective states that must be expressed, and the normative agreements that can be forged. Thus, the more an exchange of resources is stabilized, the fewer are the claiming options of actors, the easier is the mutual validation of claims, and as a consequence the more focused is the imposition of frames by actors.

With respect to staging processes, stabilization of resource transfers defines the relative values of material objects and props, the importance of varying regions, and the significance of spacing arrangements in a situation; and in so doing, it circumscribes staging activities. Hence, the more an exchange of resources is stabilized, the more clearly defined are the meanings and values of objects, props, regions, and spacing in a situation, the fewer are the staging options of actors, and as a further result the more delimited are the role-making options of actors.

Resource stabilization also influences motivational processes directly, as well as indirectly through its effects on ritual, staging, and claiming procedures. The most important direct causal effect of stabilization is on needs for symbolic and material gratification, where established transfers dictate the nature and amount of material and symbolic resources that actors can receive. And though some actors may feel somewhat deprived as they consistently come out on the short end of exchanges, needs for gratification are still being met, at least to some degree, because actors "know" what resources and how much of these resources they can expect to receive. More indirectly, as resource stabilization works to define the respective levels of gratification for actors and to dictate the nature of their ritual and staging activities, it operates to meet needs for group inclusion by informing actors where they stand with respect to their place in the spatial distribution of group members, their control of group resources, and their obligations for emitting rituals reaffirming group involvement. Thus, it is reasonable to hypothesize that the more stabilized the transfer of resources, the more clearly defined are the symbols, props, and objects of the group, the more explicit are the necessary interpersonal procedures for realizing a sense of group inclusion, and as a consequence the easier it is for actors to meet needs for group inclusion.

The stabilization of resource transfers also has implications for other motive states, although I suspect that these effects are less than those described above. Phrasing these additional implications propositionally, let me offer the following hypotheses. First, the more stabilized is the transfer of resources in a situation, the more clearly defined are the symbols, objects, and procedures for self-definitions, and hence, the more readily can actors meet needs for self-confirmation/affirmation. However, if an existing exchange does not allow for self-confirmation or affirmation, especially because of great inequality in the ratio of payoffs, then the less will needs for self-maintenance be met by the stabilization of resources and the greater will be pressures for change in the ratio of payoffs. Second, the more stabilized is the transfer of resources in a situation, the more defined are the symbols, objects, and procedures that can be used to create a sense of facticity, and as a result the more readily can actors meet needs for both facticity and ontological security. Third, the more stabilized is the transfer of resources in a situation, the more predictable are the responses of each actor as well as the resource payoffs, and therefore the more likely are needs for trust to be met. And finally, the more stabilized is the transfer of resources in a situation and the more such stabilization meets other needs, the more likely are needs to avoid diffuse anxiety to be realized.

The effects of routinizing. As routines come to dictate what individuals are to do in space, what ritual sequences they are to follow, what procedures they are to use in developing accounts, and what claims they are to validate, the processes of framing and role-making/taking are facilitated and simplified. Indeed, people hardly need to think about frames and roles as they go about their routinized responses; as a result, staging, ritual, accounting, and validating activities are also emitted without great deliberation. Thus, the more a situation is routinized, the more all interpersonal processes become unconscious and predictable.

In making each actor's responses predictable, routinizing increases actors' sense of trust, which, in turn, reduces their level of anxiety and their needs for facticity. Moreover, routines create a sense that "things are as they appear," since interacting in the same manner at each encounter gives a situation a sense of being real and secure. As routines meet needs for security, they also reinforce needs for facticity by providing actors with a sense that, for the purposes at hand, they share common subjective and intersubjective worlds. To a lesser extent, routines help meet other needs by making habitual the material/symbolic resources received in a situation, by creating a sense that they are plugged into the habitual pattern of ongoing activity, and by providing stable responses from others that can be used for consistent self-evaluation. Hence, the more a situation is routinized, the greater is the predictability of responses from others, and hence, the more readily are all basic motivational needs realized.

Conclusion

I have now completed what may seem like a tedious review of the various causal paths among motivational, interactional, and structuring processes. Yet, even with this rather long review, it is evident that only the surface of these causal links has been touched. Considerably more could be said, but for my purposes, the hypotheses presented discursively in this chapter can illustrate the utility of analytical models for generating testable statements. Of course, as is also evident, the juxtaposing of three complex models perhaps generates too many hypotheses. In systematically delineating all of the causal linkages in Figs. 5.1, 8.1, and 11.3, I run the risk of creating an unmanageable number of propositions. And, when coupled with those presented at the conclusion of Chapters 5, 8, and 11, the inventory of propositions is now becoming somewhat unwieldy.

There is, then, still some theoretical work to be done. Simply using the models as "hypothesis generating machines" is not enough. Such a tactic may represent one place to begin developing laws of human social interaction, but it should not be the end product. A *selective* reorganization of propositions into a more coherent inventory is also necessary. This inventory should stress those properties of social interaction that are considered particularly important. Such an exercise involves adding theoretical content, since it will be necessary to assert which processes are more important than others.

Thus, in the next and last chapter, I will conclude by emphasizing certain processes and presenting what I see as the most crucial propositions. Some may disagree with my selection and ordering of propositions; if this is the case, the models presented in previous chapters can at least serve as a guideline for developing a better inventory of abstract propositions. My conclusions in the next chapter are only preliminary; I invite others to use the models developed in earlier chapters and the summaries presented in this chapter as a place to begin taking the next theoretical step: creating laws of social interaction.

13

Speculation on the Critical Micro Dynamics

I HAVE ALWAYS ENJOYED the last chapter in books by George Homans because, as he noted in the first edition of his *Social Behavior* (1961: 378), "a last chapter should resemble a primitive orgy after harvest. The work may have come to an end, but the worker cannot let go all at once." I have also admired anyone who has excess energy at the end of a book. Personally, I always find myself tired, staggering to the finish line. Such is the case for this book, but I am also worried about what I have promised: some laws of social interaction. Since I am the author, I could go back and edit these promises out, but duty and honor force me to do something more along these lines.

I am not going to be highly systematic, however, as I was in the last chapter, following each arrow back and forth across Figs. 5.1, 8.1, and 11.3. Rather, in the spirit of a Homansian harvest orgy—hopefully not too primitive—what I see as the most critical processes of social interaction will be outlined. This selectivity can be excused in light of the fact that systematic lists of principles in Chapters 5, 8, and 11, as well as a series of less formal hypotheses in the last chapter, have already been presented. What I offer here, then, are hunches about the most basic microdynamics.

The Fundamental Micro Processes

The Importance of Self

People's self-conception is a crucial force in interpersonal affairs. I argue that humans possess a core self-conception composed not only of cognitive definitions but also of powerful feelings and emotions about themselves. Usually, these emotions are buried somewhat beneath the surface of consciousness, although individuals vary in their level of awareness of these most fundamental self-feelings. Thus, contrary to some interactionist positions, the core self is not conceptualized as a linguistic construct; if anything, it is a feeling construct and consists of a field or configuration of self-feelings about oneself as an object. Of course, when pressed by others, or when subject to various introspective procedures, people can usually articulate at least some of these self-feelings. Moreover, I visualize this core of self-feelings as transsituational; people carry them from context to context as part of their emotional baggage. At the same time, people also have situational and peripheral selves composed of more conscious and easily articulated attitudes and images of themselves as a certain kind of person in particular types of situations.

My belief is that many of the dynamics of self revolve around the interplay between core and transsituational emotions, on the one side, and peripheral and situational cognitions, on the other. Thus, I am decidedly more Freudian than interactionist in my view of self, although I do not see great incompatibility between my views and more traditional mainstream perspectives. I would argue further that the often debated issue of which is more important—maintaining consistency or esteem in the elements of self[1]—depends upon the self in question, whether core or peripheral, the relations between these levels of self, and the use of defense mechanisms, particularly repression. How, then, do we sort all of these forces out?

My answer is that people enter interactions with a relatively stable level of self-esteem, which has been acquired in past socialization and which is the organizing principle of their core emotions and feelings about themselves. Moreover, people typically seek to maintain consistency among these core feelings, while at the same time they attempt to sustain consistency between this core self and their various situational selves. Greater inconsistency can be tolerated, without the use of defense mechanisms, at the peripheral-self level than at the core-self level, although one's core-self feelings impose a limit as to how much inconsistency among peripheral selves can be tolerated. Defense mechanisms are, I further hypothesize, most likely to be invoked when people have very low levels of self-esteem and when there are high levels of inconsistency among and between the elements of either the core or the peripheral self (indeed, I suspect that high inconsistency produces low self-esteem, especially at the core-feeling level).

The use or nonuse of defense mechanisms complicates the dynamics of motivational energy for a person, in several respects.[2] Once such mechanisms become a habitual part of people's behavioral repertoire, they will often appear to themselves and outsiders as consistent in their self-feelings and self-definitions, when in fact they have merely masked these incongruities. Moreover, defense mechanisms will typically create a sense of raised

---

[1] See Chapter 4's discussion of the interactionist model.

[2] As a general hunch, I think the use of defense mechanisms is curvilinear: they are not needed until certain levels of inconsistency and low esteem are reached; they then kick in and enable people to cope (although others are usually very aware of their conflict and torment); and at some point, or during certain moments, these mechanisms can collapse, although this usually takes a major life crisis. Sociologists do not like to hear about such complications because they like to use survey research techniques, which are unsuitable for uncovering these dynamics (also they do not like nonlinear relations, especially those that probably involve threshold effects, since they make "explaining variance" difficult).

self-esteem, thereby making people feel more comfortable with themselves, at least at the surface, verbal level. Yet the use of defense mechanisms creates ever-increasing levels of emotional energy that, in the end, will become manifest in both the cognitions and behavior of an individual. This release of repressed energy, however, can often become a basis for further use of defense mechanisms, which merely postpones the emotional reckoning at even greater levels of intensity.

Thus, one's "need to sustain self-conception," as Fig. 5.1 so simply summarized all this, is complicated, especially if one is trying to determine how this need influences the release of energy that people use to signal, interpret, and structure social relations. Despite these complications, my conclusion is actually rather simple: people try to avoid the anxiety that comes with low self-esteem and inconsistency in both their core and peripheral self. The result is that people's overall level of energy for confirming self will be an inverse and additive function of their level of esteem and consistency in the elements of their self-conception, especially for core self-feelings. The use of defense mechanisms can delay, distort, and deflect this energy, but in the long run, it will be released, at least up to the point of complete emotional disruption where social interaction becomes virtually impossible or so deviant that it is no longer possible to participate in normal social circles.

This conclusion, which of course is much the same as that among sociologically oriented psychoanalysts (e.g., Sullivan, 1953), argues that the intensity of, and the emotion surrounding, the processes of signaling, interpreting, and structuring are a gradual s-function of the degree to which a person enters an interaction with a low level of esteem and inconsistent core self-feelings and of the degree to which the gestures of others disconfirm a given level of esteem or consistency in either core or peripheral selves. Since these relations are an s-function, I am asserting that people with chronically low self-esteem and inconsistent feelings or cognitions will "work harder" during signaling and interpreting, at least up to the point where they withdraw or invoke defense mechanisms. Moreover, I am also arguing that individuals with chronic anxiety, as well as those without these chronic problems, will find themselves anxious and will be mobilized when the gestures of others in a situation are interpreted in ways that contradict a given level of esteem or a crucial component of self.

The above proposition leads to several corollary points that should at least be listed. First, individuals with high esteem and consistency are less likely to use defense mechanisms and emit inconsistent gestures towards others. As a result, the responses of others toward them will also tend to be noncontradictory; when such is not the case, these individuals will become highly mobilized "to do something about" contradictions to their existing esteem as well as their core and peripheral self-conceptions. Second, because people with low esteem and inconsistent self-feelings and cognitions are more likely to use defense mechanisms to hide their true feelings and because they are often inconsistent in the messages that they signal others, it is more likely that the gestures of others will produce contradictions to their sense of self. The result is that these individuals will be mobilized by anxiety to cope with their self-doubts. Such is the case, I would argue, even when the contradictory information from others is positive and counters a low level of esteem; it will nonetheless produce anxiety and mobilize the individual in interaction.[3]

As needs to sustain self are mobilized through the dynamics described above, signaling and interpreting will increase. That is, people will offer more gestures to others, while reading and interpreting the latter's gestures with greater care. Moreover, when needs for self-confirmation and affirmation are the motivating force, people signal and interpret primarily with respect to staging and ritual cues. Therefore, individuals who experience anxiety over self-feelings and definitions will become particularly concerned about role-making and taking in terms of stagecraft (positioning, props, objects, movements) and ritual (openings, closings, totemizing, and repairs).[4]

In turn, to the extent that an interaction endures and is repeated, people's anxiety over self will be reduced, as they use staging cues to organize props and space (regionalize), while at the same time employing rituals to standardize and sequence time with clear openings, closings, repairs, and totems (ritualize). Such regionalization and ritualization will also facilitate the stabilization of the resource transfers that are used to confirm self. Thus, I believe that needs to sustain consistent definitions and feelings about self, especially core feelings about one's worth and esteem, are one of the primary motivating forces behind the regionalization, ritualization, and stabilization of the interaction.[5] Social structure must, at the micro level, be able to confirm self; and if such is not the case, then individuals will seek to change or leave a structured interaction.[6]

Such are my views on the importance of self. Let me now formalize these observations into a few elementary principles.

---

[3] Erving Goffman (1959) and others who ignore core self have, I believe, simply captured the surface dynamics of self.

[4] The often-noted folk observation that "insecure people are overly concerned with status" is another way of saying that they are very attuned to props and rituals denoting their role in ongoing activity.

[5] Of course, the macrostructure often sets the parameters within which these micro efforts at regionalization, ritualization, and stabilization occur.

[6] Naturally, this is not always possible, since micro encounters often occur in macrostructural contexts where power, authority, and other resource inequalities limit an individual's options.

1. The level of motivational energy produced by needs for self-confirmation and affirmation is an inverse and additive function of the level of self-esteem possessed by that person, the degree of consistency in self-feelings and cognitions of that person, the ability to avoid use of defense mechanisms, and the degree of concordance between self-references and the responses of others.

2. The degree of role-making and role-taking through staging and ritual cues in an interaction is a partial function of the level of motivational energy produced by needs for self-confirmation and affirmation.

3. The degree of regionalization, ritualization, and stabilization of resource transfers in an interaction is a partial function of the extent to which staging and ritual are successful in sustaining self-feelings and cognitions.

The Importance of Feeling Involved

People want to feel that they are part of events. This desire can range from a sense of close solidarity with others to a perception of being loosely in touch with the flow of events. Much of what is gratifying for humans, I believe, revolves around the exchange of symbols and material things that mark this inclusion in ongoing collective activities. Randall Collins (1986, 1981, 1975) has, of course, built his theory of interaction rituals around the process of actors developing a common focus, mood, and sense of solidarity. Indeed, he appears to define ritual only in terms of its solidarity-producing functions. My view is that rituals may or may not have these consequences for solidarity; it depends upon the motives driving the use of rituals as well as the macrostructural circumstances within which the ritual is emitted. Many rituals do nothing but mark the flow of interaction; others mobilize emotions and infuse the interactions with special significance; and still others close or break off an interaction, and thereby reduce solidarity.

In my view, rituals will produce solidarity when actors' needs for inclusion are very strong. Such rituals use symbols—mostly words but other gestures also—to create the sense of focus, mood, and solidarity that Collins sees as essential to social structure. But high needs for group inclusion also create needs for material signs—positioning, situational props, objects, and other staging techniques—to denote one's place in a larger solidarity. Thus, people's needs for group inclusion create needs for both symbols and material objects that signify involvement and, if the need for inclusion is strong enough, solidarity with others in a situation.[7]

Such needs for inclusion are, as Fig. 5.1 underscores, mediated by a need for trust or predictability, which in turn is connected to the anxiety that

[7] Needs for self-confirmation also exert this influence, but not to the same extent.

comes when the symbols and objects denoting inclusion are not forthcoming. Thus, group inclusion involves more than achieving a common mood, focus, and feelings of solidarity; it also revolves around a need to trust others, in the sense that their responses are predictable. Indeed, I would argue that in most interaction contexts, people do not need solidarity, but rather seek a relatively unemotional sense that they are "part of things" and an implicit presumption that they can rely upon others to do as expected. In my view, then, human life is considerably more low key and blasé than in Durkheim's (1912) notion of ritual effervescence or Collins's (1975, 1986) conception of interaction ritual chains.

Needs for inclusion are met primarily through role-making (and taking) through attention to staging and ritual cues. In turn, from mutual acts of staging, actors regionalize their interaction in space and around physical props and objects that mark their places and positions in a group. From the use of ritual, especially totemizing rituals, actors symbolize their involvement with each other, and as a result, they come to view the group, and their involvement in it, as a quasi-sacred "thing" and an emotional "force" external to them (this is, of course, Durkheim's argument, as it was adopted by Collins). Such outcomes of ritual assume, however, very high needs for inclusion and extensive use of ritual, but as Luhmann (1982) emphasizes, this state of affairs is rather rare in complex and differentiated systems. Instead, rituals are more perfunctory and operate to open, close, and repair rather uninvolving social relations.[8]

Yet, even in these relations, people want to feel that they are at least "in touch with" and "a part of" what's going on. If regionalization and ritualization can successfully mark an individual's place and position in the group and, at the same time, symbolize group involvement, then other structuring processes are facilitated. Exchanges of symbols and materials can be more readily stabilized, since each party knows the other's bargaining position while, at the same time, feeling mutually committed to the group within which the exchange is occurring. Moreover, routinization is facilitated by ritualized exchanges of group membership, since each actor can know and predict what is likely to occur in their group. And, when this structuring of staging and ritual meets needs for the symbols and objects

---

[8] Indeed, as almost all of the early masters of social theory worried, modern society does not operate to meet basic "needs" for a sense of "community." Despite results of survey research (and I emphasize the inadequacy of this methodology for penetrating deeper emotional levels in people) indicating that people are indeed plugged into family and friendship networks, and hence, happy, I do not think that such is really the case. A macrostructure that "prepackages" space and ritual, while limiting the use of totemizing rituals, is not one that promotes feelings of group inclusion. As Luhmann emphasizes, we can all "get along" under these circumstances, but some very basic needs in humans are denied, or at least only partially fulfilled, in the bargain.

of group involvement, actors will want to reproduce these structuring processes. Thus, to a great extent, regionalization, ritualization, and routinization are possible because they increase the likelihood that individuals will receive material and symbolic payoffs that meet powerful needs for group inclusion as mediated by needs for trust or predictability. Let me phrase this line of argument more formally.

1. The greater are needs for group inclusion among individuals in an interaction, the greater are needs for predictable responses denoting group involvement and activity.

2. The level of need for symbolic and material gratification in an interaction is a partial and additive function of the intensity of needs for denoting group inclusion and for predictability in the responses of others.

3. The degree of role-making and role-taking through staging and ritual cues in an interaction is a partial function of the level of motivational energy produced by needs for symbols and objects that denote group inclusion and mark the predictable flow of group activity.

4. The degree of ritualization, internalization, and stabilization of an interaction is a partial function of the extent to which staging and ritual can successfully meet needs for group inclusion and for trust.

The Importance of Feeling Right About Things

People need to feel and sense that "things are as they seem," that there is a pattern, not only to the world "out there," but also to intersubjective states, and that others are predictable and hence trustworthy. Most of this sense of security, facticity, and trust, as it was termed in Fig. 5.1, is implicit, and perhaps much of it is illusionary. But without it people feel that social interaction is "awkward," "out of sync," "without rhythm," "not quite right," and have other anxiety-provoking feelings about what's real, factual, and predictable. In a word, it is important for people to "feel right about" their dealings with each other, not so much in a moralistic sense, but rather in terms of sensing a rhythm, flow, and predictability. Moreover, other basic motivational dimensions of interaction, particularly confirming one's sense of self and feeling included in the ongoing flow of interaction, rely upon this implicit sense of security. For without it we have trouble really believing and accepting the symbols and objects that mark inclusion as well as the gestures that would seem to confirm self.

Needs for ontological security and facticity, as mediated by needs for trust, are the major causal forces behind frame-making and taking. By framing a situation, we have gone a long way toward achieving an interpersonal ontology that "things are as they seem" and toward creating a factual presumption that the world "out there" is the same as the world "inside of us." More specifically, we use ethnomethods primarily to construct accounts in order to make the external and intersubjective worlds seem factual, while we rely upon reciprocal claiming-validating to promote a sense that, indeed, matters are as they seem and that they are predictable. Of course, claiming also helps in the construction of an account, and vice versa, but neither can substitute for the other in creating feelings of facticity, security, or trust.

The key problem with most phenomenological analyses of these dynamics is that scholars are often intellectual bigots, claiming that there is no "really real" world and that the universe is a relativistic construct of illusionary meanings. It is little wonder that we "normal sociologists" were offended by these polemics and that, as a result, many of the more creative scholars in this new tradition, such as ethnomethodologists, have been forced to retreat into their own cult fringe in linguistics and other highly specialized fields. As ethnomethodologists learned, their "breaching experiment" with an entire field or discipline (whose power structure was, after all, only an illusion!) has generated a hostile reaction. My feeling is that many in this camp deserve some of this hostility from "normal sociology"; at the same time, we should not forget the incredibly important insight that phenomenologically inspired sociology has presented us. It requires not an intellectual retreat, but incorporation into the mainstream of sociology.

How is this to be done? My belief is that not only are accounting and claiming important in helping people meet other basic needs, but they are also essential dynamics in creating and sustaining social structures—not just the illusion of structure, but the real thing! That is, as contradictory as it may initially seem, people need to create a sense of structure, even an illusionary one, for such structures to be viable. The structure itself is real—after all, people do pattern and reproduce their interactions in space and across time—but part of this structuring depends upon implicit accounts and claims of "what's real," "what's what," and "what's likely to happen." Even if these accounts and claims are factually wrong, they are nonetheless crucial to structuring, because they give people the confidence to continue interacting and to resume or reproduce the interaction. The problem with the extreme ethnomethodological critique, then, is that in presuming accounts to be about illusionary structures, it is also assumed that social structures themselves are illusionary. This conclusion is utter nonsense, and so my efforts have been directed at using the key insights of phenomenology to build something other than a sociological cult committed to a solipsistic relativism.

The use of ethnomethods to construct accounts is essential to categorizing situations, whereas validating activities through implicit (not explicit, as Habermas would argue) discourse is critical to normatizing a situation. As people use ethnomethods, they create a "factual" world (or, at least, think that they do) by classifying others and situations; and on the basis of this categorization, they then proceed to develop a more fine-tuned version of "what's real" in the situation. As people make claims about means-ends, sincerity, and normative appropriateness, they forge agreements over rights, duties, appropriate interpretations, and how to go about negotiating over these normative issues. And on the basis of this normatizing they create a predictable reality. Moreover, categorizing and normatizing are very much interrelated: an account not only facilitates categorizing a situation, it also helps determine rights, duties, and the interpretative schemata employed by actors. Similarly, implicit discourse over claims not only helps normatize a situation, it encourages typification of individuals and the nature of their interrelations. Contrary to much ethnomethodological and critical theory, then, I see the interpersonal processes of accounting and validating as very much within a mainstream analysis of structuring. Indeed, although role-making and taking also have some effects (see Chapter 12 for details), two essential structural processes—normatizing[9] and categorizing—depend upon accounting and validating practices; or, in other words, they depend upon the use, respectively, of ethnomethods and of implicit discourse over validity claims.

Other aspects of structuring also depend on accounting and claiming, since categorizing and normatizing have effects on, and are affected by, other structuring processes (see Fig. 11.3 and text of Chapter 12). But I want to emphasize one in particular: routinization. This structuring process is directly produced by role-making and taking, as actors seek to meet needs for group inclusion and self-confirmation. Yet, to the extent that claiming and accounting influence people's sense of trust through their effects on facticity and security, then such claiming and accounting will have very powerful indirect effects on routinization. For routines are critical in creating the sense of predictability or trust that will, in turn, influence a person's sense of facticity and security. Thus, much of "feeling right about" a situation is related to people's capacity to create routines.

Therefore, in conjunction with other structuring processes, primarily routinization, the processes of categorizing and normatizing promote security, facticity, and predictability. In so doing, they meet fundamental human needs, encouraging the further conclusion that structuring is possible

---

[9] This argument runs counter to Thomas Wilson's (1970) well-known juxtaposition of ethnomethodology and normative sociology on opposite sides. But Wilson uses a Parsonized version of "normative sociology" to make his ethnomethodological critique. My normative theory, as expressed in Chapter 11, is more in tune with ethnomethodological challenges, although I doubt if most ethnomethodologists would admit it.

because it has reinforcement value for humans' basic needs. With that conclusion in mind, let me now summarize the above argument more formally.

1. The greater are needs for ontological security, facticity, and trust among individuals in an interaction, the greater are their efforts at framing the interaction.

2. The level of framing activity in an interaction revolving around account-making and taking is primarily a function of needs for a sense of facticity as influenced by needs for trust, whereas the level of framing activity revolving around claim-making and taking is primarily a function of needs for a sense of ontological security as these influence the level of needs for trust.

3. The degree of categorization of an interaction is a primary function of the extent to which account-making and taking are successful in meeting needs for facticity and a secondary function of the extent to which claim-making and taking are successful in meeting needs for ontological security and trust.

4. The degree of normatization of an interaction is a primary function of the extent to which claim-making and taking are successful in meeting needs for ontological security and trust and a secondary function of the extent to which account-making and taking are successful in meeting needs for facticity.

5. The degree of routinization of an interaction is a partial function of the extent to which claiming and accounting are successful, both directly and indirectly through their effects on other structuring processes, in meeting needs for facticity, security, and trust.

Constraints on the Structure of Social Interaction

The Behavioral Basis of Social Interaction and Structures

In the earlier analysis of motivation in Chapters 3–5, I concluded that the basic needs outlined in Fig. 5.1 could be seen as the "domains of value" that determine just what individuals find rewarding.[10] These domains are the energetic "force" that directs signaling and interpreting and that determines the viability of structuring. When Mead (1934) proposed his "social behaviorism" as an alternative to the extreme behaviorism of J. B. Watson (1913) and, I am sure, the subsequent advocacy of B. F. Skinner (1938, 1953), he wanted to emphasize that both the overt and covert behavioral capacities of humans, as well as the structures of society reproduced by

[10] Rather than conceptualize "hierarchies of value," as most utilitarian theories imply, it is better to see these in more gestalt terms, as loose configurations and clusters of value.

virtue of these capacities, are sustained through reinforcement dynamics. George Homans (1961) reintroduced this line of argument into sociology, and I think that he deserves credit on this score. Moreover, his assertion that the institutions of society ultimately rest on their capacity to provide at least some rewards for individuals is true, although it is not the whole story.

I am drawing a similar conclusion, but in greatly qualified form: to the extent that structured interactions meet humans' basic needs, their persistence over time and space becomes increasingly more likely. But I should also emphasize the converse or "dark side" of these reinforcement processes: to the extent that structured interactions cannot meet some or all of humans' basic needs, as outlined in Fig. 5.1, then structuring becomes progressively less viable and less likely to persist over time. If they can—and this is an important qualification—people will try to change those structures that deny them symbolic and material gratification (especially with respect to needs for group inclusion, trust, and self-confirmation) and that keep them from achieving a sense of facticity, security, and trust. Society ultimately rests on this behavioral base, and in the long run, powerful pressures will build to change those structures that deny humans the ability to meet basic needs. Indeed, the history of human organization is scattered with the remains of societies that failed in this most fundamental sense.

Yet Homans and others who have drawn this same conclusion have underemphasized an important point: people are often constrained by the very macrostructures that they have created or that their ancestors and predecessors have constructed. Individuals often do not have a say in the conditions under which they interact; even if these conditions are unrewarding, they frequently can do little but grumble and feel humble. Moreover, highly oppressive social arrangements, or just boring or ungratifying ones, often persist because people can find sources of reward "between the cracks." Humans are amazingly flexible; even in the midst of despair, they typically find a way to meet at least some basic needs to some degree. This flexibility is often a conservative force, preventing people from rising up in rebellion against unpleasant social structures. But, in the long run, I believe (perhaps too optimistically) that resentment of those structures that fail to meet the basic needs portrayed in Fig. 5.1 will mobilize people to create the conditions favorable to change, even against massive macrostructures held together by concentrated power. Thus, there is a behavioral basis for the production and reproduction as well as the reorganization of society.

The Structural Basis of Social Behavior and Interaction

I promised not to get pulled into the micro-macro gap issue, but I will indulge myself with a few observations. One of the problems with much behaviorist sociology is that it misses a crucial point: macrostructures are like a "Skinner's box"; they frequently determine the conditions and nature of the reinforcement schedule. Indeed, the reductionist position of many thinkers often fails to recognize that macrostructures constrain just about every interaction. For example, the symbolic and material resources available to individuals, the placement of people in space, the amount of time people have, the options that are realistically available, and just about everything that is possible in a micro encounter are all dictated by macrostructure. Indeed, contrary to much micro-chauvinism, I think that we will learn more about interaction by examining macrostructural constraints than we will ever learn about macrostructure by exploring the dynamics of micro interaction.

How can I draw such a conclusion, especially after analyzing micro processes in such detail? My answer takes two different, though related, directions. First, let me assert that if we only study micro processes, as I have done in these pages, we will never see the forest for the trees. We will become conceptually myopic and fail to observe one of the most basic parameters of our daily lives: macrostructures. We cannot simply "translate" the macro into micro encounters, as Randall Collins (1981) once suggested. We cannot continue to conceptualize in a vague manner that the macro is composed of aggregated micro encounters, as so many micro theorists have done. Such assertions are not only vague, but they also ignore the issue of emergent properties.

Secondly, and perhaps this is why Collins and others have altered somewhat their once extreme positions, we cannot even fully understand the micro without some knowledge of the macrostructural parameters that order micro encounters. To take a somewhat "theory-construction" tack on this basic line of argument, what determines the values or content of the variables in the micro models presented in these pages? If one looks at the models individually or together, as I did in Chapter 12 and more selectively in this chapter, one does not find power, money, authority, coercion, inequality, and other forces that we know, as sociologists and as human beings living in society, are important parts of social life, especially our daily interactions. Have I made a big conceptual blunder here? I think not, but I should elaborate upon the discussion in Chapter 2.

As I indicated there, much sociology has mixed micro and macro concepts together—often in very creative ways, I should add. Yet this mixing has persistently confused matters to such an extent that neither the micro or macro realms are adequately conceptualized. In this book I have attempted to use the important insights of others in order to reconceptualize the micro so that it might be possible to make conceptual liaisons with more macro analysis. One such liaison is to see macrostructural variables—size, density, resource distributions, differentiation, and the like—as determining the values for the variables in the micro models and propositions presented in this book. Rather than try a "decomposition" strategy of viewing macro as nothing more than aggregated micro events, we should conceptualize both micro and macro in terms of *their own distinctive properties* and, when relevant, in terms of their variable states. In this way, it becomes possible to reconcile the two, not by blending them together but by seeing certain variable states of one influencing the variable states of the other. Let me offer an example of how to use macrostructural variables in my analysis: in a structure revealing high inequality of resources (the macrostructural variable), the ritual-making activities (the micro-interpersonal variable) between those high and low in resources will emphasize opening, closing, and sequencing cues, while de-emphasizing totemizing cues. I do not know if this proposition is correct, but the logic is still important. What I am arguing is this: visualize a macrostructural variable as loading a micro variable so as to produce a given interaction (in this example, certain patterns of ritual-making).

To a great extent, this strategy is implicitly performed by many theorists; I argue that it should be more explicit. For then it is more likely that precise models and propositions about both micro and macro processes will be developed *before* we rush headlong into premature conceptual marriages. Of course, we will always think about how micro and macro interface with each other; but when seriously *doing* theory, we should concentrate on developing precise and explicit theories of micro and macro dynamics that, with all of the conceptual leads available, we can eventually reconcile. This reconciliation will, I am positive, reveal that both micro and macro analysis must still be understood in their own terms. There will, however, be useful points of theoretical cross-fertilization when the variable state of a concept in a macro model will determine the variable state of another concept in a micro model, and vice versa (although I would guess that the macro will better inform the micro than the other way around).[11]

Concluding Remarks

In closing, I should emphasize again that the models and propositions presented in these pages are only provisional. They represent my best guess

[11] The reason for this hunch is this: vague references to "system reproduction" aside, how does one conceptualize the enormous number of micro events that are involved in macrostructures? What rules of aggregation of these events does one use to explain variable states of social differentiation, inequality, resource distributions, ecological distributions, and other macro-level processes? It is a lot easier, I think, to see how one of these macro-level processes constrains the processes that I have outlined in this book than it is to do the converse—that is, to see how motivational, interactional, and structuring processes produce and reproduce macrostructures.

about the processes of motivation, signaling/interpreting, and structuring. I invite criticism, revision, and debate on the issues that have been raised.

The goal of this book has been to change the nature of theoretical dialogue, to move away from the philosophical questions over suppositions and toward figuring out what people actually do during interaction. Moreover, I hope that my eclecticism will also be emulated, since for too long, sociologists have argued from doctrinaire positions associated with this or that intellectual camp. No one approach has captured all of the micro dynamics of the social world; we need to be more tolerant of, and receptive to, ideas in what are usually considered incompatible approaches. Taken together, as I have done in this book, these approaches go a long way in isolating the key processes involved in human interaction.

References

Alexander, Jeffrey C. 1987. *Twenty Lectures: Sociological Theory Since World War II.* New York.

———. 1984. *Theoretical Logic in Sociology,* vol. 4: *The Modern Reconstruction of Classical Thought: Talcott Parsons.* Berkeley, Calif.

Allport, Gordon W. 1943. "The ego in contemporary psychology," *Psychological Review,* 50 (Fall): 451–78.

Baldwin, John D. 1986. *George Herbert Mead.* Beverly Hills.

Berger, Joseph, Bernard P. Cohen, and Morris Zelditch, Jr. 1972. "Status characteristics and social interaction," *American Sociological Review,* 37 (4): 241–55.

Berger, Joseph, Thomas L. Conner, and M. H. Fisek, eds. 1974. *Expectations States Theory: A Theoretical Research Program.* Cambridge, Mass.

Berger, Joseph, and Morris Zelditch, Jr. 1985. *Status, Rewards and Influence.* San Francisco.

Biddle, Bruce J., and Edwin Thomas. 1966. *Role Theory: Concepts and Research.* New York.

Blalock, Herbert M. 1964. *Causal Inferences in Nonexperimental Research.* Chapel Hill, N.C.

Blau, Peter M. 1977. *Inequality and Heterogeneity: A Primitive Theory of Social Structure.* New York.

———. 1964. *Exchange and Power in Social Life.* New York.

Blumer, Hubert. 1969. *Symbolic Interactionism: Perspective and Method.* Englewood Cliffs, N.J.

Cicourel, A. V. 1973. *Cognitive Sociology.* London.

Coleman, James S. 1986. "Social theory, research, and a theory of action," *American Journal of Sociology,* 91 (May): 1309–36.

———. 1975. "Social structure and theory of action," in P. M. Blau, ed., *Approaches to the Study of Structure.* New York.

———. 1973. *The Mathematics of Collective Action.* London.

———. 1972. "Systems of social exchange," *Journal of Mathematical Sociology,* 2 (1): 145–63.

———. 1966. "The possibility of a social welfare function," *American Sociological Review,* 31 (4): 1105–22.

Collins, Randall. 1986. "Interaction ritual chains, power, and property," in J. Alexander, Richard Munch, Neil J. Smelser, and Bernard Giessen, eds., *The Micro-Macro Link.* Berkeley, Calif.

———. 1985. *Three Sociological Traditions.* New York.

———. 1984. "Statistics versus words," *Sociological Theory,* 2: 329–62.

———. 1981. "On the micro-foundations of macro-sociology," *American Journal of Sociology*, 86 (Mar.): 984–1014.

———. 1975. *Conflict Sociology: Toward an Explanatory Science*. New York.

Cook, Karen S., and Richard Emerson. 1978. "Power, equity, and commitment in exchange networks," *American Sociological Review*, 43 (3): 712–39.

Cook, Karen S., and Karen A. Hegtvedt. 1983. "Distributive justice, equity, and equality," *American Sociological Review*, 48 (1): 217–41.

Cooley, Charles Horton. 1902. *Human Nature and the Social Order*. New York.

Duncan, Otis Dudley. 1966. "Path analysis: sociological examples," *American Sociological Review*, 31 (1): 1–16.

Durkheim, Emile. 1912. *Elementary Forms of Religious Life*. New York.

———. 1895. *The Rules of the Sociological Method*. Reprinted New York, 1938.

———. 1893. *The Division of Labor in Society*. Reprinted New York, 1933.

Durkheim, Emile, and Marcel Mauss. 1903. *Primitive Classification*. London.

Emerson, Richard. 1986. "Toward a theory of value in social exchange," in K. S. Cook, ed., *Social Exchange Theory*. Beverly Hills.

———. 1972a. "Exchange theory, part I: a psychological basis for social exchange," in J. Berger, M. Zelditch, and B. Anderson, eds., *Sociological Theories in Progress*, vol. 2. Boston.

———. 1972b. "Exchange theory, part II," in Berger, Zelditch, and Anderson.

———. 1962. "Power-dependence relations," *American Sociological Review*, 27 (1): 31–41.

Erikson, Erik. 1950. *Childhood and Society*. New York.

Festinger, Leon. 1957. *A Theory of Cognitive Dissonance*. Evanston, Ill. Reprinted Stanford, Calif., 1962.

Freese, Lee. 1987. "What is interaction?" *Advances in Group Processes*, 4, in press.

Freud, Sigmund. 1900. "The interpretation of dreams," in *The Complete Psychological Works of Sigmund Freud*, vol. 4. Reprinted London, 1953.

Fuchs, Stephan, and Jonathan H. Turner. 1987. "What makes a science mature? Organizational control in scientific production," *Sociological Theory*, 4 (Fall): 143–50.

Garfinkel, Harold. 1967. *Studies in Ethnomethodology*. Englewood Cliffs, N.J.

———. 1963. "A conception of, and experiments with, 'trust' as a condition of stable concerted actions," in O. J. Harvey, ed., *Motivation and Social Interaction*. New York.

Gecas, Viktor. 1986. "The motivational significance of self-concept for socialization theory," *Advances in Group Processes*, 3: 131–56.

———. 1982. "The self-concept," in R. H. Turner and J. F. Short, eds., *Annual Review of Sociology*, vol. 8. Palo Alto, Calif.

Gergen, Kenneth J., and Stanley J. Morse. 1967. "Self-consistency: measurement and validation," in *Proceedings of the 75th Annual Convention, American Psychological Association*, pp. 207–8.

Gerstein, Dean R. 1976. "A note on the continuity of Parsonian action theory," *Sociological Inquiry*, 46 (Winter): 110–26.

Giddens, Anthony. 1984. *The Constitution of Society: Outline of the Theory of Structuration*. Berkeley, Calif.

———. 1979. *Central Problems in Social Theory*. London.

Goffman, Erving. 1974. *Frame Analysis*. New York.

———. 1967. *Interaction Ritual*. Garden City, N.Y.

———. 1959. *The Presentation of Self in Everyday Life*. New York.

Granovetter, Mark. 1986. "Economic action and social structure," *American Journal of Sociology*, 91 (July): 481–510.

Habermas, Jürgen. 1984. *The Theory of Communicative Action*, vol. 1. London (original German publication, 1981, 2 vols.).

———. 1979. *Communication and the Evolution of Society*. London.

———. 1976a. *Legitimation Crisis*. London.

———. 1976b. "Some distinctions in universal pragmatics: a working paper," *Theory and Society*, 3: 155–67.

———. 1970a. "On systematically distorted communication," *Inquiry*, 13: 205–18.

———. 1970b. "Toward a theory of communicative competence," *Inquiry*, 13: 360–75.

———. 1970c. *Knowledge and Human Interest*. London.

Heiss, Jerold. 1981. "Social roles," in M. Rosenberg and R. H. Turner, eds., *Social Psychology: Sociological Perspectives*. New York.

Heritage, John. 1984. *Garfinkel and Ethnomethodology*. Cambridge, Eng.

Homans, George C. 1974. *Social Behavior: Its Elementary Forms*, rev. ed. New York.

———. 1961. *Social Behavior: Its Elementary Forms*. New York.

Husserl, Edmund. 1913. *Ideas: General Introduction to Pure Phenomenology*. Reprinted London, 1969.

James, William. 1890. *The Principles of Psychology*, vol. 1. New York.

Knorr-Cetina, Karin, and Aaron V. Cicourel, eds. 1981. *Advances in Social Theory and Methodology, Toward an Integration of Micro- and Macro-Sociologies*. Boston.

Kuhn, Manford H., and T. S. McPartland. 1954. "An empirical investigation of self-attitude," *American Sociological Review*, 19 (1): 68–76.

Lecky, Prescott. 1945. *Self-Consistency*. New York.

Lévi-Strauss, Claude. 1963. *Structural Anthropology*. New York.

Lieberson, Stanley. 1986. *Making It Count*. Berkeley, Calif.

Linton, Ralph. 1936. *The Study of Man*. New York.

Luhmann, Niklas. 1982. *The Differentiation of Society*. New York.

McCall, George J., and J. L. Simmons. 1966. *Identities and Interactions*. New York.

Manis, Jerome G., and B. N. Meltzer, eds. 1978. *Symbolic Interaction*. Boston.

Mayhew, Bruce H. 1981. "Structuralism versus individualism," *Social Forces*, 59 (3): 627–48.

———. 1972. "Growth and decay of structure in interaction," *Comparative Studies*, 3 (Spring): 131–60.

Mead, George Herbert. 1938. *The Philosophy of the Act*. Chicago.

———. 1934. *Mind, Self, and Society*. Chicago.

Mehan, Hugh, and Houston Wood. 1975. *The Reality of Ethnomethodology*. New York.

Miyamoto, F. S. 1970. "Self, motivation, and symbolic interaction theory," in T. Shibutani, ed., *Human Nature and Collective Behavior*. Englewood Cliffs, N.J.

Miyamoto, F. S., and Sanford Dornbusch. 1956. "A test of interactionist hypotheses of self-conception," *American Journal of Sociology*, 61 (Mar.): 399–403.

Münch, Richard. 1982a. *Theory of Action: Reconstructing the Contributions of Talcott Parsons, Emile Durkheim, and Max Weber*, 2 vols. Frankfurt.

———. 1982b. "Talcott Parsons and the theory of action II," *American Journal of Sociology*, 87 (Feb.): 771–826.

———. 1981. "Talcott Parsons and the theory of action I," *American Journal of Sociology*, 86 (Dec.): 709–39.

Osgood, C. E., and P. H. Tannenbaum. 1955. "The principle of congruity in the prediction of attitude change," *Psychological Review*, 62 (Jan.): 42–55.

Parsons, Talcott. 1978. *Action Theory and the Human Condition*. New York.

———. 1970. "Some problems of general theory," in J. C. McKinney and E. A. Tiryakian, eds., *Theoretical Sociology: Perspectives and Developments*. New York.

———. 1963a. "On the concept of political power," *Proceedings of the American Philosophical Society*, 107 (June): 232–62.

———. 1963b. "On the concept of influence," *Public Opinion Quarterly*, 27 (Spring): 37–62.

———. 1961. "An outline of the social system," in T. Parsons et. al., eds., *Theories of Society*. New York.

———. 1958. "An approach to psychological theory in terms of the theory of action," in S. Koch, ed., *Psychology: A Science*, vol. 3. New York.

———. 1951. *The Social System*. New York.

———. 1949. "The present position and prospect of systemic theory in sociology," in T. Parsons, *Essays in Sociological Theory*. New York.

———. 1937. *The Structure of Social Action*. New York.

Parsons, Talcott, Robert F. Bales, and Edward Shils. 1953. *Working Papers in the Theory of Action*. Glencoe, Ill.

Parsons, Talcott, and Gerald M. Platt. 1975. *The American University*. Cambridge, Mass.

Parsons, Talcott, and Edward A. Shils, eds. 1951. *Towards a General Theory of Action*. New York.

Pavlov, Ivan Petrovich. 1928. *Lectures on Conditioned Reflexes*. 3d ed. New York.

Perinbanayagam, R. S. 1975. "The significance of others in the thought of Alfred Schutz, G. H. Mead, and C. H. Cooley," *The Sociological Quarterly*, 16 (Autumn): 500–521.

Rosenberg, Morris. 1979. *Conceiving the Self*. New York.

Sacks, Harvey. 1972. "An initial investigation of the usability of conversational data," in D. Sundow, ed., *Studies in Interaction*. New York.

Sacks, Harvey, Emmanuel Schegloff, and Gail Jefferson. 1974. "A simplest systematics for the analysis of turn taking in conversation," *Language*, 50 (Fall): 696–735.

Saussure, Ferdinand de. 1915. *Course in General Linguistics*. Reprinted New York, 1966.

Schutz, Alfred. 1932. *The Phenomenology of the Social World*. Reprinted Evanston, Ill., 1967.

Schutz, Alfred, and Thomas Luckman. 1974. *The Structures of the Life World*. London.

Scott, John Finely. 1963. "The changing foundations of the Parsonian action scheme," *American Sociological Review*, 28 (Oct.): 716–35.

Shibutani, Tamotsu. 1986. *Social Processes*. Berkeley, Calif.

———. 1968. "A cybernetic approach to motivation," in W. Buckley, ed., *Modern Systems Research for the Behavioral Scientist: A Sourcebook*. Chicago.

———. 1961. *Society and Personality: An Interactionist Perspective*. Englewood Cliffs, N.J.

Simmel, Georg. 1907. *The Philosophy of Money*. Reprinted Boston, 1978.

Skinner, B. F. 1953. *Science and Human Behavior*. New York.

———. 1938. *The Behavior of Organisms: An Experimental Analysis*. New York.

Spencer, Herbert. 1874–96. *Principles of Sociology*, 3 vols. Reprinted New York, 1905.

Strauss, Anselm L. 1959. *Mirrors and Masks: The Search for Identity*. New York.

Stryker, Sheldon. 1980. *Symbolic Interactionism*. Menlo Park, Calif.

Sullivan, Harry Stack. 1953. *The Interpersonal Theory of Psychiatry*. New York.

Swann, William B. 1983. "Self-verification: bringing social reality into harmony with the self," in J. Suls and A. Greenwald, eds., *Psychological Perspectives on the Self*, vol. 2. Hillsdale, N.J.

Thomas, W. I., and Florian Znaniecki. 1927. *The Polish Peasant in Europe and America*. New York.

Thorndike, Edward Lee. 1932. *The Fundamentals of Learning*. New York.

Turner, Jonathan H. N.d.*a*. *A Theory of Social Organization*. In preparation, ca. 1989.

———. N.d.*b*. "A theory of macrostructural dynamics," in M. Zelditch and J. Berger, eds., *Sociological Theories in Progress*, vol. 3. Pittsburgh, in press.

———. 1987. "Toward a sociological theory of motivation," *American Sociological Review*, 52 (1): 15–27.

———. 1986a. "Analytical theorizing," in A. Giddens and J. H. Turner, eds., *Social Theory Today*. Stanford, Calif.

———. 1986b. *The Structure of Sociological Theory*, 4th ed. Chicago.

———. 1986c. "The mechanics of social interaction: toward a composite model of signaling and interpreting," *Sociological Theory*, 4 (Spring): 95–105.

———. 1986d. "Problems and prospects of exchange theory," in K. S. Cook, ed., *Social Exchange Theory*. Beverly Hills.

———. 1985a. "In defense of positivism," *Sociological Theory*, 4 (Fall): 32–44.

———. 1985b. *Herbert Spencer: Toward a Renewed Appreciation*. Beverly Hills.

———. 1985c. "The concept of action in sociological analysis," in G. Seebass and R. Toumea, eds., *Analytical and Sociological Theories of Action*. Dordrecht, Holland.

———. 1984a. *Societal Stratification: A Theoretical Analysis*. New York.

———. 1984b. "Durkheim's and Spencer's principles of social organization," *Sociological Perspectives*, 27 (Jan.): 21–32.

———. 1983a. "Theoretical strategies for linking micro and macro processes: an evaluation of seven approaches," *Western Sociological Review*, 14 (1): 4–15.

———. 1983b. "The structure of social action: an alternative approach," *Current Perspectives in Social Theory*, 4: 225–35.

———. 1982. "A note on G. H. Mead's behavioristic theory of social structure," *Journal for the Theory of Social Behavior*, 12 (July): 213–22.

———. 1981. "Returning to 'social physics': illustrations for the work of George Herbert Mead," *Current Perspectives in Social Theory*, 2: 153–86.

———. 1979. "Toward a social physics." *Humboldt Journal of Social Relations*, 7 (Fall/Winter): 123–39.

Turner, Jonathan H., and Leonard Beeghley. 1981. *The Emergence of Sociological Theory*. Chicago.

———. 1974. "Current folklore in the criticisms of Parsonian action theory," *Sociological Inquiry*, 44 (Winter): 47–63.

Turner, Jonathan H., and Alexandra Maryanski. 1978. *Functionalism*. Menlo Park, Calif.

Turner, Ralph H. 1979. "Strategy for developing an integrated role theory," *Humboldt Journal of Social Relations*, 7 (Fall/Winter): 114–22.

———. 1978. "The role of the person," *American Journal of Sociology*, 84 (July): 1–23.

———. 1968. "Social roles: sociological aspects," in *International Encyclopedia of the Social Sciences*. New York.

———. 1962. "Role-taking vs. conformity," in A. M. Rose, ed., *Human Behavior and Social Processes*. Boston.

Watson, John B. 1919. *Psychology from the Standpoint of a Behaviorist*. Philadelphia.

———. 1913. "Psychology as the behaviorist views it," *Psychological Review*, 20 (1): 158–77.

Weber, Max. 1978. *Economy and Society: An Outline of Interpretive Sociology*, G. Roth and C. Wittich, eds. Berkeley, Calif.

Webster, Murray A., and James E. Driskell. 1978. "Status generalization: a review and some new data," *American Sociological Review*, 43 (2): 220–36.

Weigert, Andrew J., J. Smith Teitge, and Dennis Teitge. 1986. *Society and Identity*. Cambridge, Eng.

Willer, David. 1981. "The basic concepts of elementary theory," in D. Willer and B. Anderson, eds., *Networks, Exchange, and Coercion*. New York.

Wilson, Thomas. 1970. "Normative and interpretative paradigms in sociology," in J. Douglas, ed., *Understanding Everyday Life*. London.

Wundt, Wilhelm. 1916. *Elements of Folk Psychology*. London.

Index of Names

General Index